Date Due

			M.
			5

BRODART, INC.   Cat. No. 23 233   Printed in U.S.A.

© THE BAKER & TAYLOR CO.

Masquerade Peace

Masquerade Peace

America's UN Policy, 1944–1945

Thomas M. Campbell

Florida State University Press
Tallahassee

PRINTED BY
STORTER PRINTING COMPANY, INCORPORATED
GAINESVILLE, FLORIDA

This copyrighted work was promulgated at a cost of $3.58 per copy for the purpose of advancing learning.

Preface

THIS BOOK DESCRIBES HOW AMERICAN LEADERS TRIED
to use the conditions of World War II as a crucible out of which
they could bring a new international order. By this UN policy the
Roosevelt administration hoped to bring the nations of the world
to accept American political traditions, thereby fulfilling Wilson's
dream of making the world safe for democracy. This policy would
provide, at long last, the orderly international setting that America's
open-market economy demanded for continued success. Because
this UN policy had a central role in American diplomacy, it influenced the beginnings of the cold war. A significant shift in policy
occurred after Truman succeeded Roosevelt.

The origins of the cold war cannot be understood without a
knowledge of the beginnings of UN policies. The story of the
changing policies is seen here from the perspective of Edward R.
Stettinius, Jr., whose tenure as Secretary of State spanned the late
Roosevelt and early Truman administrations. Stettinius had a pivotal role in making the UN policies, and his papers throw new light
on the whole period.

The UN policy went through several phases in the twelve
months before the UN Charter was signed on June 26, 1945. The

initial period, one of optimism, culminated in the Dumbarton Oaks Proposals in October, 1944. Throughout this phase Allied relations were still relatively stable and were strengthened by the Allies' military successes in Europe. The second phase saw the U.S. government launch a vigorous campaign to rally public support for the United Nations. This coincided with serious rifts among the Allies over their respective policies toward defeated Axis states and liberated nations of Europe. In the United States criticism of Soviet and British actions resulted in a revival of isolationist thinking among the people. This placed the Roosevelt administration in a bad position as the president prepared for the Yalta Conference. The third phase was the brief period associated with the Yalta meeting, where the American government made its most determined bid to integrate political compromise on Europe and Asia with the UN policy and to bind Britain and Russia to the American conception of the postwar world. At home there was a renewed faith that the UN policy would succeed. This period marked a major turning point in the U.S. commitment to the UN policy. For, thereafter, the cost of abandoning that policy would be regarded as politically too great to pay: telling the people that each great power sought to satisfy its own political and territorial objectives. The fourth phase witnessed the renewal of serious friction among the Allies. This prompted an intensive review among American leaders of policy toward Russia. Not ordered by Roosevelt, whose grip on power quickly slipped after Yalta, this rethinking of U.S. commitments brought together top officials of the State, War, and Navy departments whose common link was fear of and hostility toward communism. Yet neither the government nor the people long considered canceling the UN Conference, slated to begin April 25.

It was during the fifth phase that a most significant point was reached. This was the period of the San Francisco Conference. It marked the widest gap in U.S. praise of UN policy and keynoted the deteriorated state of Allied relations. The UN Conference captured headlines along with the deathrattle coming from Germany. The prognosis on the Charter, despite conference crises, was officially optimistic. The government's public relations campaign to sell the merits of the UN policy peaked at this time. Yet decisions by the new Truman administration indicated that America was moving into a new position where cooperation with Russia was still a goal. America, then, would insist on a relationship in which Russia was made to realize that cooperation, in Truman's words, was "a two-way street."

This final phase has figured prominently in revisionist accounts of American policy and the cold war. Historians certainly owe a debt to the revisionists, whose searching questions have brought vigor to the historiography of the war period. The revisionists find much fault with President Truman. The work of Gar Alperovitz particularly has been widely circulated, giving popular credence to the idea that Truman, in the early days of his presidency, employed "atomic diplomacy" against Russia. The object, according to this thesis, was to make Russia more agreeable to American goals, chief among which was to gain a voice in Eastern Europe in the postwar years.

This book seeks to show that an improper emphasis has been placed on atomic diplomacy, that Truman's thinking in the spring and summer of 1945 placed as much emphasis on the UN as on the atomic bomb. Truman was, however, primarily concerned about achieving American security, which he saw as postwar domination of the Pacific, sole responsibility for deciding Japan's future, and keeping Western Europe and the Mediterranean safe from communism. In pursuing these objectives, Truman altered Roosevelt's UN policy by his willingness to employ the UN as part of the masquerade peace behind which America and Russia engaged in a struggle for power.

I would like to express appreciation to the American Philosophical Society, the Stettinius Fund, and the Florida State University Research Council for financial support of my research. To my colleagues, C. Jay Smith, George Lensen, Richard Bartlett, and Vincent Thursby of Florida State University and to Edward Younger of the University of Virginia, I am indebted for perceptive criticisms and suggestions. I particularly appreciate the support of Mrs. O. Witcher Dudley (Mr. Stettinius's widow) and her sons in making this work possible in its initial stages.

Thomas M. Campbell

Contents

At least such subtile covenants shall be made,
Till peace itself is war in masquerade.

JOHN DRYDEN
Absalom and Achitophel

1

Politics of Postwar Policy

MUCH OF THE DIFFICULTY THAT SURROUNDS OUR EF-
forts to understand the collapse of the wartime alliance of the
United States and the Soviet Union and the onset of the cold war
stems from many historians' treatment of international organization as an issue largely isolated from the mainstream of wartime relations.[1] The record shows that the idealistic program for the United
Nations, which Secretary of State Cordell Hull injected so forcefully
into the proceedings of the Moscow Conference of Foreign Ministers in October, 1943, was a vital part of a bipolar American foreign
policy. The promise of the great powers to establish a world organization "at the earliest practicable date" for "the maintenance
of international peace and security," and their reaffirmation of the
UN Declaration was widely hailed in America as ensuring the triumph of the Wilsonian program of political self-determination.[2]

At the other pole was the pragmatism of President Roosevelt's

1. Herbert Feis, *Churchill, Roosevelt, and Stalin: The War They Waged
and the Peace They Sought,* pp. 426–428. This pioneer work largely neglects
the UN as an integral objective of wartime diplomacy.
2. U.S., Department of State, *Foreign Relations of the United States,
1943,* Vol. 1, *General* (Washington, 1963), p. 756. [Hereafter: *FRUS.*]

performance at the Tehran Conference the following month, where he realistically laid the basis for the important postwar territorial changes agreed upon at Yalta fourteen months later. These concerned the Far East, where Roosevelt expressed a willingness to negotiate with Stalin regarding Russia's claims. Out of the subsequent talks between Ambassador Averell Harriman and Soviet Foreign Minister V. M. Molotov emerged the specific territorial concessions that the United States recognized at Yalta. Also at Tehran the discussions of Poland among the Big Three could be interpreted by Stalin as indicating Roosevelt's support for Russia's claim to moving her frontier with Poland westward.[3]

The Roosevelt administration continually fluctuated between these two conflicting policies: the idealistic one, the UN policy more visible to the public eye; the pragmatic one, Roosevelt's willingness to act according to the precepts of power politics, largely hidden from popular scrutiny. The American public did not begin to perceive the contradiction in Roosevelt's policy until after the Moscow and Tehran Conferences. Then the tension generated by Roosevelt's dual policy began to manifest itself. The American government's efforts to make the UN policy cover allied power politics with a Wilsonian coating palatable to the American people were the chief preoccupation of American diplomats in 1944 and 1945. These efforts brought Roosevelt to a nearly impossible position from which death delivered him. His subordinates found in President Truman a leader who was willing to use the UN as a mask for building an anticommunist Western entente.

The pivotal year in America's integration of military campaigns and plans for the postwar world was 1944. As the Western Allies launched the second front in Europe, questions concerning territorial and governmental changes in Europe pressed to the forefront of their relations. The Roosevelt administration found it increasingly difficult to delay facing the political consequences of impending victory. Yet it continued to delay because American hopes were pinned to the overall goal of creating the United Nations which would adjudicate political matters. Thus the Americans put their UN strategy into operation by exchanging views with the major

3. *FRUS, Cairo and Teheran*, pp. 847–848, 869, 512, 598–604; Adam B. Ulam, *Expansion and Coexistence, The History of Soviet Foreign Policy, 1917–1967* (New York, 1968), p. 351; Feis, *Churchill, Roosevelt and Stalin*, p. 255.

Allies about postwar international organization. The dual challenge of delaying political decisions while trying to win over the powers to the UN policy provided the greatest test of Roosevelt's wartime leadership; his inability to achieve a successful balance in executing this dual policy was his chief failure.

Many elements contributed to the malaise that existed by the end of 1944, but underlying all of them was Roosevelt's reluctance to tell Americans about the political realities of the wartime alliance. The President's caution was greatly influenced by his view of America's interest as of limited scope in postwar involvements. The American rejection of Wilson's broad plans in 1919 was a specter that haunted Roosevelt. He feared that too vigorous leadership, along Wilsonian lines, would stir the political maelstrom which had swamped Wilson. Roosevelt realized, too, that the people were not agreed on any firm strategy for implementing the war goals that the Atlantic Charter had nebulously expressed.[4]

Roosevelt had deliberately sought a vague statement. He wanted a document that called America to a joust of principle as the best way to rally public support for war. Secondly he wanted to concentrate on victory and to avoid specific statements that might arouse difficulties among the Allies during the war. He recognized the alliance with Russia and Britain as a matter of necessity that might quickly dissolve when Germany had been defeated. He appreciated the animosities between Russia and the West, and he regarded British imperial policies as different from American interests.[5]

Roosevelt successfully kept the differences subdued in the early war years. This was more easily accomplished because the Allies were on the defensive; political issues could be left for a later time. Up to the end of 1943, the president successfully warded off efforts by Congress and the public to elicit a clear administration statement on the political questions of the war and postwar period. When the internationalist element in America stirred Congress into debate over America's postwar commitment, in the strong resolution introduced by Senators Ball, Burton, Hatch and Hill in the

4. Robert A. Divine, *Roosevelt and World War II*, pp. 58–59; James MacGregor Burns, *Roosevelt: The Soldier of Freedom, 1940–1945*, pp. 606–607.
5. Burns, *Roosevelt: The Soldier of Freedom*, pp. 591–593.

spring of 1943, the government pushed through Congress resolutions much less explicit as to America's postwar involvements.[6]

Roosevelt's policy of postponement has frequently led to the unfounded conclusion that the American government, as a whole, drifted through the war. The opposite is the case, for wartime Washington pulsed with the intense planning to turn the war to America's national advantage. Even as the war shook the moorings of world society in an unprecedented fashion, it was also the midwife of America's world leadership. Taken as a whole, the Roosevelt administration's preparation for this postwar role was impressive and thorough.

Much of the credit belongs to the leadership of Cordell Hull and the State Department. It is a myth that during the war Roosevelt was his own Secretary of State. This false picture was born during the war from the popular view of Roosevelt's war leadership. Certainly Roosevelt exercised his powers as Commander-in-Chief in a forceful and highly personalized way. And he did make the final decisions—at times capriciously. But the president's visibility must not be equated with dominance over all policy planning. American war goals received their essential imprint from Cordell Hull, who saw the war as an opportunity to remold the world along lines that would aggrandize the national economy and spread democratic ideology. Hull was much more of a Wilson disciple than Roosevelt and aggressively pursued his program.[7]

The heart of the State Department program is found in its UN policy. Political internationalization of the American system had been the elusive quest of statesmen since the turn of the century. It was most ambitiously outlined by Wilson, who foresaw that American economic growth would best be secured and protected through a community of nations that accepted American democratic values in the political sphere. It is simply putting the cart before the horse to claim, as Gabriel Kolko did in *The Politics of War*, that economic considerations dominated American diplomacy during the war.[8] The mass of documents, the large amount of time

6. Robert A. Divine, *Second Chance, The Triumph of Internationalism in America during World War II,* chaps. 5 and 6.
7. Gabriel Kolko, *The Politics of War, the World and United States Foreign Policy, 1943–1945,* pp. 243–244, 348–350.
8. Ibid., pp. 242, 266.

devoted at the top level of government, and the focus of negotiations was primarily concerned with effecting the UN policy. This is not to minimize Hull's concern with America's economic goals, but the economy had operated effectively (in terms of the business community's ability to penetrate international markets) for years. The essential problem facing America, in both World Wars, was how to build an international political framework to assure stability of already existing economic ties.

A major American political goal in the war was to insure the emergence of democratically oriented governments in the liberated nations of Europe. So far as possible, the hope of ending colonialism was important. This would undermine the British Empire and increase American influence in Britain's place, which, as Gaddis Smith has suggested, was a major interest of the Roosevelt administration.[9] The most ambitious part of the program was the conversion of Russia. While American leaders realized the dim chance of Russia becoming a democracy by the end of the war, it was worthwhile to plant the seeds of democracy, which would be watered by the United Nations in years to come. Additionally, they envisioned the regeneration of Germany and Japan along democratic lines.

The realization of these goals would come through implementation of the UN policy in three stages. One was detailed planning, done in the Department of State, on a scale far surpassing Wilson's restricted approach. The plan for the UN would then be discussed among the Allies. This part of the process envisioned the major Allies, Russia and Britain, being influenced to accept the democratic institutions that operated in America. The second, and partly concurrent stage, was to win the allegiance of the American people to the internationalization of democracy. The third step was to establish the UN which would become the permanent agency for democratizing the world community.

Development of the UN policy was the main consideration of the State Department, Hull having started initial work in 1939. Roosevelt wavered in his thinking about postwar security. He initially favored his four-policemen idea of great power regional rule, but by mid 1944 the president had accepted Hull's concept of a

9. Gaddis Smith, *American Diplomacy during the Second World War, 1941–1945,* chap. 5.

more broadly based international organization.[10] By the end of 1943 Roosevelt had approved a plan that incorporated many features of the old League of Nations, including a General Assembly, Security Council, Secretariat, and International Court. In addition to a Trusteeship Council, which would replace the old Dependent Areas mandates, there was an Economic and Social Council. This was a major innovation, reflecting the American interest in rooting out the problems which, left unattended, sparked political disputes and led to wars. Perhaps the most basic change in the American plan was the clear demarcation of the Security Council's exclusive responsibility for maintaining peace. Under the League this power belonged jointly to the Council and Assembly, thus making it difficult to achieve rapid action. The old requirement of unanimity in decisions was now to be confined to the great powers, preventing a small state from blocking enforcement action.

The area of real innovation lay less in structural changes, significant though some were, than in the American program of implementing the UN policy. This was the field where the battle would be won or lost. Here, too, came the greatest contrast between the strategy of Roosevelt and Wilson. The earlier president had dramatically outlined a Fourteen-Point peace program, then neglected to build a base of solid support. Roosevelt and Hull avoided clear-cut statements to the point of equivocation. But the administration, and Hull in particular, cultivated bipartisan political involvement energetically, although without great fanfare. And during 1944 the State Department laid the groundwork for a public relations blitzkrieg to insure public support for the UN policy.

A task fraught with greater political peril could hardly be imagined. Emotions in America ran deep throughout the war. And contrary to popular belief, the only significant unity produced by the Pearl Harbor attack was America's declaration of war. Support for the war effort was basically that of survival and victory. There agreement stopped. During 1943, debate over war goals became intense and widespread. On the left, the advocates of "one world" proclaimed the necessity of fundamental changes in postwar governments. The proposals ranged from plans for world government to blueprints of a powerful international organization to which

10. Divine, *Roosevelt and World War II*, pp. 65–66.

member states would surrender direction of their national security. Such prestigious figures as Vice President Henry A. Wallace and Republican presidential candidate Wendell L. Willkie commanded wide popular support for their views.

Many other Americans looked with alarm on suggestions to dilute national sovereignty. Leaders and writers, who viewed themselves as realists, preferred a world policed by the great powers. Well-known writers such as Raymond Moley, Henry J. Taylor, and Walter Lippmann advocated division of the world into security regions, each kept at peace by a great nation.[11] This regional approach found warm response among conservative Republicans, especially former President Hoover.

While opinion polls showed that Americans believed firmly in postwar cooperation with other nations, there was thus no agreement on basic strategy. This division indicated a fundamental weakness in the extent of public commitment to world involvement. Moreover, writing about the "wartime triumph of internationalism in America," as Robert Divine has done, tends to obscure this essential point.

If the State Department was to win acceptance of its UN policy, it had to steer between the internationalists and regionalists. This challenge, as early as the fall of 1943, had begun to concern Roosevelt and Hull. The president believed that the State Department was ill-equipped to handle such an assignment. The power of the department had been diluted by the war, which had called into being new agencies, such as Lend-Lease, whose functions were partly diplomatic. The military leaders held center stage. Also, there had been a bewildering diversification of activities in the State Department, and Hull lacked the administrative ability to run his department efficiently. The State Department enjoyed the dubious reputation of being the capital's worst run, most antiquated agency. "Foggy Bottom" was the frequent butt of caustic comment in magazines and newspapers, and public confidence in the department's ability to provide leadership was negligible.[12]

11. Divine, *Second Chance,* pp. 104–105, 172–182.
12. Donald F. Drummond, "Cordell Hull," in Norman Graebner, ed., *An Uncertain Tradition, American Secretaries of State in the Twentieth Century,* pp. 189–190.

Matters came to a head in the late summer of 1943. As part of Hull's scheme to revive the department, he forced the resignation of Undersecretary Sumner Welles. This action removed a rallying point for internal opposition to Hull but left unanswered the major question of obtaining new leadership. Indeed the popularity of Welles with the regionalists increased their criticism of the poor management of the State Department.[13]

In filling the vacancy created by Welles's departure, Roosevelt made a selection that, unknown to him at the time, was to have far-reaching significance in the course of the UN policy. His choice was Edward R. Stettinius, Jr., then serving as head of the Lend-Lease Administration. Stettinius had entered the government from the chairmanship of the U.S. Steel Co. in June, 1940. He served in various defense mobilization agencies until Roosevelt moved him into the new Lend-Lease post in the fall of 1941. Over the next two years, Stettinius earned distinction as one of the ablest administrators in Washington, and his work drew wide praise, especially from Congress.[14]

This record caught the president's attention. Stettinius had a reputation for great skill in public relations in the business world before the war, and he proved this reputation in representing administration views to Congress on the difficult subject of foreign aid. Roosevelt picked Stettinius to assist Hull in reforming the State Department's chaotic administration and refurbishing its public image. He expected that Stettinius's youth (he was only 42) would add an energetic quality and that he would be valuable to Hull in promoting the UN policy.[15]

Public acceptance of the new Undersecretary was almost wholly favorable. Stettinius breezed through a perfunctory hear-

13. Fred L. Israel, ed., *The War Diary of Breckinridge Long*, pp. 322–329; *Washington Star*, Aug. 24, 1943, *New York Times*, Aug. 4, 5, 6, and 25, 1943; *Newsweek*, 22 (Sept. 6, 1943), 48; Atlantic Monthly, 172 (Oct., 1943), 21; Julius W. Pratt, *Cordell Hull*, 2 vols. (vol. 12 of *The American Secretaries of State and Their Diplomacy*, ed. by Robert H. Ferrell) 2: 616–617, 802.

14. *New York Times*, Mar. 12, 1943; *St. Louis Post-Dispatch*, Apr. 19, 1943; *Washington Post*, Jan. 10, 1944; U.S., Congress, Senate, *Congressional Record*, 78th Cong., 1st sess., 1944, pts. 2, 4 and 6: 1658, 1745, 2049, 4731, 7821.

15. Mrs. Stettinius to Edward R. Stettinius, III, Oct. 12, 1943, The Edward R. Stettinius, Jr. Papers, University of Virginia Library, Charlottesville. [Hereinafter cited as *SP*.].

ing of the Foreign Relations Committee and received overwhelming Senate approval. By October he was already immersed in his first assignment, the reorganization of the department.[16]

While Stettinius was brought into the Department of State as a troubleshooter rather than as a policymaker, Hull's age and infirmities forced him to rely heavily on Stettinius for help on substantive issues, particularly the UN policy. Because Roosevelt left postwar policy largely up to the department and owing to the limits that his health imposed, Stettinius came into a much more prominent policy role in 1944 and 1945 than had been envisioned.

Unfortunately Stettinius had serious limitations as a policymaker. He had moved into American society from a high rung on the ladder of success by virtue of his father's achievements in J. P. Morgan & Co. While he had real talents, the most noteworthy being his ability as a reconciler and organizer, Stettinius was intellectually shallow and poorly read. Stettinius never developed the disciplined mind that serious academic work demanded. His preference was for direct, practical human relationships.[17] His experience in diplomacy was meager, his slight knowledge of international affairs having come indirectly through his involvement with the Lend-Lease program. Stettinius was thus of limited value in providing Hull or the president with penetrating analyses of foreign policy problems.

After Stettinius completed his departmental reorganization program, Roosevelt dispatched him to London in April, 1944, to coordinate Anglo-American diplomacy prior to the Normandy invasion. While several important economic issues were to be raised, the central purpose of the Stettinius mission was to wean Churchill from his support of the regional concept of postwar security and convince him that the universalist position of America's UN policy was correct.

By early March position papers were available for Stettinius covering every aspect of Anglo-American relations. The president had cautioned against hard commitments, so it was agreed that the

16. Stettinius, "Last Best Hope" (chap. 1 of an incomplete memoir of founding of the UN in *SP*), p. 3.
17. Transcript of college record of Edward R. Stettinius, Jr., University of Virginia, Office of the Registrar. Stettinius spent three and a half years at Virginia but earned only six hours toward a degree; interview with John Lee Pratt, June 5, 1962.

mission would exchange no documents with the British. The mission was compact, with only seven experts who would conduct technical conversations with Foreign Office officials. Stettinius was to range over the entire field in talks with Churchill and Eden.[18]

In late March the undersecretary left New York aboard the *Queen Mary*, its decks crammed with soldiers destined for the European invasion. The hard pace of preparation continued during the voyage, the mission reaching England on April 7. Stettinius spent the weekend with Churchill at Chequers, the prime minister's country retreat near London. The subject of international organization arose during the second round of talks with Churchill at Chequers. Expecting to focus on the subject of international organization, Stettinius took Isaiah Bowman, the mission's technical expert on the UN, with him. Churchill received them warmly. But the first mention of a postwar international organization brought a dour expression to the prime minister's face. With "great operations" on the horizon, Churchill termed the time inopportune for discussion of such an organization. "We had to see the war through first and take up world organization afterward," Stettinius later reported the prime minister saying. Besides, no one could predict what the world situation would be at the war's end. Life was unsure, he had no assurance of his own, and he might not even be present at the peacemaking. If he seemed less than enthusiastic, Churchill added, they must realize that the war had greatly influenced his thinking. In the dark days of Dunkirk, Britain had held "the baby" alone. He was unsure that Britain could place her security in a vague league to keep the peace. Would it work for future "Dunkirks"?[19]

Bowman played on Churchill's interest in military developments. What about the future of Germany? How would current military operations affect that? By such questions Bowman turned Churchill again to international organization, and the prime minister proceeded to outline his ideas about how a league might keep the peace. He took a piece of scrap paper and outlined "the tripod

18. Stettinius, calendar notes, conversation with Roosevelt, Jan. 17, 1944, *SP;* Harley A. Notter, *Postwar Foreign Policy Preparation, 1939–1945,* pp. 231–232.
19. Stettinius Mission to London, minutes, Mar. 10, 1944, Apr. 3, 1944; Stettinius, London Mission Diary, Mar. 17, 1944, *SP.*

upon which peace depends." At the top he marked the Big Three Allied powers and China, then came the "Supreme Council." Under this he drew circles representing regional councils. The Supreme Council would draw its power from continued Allied cooperation. It would have the force to preserve the peace. The regional councils, however, should assist the Supreme Council; each regional council would have primary responsibility for its area. They would settle issues at the local level to "avoid having every nation poking its finger into every other nation's business around the world." He suggested the utilization of troops, wearing their own "distinctive insignia." The regional councils could dispatch them in event of trouble. He handed the sketch to Bowman; then, as an afterthought, he took it back and added a world court.

Suppose a conflict involved nations of different regions, Bowman inquired. Then, Churchill replied, the council would step in directly, or establish a commission from the regional councils involved, to examine the case. The main point to keep in mind was the overriding importance of continued cooperation between America and Britain. Future peace depended on such an alliance.[20]

The problem was how to work out the machinery of Allied political cooperation prior to establishing the UN, and here a serious rift existed between the British and Americans. The October, 1943, Moscow Conference had created the European Advisory Commission (EAC) which the British hoped would oversee the coordination of Allied policies for liberated European nations. Hull and Secretary of War Henry L. Stimson, fearing possible British domination of the EAC because of its London headquarters, opposed its having a broad role.[21] The American government insisted that the EAC limit its actions primarily to drafting German surrender terms, an attitude that had greatly disturbed the British.[22]

Eden and the Foreign Office favored a universalist rather than a regional approach to the UN, but they believed that American intransigence on the EAC was threatening Allied cooperation. Eden gave Stettinius a memorandum contending the original purpose of

20. Stettinius, London Mission Diary, Apr. 15, 1944, SP.
21. Stettinius, London Mission Diary, Apr. 15, 1944; Isaiah Bowman, memorandum of conversation at Chequers, Apr. 15, 1944, SP.
22. FRUS, Cairo and Teheran, p. 616; FRUS, 1943, vol. I, General, pp. 812–813.

EAC was to review the situation in each country of Europe. The American government's negative attitude "tends to stultify one of the main objects for which the Commission was established . . . [and could] well cause a serious setback to collaboration between the Western democracies and the Soviet Union." Eden feared that, unless EAC were made effective, Russia would adopt a unilateral policy toward postwar problems.[23]

Although Hull's opposition to British ideas limited Stettinius's flexibility, he was determined to press for an early UN conference, despite the differences in British and American thinking about postwar organization. He minimized these in his cables to Hull and stressed the need for speed. He recommended that Russia and China be consulted immediately about beginning formal talks in late May.[24]

The Secretary's reply punctured Stettinius's idea of rapidly pushing ahead. Hull pointed out that he had just begun conversations with Senate and House leaders to inform Congress of the American proposals for international organization and secure advance support for them. A number of complex problems were involved, and the Secretary did not want Stettinius making commitments to the British because such actions might give Congressmen the impression that the State Department was trying to bring pressure for support of its program. When Hull instructed Stettinius to be cautious, talk of a spring conference was abandoned.

Stettinius's probing did produce one positive effect. He noticed in his last conversation with Churchill, on April 28, that the prime minister was more reconciled to holding a UN conference before the war's end. Stettinius noted that Churchill read from notes which bore many additions in Eden's handwriting. Churchill even suggested that talks might begin as early as June. This put Stettinius in the awkward position of saying that he could not state when the United States would be ready to proceed.[25]

Despite having some difficulties in his conversations with Churchill, Stettinius believed the mission had gathered valuable information, and he returned to America in an exuberant mood. In his report to the president and Hull, Stettinius attributed British

23. Lord Strang, *At Home and Abroad*, pp. 205–209.
24. Stettinius, "UN Record," pt. 1, chap. 3, p. 19, *SP*.
25. Stettinius to Hull, cables, Apr. 12, 18, 1944, *SP*.

divergences between the prime minister and the Foreign Office over the UN to uncertainty about how best to deal with Russia. The Americans also probed the extent of anticommunist sentiment among the British:

> We endeavored to learn whether there is any substantial body of opinion in England which believes that at some future time a stronger Germany may be necessary as a bulwark against the East and whether thinking in this direction has affected British policy. It was admitted that there exists and always has existed a minority fringe of people on the extreme Right who believe that Bolshevism is the real menace to Europe and that such people might argue for a strong Germany after the war. The vast majority of the British, however, so far as we could ascertain, are not thinking along these lines. . . .[26]

Stettinius found the British hoped for postwar cooperation:

> Given the background of Russian isolationism and suspicion over the past quarter century—not to mention traditional Anglo-Russian rivalry—the British believe that the road of cooperation will be long, slow and painful. But they feel—with occasional doubts—that the chances of ultimate success are favorable. They believe that the maximum of patience will be called for in the face of the inevitable setbacks and sudden incomprehensible Russian moves.[27]

The British belief in "ultimate success" rested on their estimate of the tremendous physical beating that Russia was absorbing in the war. Loss of manpower and economic ruin would force Russia to rely on the West for years to come. This situation would be "an important element" in persuading Stalin to cooperate with American and British plans for a new international organization.[28]

The continuing trend of British policy toward a Western European bloc to limit communism raises questions about the accomplishments of the mission. The mission did lead to better working relationships as was evidenced in the close cooperation at the Dum-

26. Stettinius, London Mission Diary, Apr. 28, 1944, SP.
27. FRUS, 1944, vol. III, The British Commonwealth, p. 10.
28. Ibid., p. 12.

barton Oaks negotiations four months later. But, by the end of the year, British officials regarded American insistence on the UN policy as endangering the forging of a Western bloc to forestall Russian domination of Europe.

Roosevelt and Hull remained opposed to any Atlantic alliance that would force Russia into a defensive stance. Roosevelt, having accepted Hull's universalist approach to the UN policy, was determined that Russia should be swayed into full partnership in the postwar community. Stettinius, who rarely questioned basic policy premises, found Hull's universalist views in harmony with his own ideals. Stettinius had regarded himself as a Wilsonian and saw in Hull "a personal link between the dream of Woodrow Wilson and the present. Even before I became undersecretary of state . . . I had begun to follow, through his eyes, the terrible and fascinating story of our century's failure to find the way to one world."[29] He found in Hull ". . . the same basic faith which I had learned from my father. I remember distinctly a day in 1919 when my father came back from France . . . and explained to me at that time Woodrow Wilson's dream of a peaceful world of a group of nations. He said the League was a very interesting evolution of society. . . . Ever since then the idea had been a germ in my mind."[30]

Although the American government made progress with the British, it neglected establishing similarly close ties with Russia. In London Stettinius had seen Ambassador Fedor T. Gusev on several occasions, but nothing of substance was discussed. In the period after the Stettinius mission, Washington contented itself with simply securing Russian agreement to meet in August in Washington to discuss postwar international organization.

The failure to pursue the political issues that had been raised at Moscow and Tehran in late 1943 was a major error on the part of the Americans. Russian armies moved into Eastern Europe in early 1944, and after the Normandy invasion political questions needed clarifying.

None was more pressing than the Polish problem. Events of the war had driven the Polish government to exile in London. The war provided the Russians an opportunity to reassert their histori-

29. Ibid.
30. Stettinius, "Last Best Hope" Draft of Foreword (in *SP*), p. 2.

cal interest in Poland, specifically to adjust the frontier westward and to work toward creation of a postwar Polish government friendly to Russia. The London Polish government, composed largely of anti-Russian political leaders, was powerless to thwart Russian ambitions. By 1944 the facade of friendship had crumbled, and Polish hopes rested squarely on Anglo-American ability to influence Stalin.[31]

This representation was severely handicapped by the American pursuit of its UN policy. This program placed chief weight on achieving great power agreement for a postwar international order maximizing democratic political practices. The Americans wanted to construct the machinery before facing the political problems of individual nations. Churchill was more willing than Roosevelt to make a wartime deal with Stalin that would salvage some degree of independence for Poland, but the president confined himself throughout most of 1944 to expressions of moral support for Polish views. The most he would do was to receive Mikolajczyk in June of 1944 and encourage Stalin to talk with the Polish leader. These talks, held in Moscow in July, settled nothing.[32]

American policy in treating the Polish issue was entirely consistent with its pursuit of the UN program. The president and Hull simply refused to act as agents for the special interests of the Poles when they were playing for much higher stakes. The criticism some writers make of Roosevelt's diplomacy toward Poland is not justifiable. To equate postponement with indecisiveness is harsh and, in part, erroneous. It can be argued, in Roosevelt's defense, that by refusing to champion the hopeless dreams of the London Poles he was pursuing, realistically, America's national interests, rather than those of Poland.

In his excellent study of the wartime alliance, William McNeill argued that American policy was adrift during much of 1944. Roosevelt, his thesis runs, took over diplomacy in the early war years, relying on special confidants and the Joint Chiefs of Staff (JCS). By 1944 Hopkins was out of favor, the JCS were preoccupied with the Pacific war, and Hull was ill. Stettinius and other State Department officials were unable to gain Roosevelt's attention

31. Ibid., p. 3.
32. William H. McNeill, *America, Britain, and Russia, Their Cooperation and Conflict, 1941–1946*, pp. 402, 407, 411–414, 429–433.

"on a regular day-to-day basis and therefore, lacking instructions from highest levels, were unable to pursue any active line of policy." McNeill says State Department officials "were in general uninterested in European political problems or were unavailable, or partially incapacitated by sickness; and there was no organization or group of individuals ready to take their place."[33]

This analysis is only accurate to the extent that he sees Roosevelt beginning to fail by 1944. In April, 1944, Roosevelt suffered heart failure and was ordered to rest for six weeks. This episode, a closely guarded secret at the time, forced the president's absence from Washington while he "vacationed" at Bernard Baruch's southern plantation, Hobcraw, in South Carolina. Thereafter Roosevelt was placed on a severely restricted schedule, although he soon ignored it.[34]

Whatever lack of direction existed, then, was attributable to the president's illness. It certainly does not follow that there was an overall disinterest in foreign policy. This error derives from McNeill's accepting too readily the wartime view that Roosevelt acted as his own Secretary of State. The facts are, to the contrary, that Hull was active and that Stettinius and other top advisers were interested and involved, as the Stettinius mission attested. Indeed American diplomacy moved along a clearly defined path in the spring and summer of 1944. Its actions were aimed at facilitating successful negotiations on international organization.

Preparation for these Allied exchanges absorbed much of Hull's time. Through Stettinius's efforts the State Department took the initiative, beginning in January, 1944, to improve its public relations. He introduced an Office of Public Information, with duties primarily to develop close relationships with groups devoted to foreign affairs.

As part of the public campaign, Hull made a major broadcast on April 9 in which he announced that plans were well along for an international organization and stressed continued great-power cooperation as the cornerstone of American policy. Hull announced formation of a bipartisan congressional committee of eight senators

---

33. Kolko, *Politics of War*, pp. 113–115.
34. McNeill, *America, Britain, and Russia*, pp. 404–405; Burns, *Roosevelt: The Soldier of Freedom*, pp. 448–450.

to consult on the details of the organization and how to implement it.[35]

Hull was acutely aware of Wilson's mishandling of Congress in 1918–1919. Further, 1944 was an election year and Hull hoped that his plan of bipartisan congressional involvement, which was more his project than the president's, would so align key senators with the administration that passage of the UN treaty would be assured.

Hull worked through Senator Tom Connally (D-Texas), chairman of the Foreign Relations Committee. Following Hull's guidance Connally approached the ranking Republican on the committee, Arthur H. Vandenberg (R-Michigan). Connally told Vandenberg that Hull wanted to consult a group of senators in a "preliminary informal discussion." The object would be to arrive at an agreed position so the State Department could tell the Allied governments that the American government was united in its attitude toward a postwar security program.[36]

There was another motivation that Hull did not stress at first to the Republicans. This was his fear of isolationism, particularly that the old American fears of involvement would be played upon by the Republicans during the coming election campaign. His interest in Vandenberg was keen because Vandenberg had been a prominent mid-western isolationist in the 1930's, but had begun changing his views after Pearl Harbor. He had played an important role in the Mackinac Declaration of August, 1943, by which the isolationist wing had joined with eastern internationalist Republicans in supporting American participation in a postwar collective security organization. Vandenberg was chairman of the GOP committee for preparing the platform's foreign policy statement. Hoping to achieve Republican cooperation through him, Hull feared that without this strange alliance the isolationists would sabotage the UN policy.[37]

Vandenberg agreed to consultations, and Connally announced formation of a committee of eight senators for talks with Hull on the UN plan. In their meetings over the next month, the committee

35. Divine, *Second Chance,* pp. 191–195.
36. Hull to Tom Connally, Apr. 17, 1944, The Cordell Hull Papers, Library of Congress, Washington, D.C.
37. Divine, *Second Chance,* pp. 131–132, 196–197.

raised two bothersome and interrelated questions. How would the UN policy be integrated with peace treaties and what evidence could Hull present to indicate Russia would cooperate after Germany fell? The first question was pursued relentlessly by Senator Vandenberg. He was favorably impressed that the State Department plan safeguarded national sovereignty, but he doubted the wisdom of establishing the UN before the peace treaties had been written. "It is impossible from my viewpoint to separate the nature of the new 'League' from the character of the 'peace' which it will assume to sustain."[38] He feared that were there an unjust peace treaty, the United States would be trapped, if she had made prior commitments to an organization designed to enforce these peace treaties. A number of senators shared this view. They wanted to know more about the shape of the postwar world before creating the security organization.

A second worry the senators expressed concerned future relations with Russia. The American plan assumed a continuing state of Allied cooperation. It was sine qua non to the organization's success, for the American plan gave each of the major Allies a right to veto action by the organization's Executive Council. This meant that any permanent member of the Council could paralyze the use of force by the organization. Might not Russia use this power to cloak aggressive designs?[39] In response Hull emphasized the importance of holding the Allies together in the difficult transition period after victory. Establishing the UN would greatly aid this task. "The malcontents," he warned the senators, were striving to "drive Russia out of the international movement by constant attacks and criticisms largely about minor incidents or acts." Press criticism over recent months had been hurtful of American policy and "has resulted in greatly confusing the minds of the public in regard to the more essential phases of the postwar situation." It was essential to keep the UN policy out of partisan politics.[40]

The sticking point in Hull's efforts to win the senators' public endorsement was Vandenberg. In a May 3 letter Vandenberg argued that the UN could not be disassociated from the peace

38. Arthur H. Vandenberg, Jr., ed., *The Private Papers of Senator Vandenberg*, pp. 92–93.
39. Cordell Hull, *The Memoirs of Cordell Hull*, 2: 1662–1664.
40. Hull, memorandum of conversation, Apr. 25, 1944, Hull Papers.

treaties, since the league must enforce its terms. "Hence it is my view that our *final and conclusive* consent to membership in the organization *cannot precede* the final and conclusive disclosure of the terms of the peace itself. Otherwise we would be signing the most colossal 'blank check' in history."[41] Vandenberg recognized the risks of waiting but had no answer. "It is in the lap of the event. . . . It seems to me that one of the lessons we should have learned from Versailles is that a League, no matter how nobly meditated, cannot cure the defects of an unsound peace."[42]

After frantic attempts to change the opinion of the Republican members of the committee of eight, Hull gave up seeking a letter he could publicize and settled for oral approval for the State Department to proceed with negotiations on the UN. The secretary announced this result to a May 29 news conference, saying he was "definitely encouraged" by the consultations. Privately he was fearful that partisan political battles might erupt over the summer.[43]

Behind Vandenberg's caution did lie a degree of political suspicion. In correspondence with Republican leaders, Vandenberg stressed that the party should make clear that nothing should impair American sovereignty. It was essential, he wrote Senator Warren Austin (R-Maine), that the party "faithfully follow the Constitution of the United States in the attainment of these international aims; and we shall vigilantly protect the essential interests and resources of the United States at all times." By this latter reference Vandenberg meant that the Democrats should be prevented from launching an international New Deal.[44] Unalterably opposed to a fourth term for Roosevelt, Vandenberg wanted a Republican victory. This might mean independent action in foreign affairs as Vandenberg saw the GOP task. "I feel," he wrote to Governor Tom Dewey, "that we must be equally plain-spoken that this contemplation [of joining an international organization] does *not* include a 'world state,' that we intend to keep the flag on the Capitol (to use the vernacular), and that we intend to protect and conserve the

41. Vandenberg to Hull, May 3, 1944, Hull Papers.
42. Divine, *Second Chance*, pp. 202–203.
43. Vandenberg to Austin, May 8, 1944 and Robert Wood to Vandenberg, Apr. 29, 1944, The Arthur H. Vandenberg Papers, Clements Library, Ann Arbor, Michigan.
44. Vandenberg to Dewey, May 10 and 22, 1944, Vandenberg Papers. Italics and parentheses in original.

legitimate self-interests of the United States precisely as Mr.
Churchill constantly asserts his primary devotion to the British
Empire." He found Dewey in complete agreement.[45]

The drift in the Republican party seemed definitely to the conservative side after Wendell Willkie's withdrawal from the primary
battles in March. The meeting of the Illinois GOP convention was
marked by heavy overtones of nationalism and isolationism. Party
leaders, spurred by Governor Dwight Green, called for retention
of large military forces after the war. America should keep all bases
it acquired in both the Pacific and the Atlantic Ocean. This way
America could be "a beacon of hope for peace and progress." In
these more conservative portions of the party, Vandenberg had
great influence, and he exerted it to moderate these ideas for sake
of party harmony. For his part, though, he agreed with this approach.[46]

Vandenberg was interested in party unity, and his spadework
in May and June went far to assuring party unity at the convention
in late June. The GOP internationalists failed to get party endorsement of the State Department's UN plan. The platform simply supported postwar cooperation "among sovereign nations" to stop aggression and attain permanent peace and justice. The elaborate
homages to national sovereignty and constitutional procedures left
little doubt that the Republicans had a limited concept of international organization.[47]

In order to keep the initiative gained from the Stettinius mission and the Congressional consultations, the administration announced on May 31 that the American proposals for the UN had
been sent to the other Big Four governments. Next Stettinius and
Leo Pasvolsky, State Department authority on the UN plan, visited
the president on June 15, after which Roosevelt released a State
Department announcement that negotiations would take place at
Dumbarton Oaks in Washington on August 14. The president also
informed the nation of the structural outlines of the proposed organization. As assurance to nationalistic elements Roosevelt took

45. 1944 Illinois State Republican Platform, copy in Vandenberg Papers;
Vandenberg to Green, June 10, 1944, Vandenberg Papers.
46. H. Bradford Westerfield, *Foreign Policy and Party Politics: Pearl
Harbor to Korea*, p. 164; *New York Times*, June 21–25, 1944.
47. *New York Times*, June 16, 1944.

pains to point out that "we are not thinking of a superstate with its own police forces and other paraphernalia of coercive power." Otherwise the outline was silent on the role of the Big Four and vague on how peace keeping would work.[48]

Commentators found the administration's statement too nebulous. The *Baltimore Sun* described the proposed United Nations as another League of Nations with an even weaker commitment. The *St. Louis Post-Dispatch* charged that America was building a great-power alliance system under the guise of international cooperation. Editorially it warned that without justice to the small nations the United Nations would amount to no more than another armistice. Reactions from some other major newspapers were more sympathetic. The *New York Times*, which enjoyed closer administration contacts than most other newspapers, termed the American planning much sounder than Wilson's had been and praised Roosevelt for his judicious approach through careful preparation and bipartisan consultation.[49]

Senate reaction was equally cautious. Vandenberg reminded reporters that the peace terms were just as vital as the UN policy. "Even a good league cannot cure a bad peace." Other Republican comment was similar, with Senator Styles Bridges (R-Vermont) voicing the widely held fear that the big powers were planning to dominate the postwar world.[50]

No one voiced this fear more eloquently than Ely Culbertson, president of the World Federation, Inc., a pressure group for world government. Writing to Roosevelt on June 16, Culbertson charged the State Department with a "cynical" resurrection of "the bullet-ridden League of Nations. . . . The old League, like the new one, is merely a screen for the war-breeding power politics of the dominating powers." Warning that the plan offered no means of enforcing peace when the great powers disagreed, Culbertson predicted that the vaunted alliance of the powers would collapse "much sooner" than the Holy Alliance.[51]

The administration was little swayed by such criticism. Roose-

48. *Baltimore Sun,* June 17, 1944; *St. Louis Post-Dispatch,* June 17, 1944; *New York Times,* June 16 and 17, 1944.

49. *New York Times,* June 16, 1944.

50. Ely Culbertson to Roosevelt, June 17, 1944, 55570F, The Franklin D. Roosevelt Papers, Roosevelt Library, Hyde Park, New York.

51. Roosevelt to Culbertson, July 12, 1944, 55570F, Roosevelt Papers.

velt simply assigned most such communications to the State Department for reply and urged critics to await the unfolding negotiations to allay fears.[52] The president was much more sensitive to
conservative opinion of the UN policy, as his dumping of Henry
Wallace for Harry Truman at the July Democratic convention
plainly showed. Wallace had become too closely identified with the
one-worlders, whereas Truman was a safe alternative.

For the next month there was vigorous public debate between
advocates of regional security and proponents of the universalist
school, but behind the scenes Republican leaders had doubts about
the direction of the administration's UN policy. GOP thinking emphasized the building of international law as the best way toward
a larger world community. John Foster Dulles, prominent lawyer
and Presbyterian lay leader, served as Dewey's foreign policy adviser. Dulles, along with Vandenberg, placed great stress on equality among the member nations of the UN. They feared that Roosevelt favored great-power dominance of the UN, and on August 16,
the eve of the Dumbarton Oaks Conference, Governor Dewey issued a sharp attack on the administration: "I have been deeply
disturbed by some of the recent reports concerning the forthcoming
conference. These indicate that it is planned to subject the nations
of the world, great and small, permanently to the coercive power
of the four nations holding this conference."[53]

The Dewey blast brought strong reaction from the State Department. Stettinius immediately discussed the situation with Senators Robert Wagner (D-New York) and Tom Connally. He told
Wagner that Dewey's charges were "uninformed" and that it was
ridiculous to think the great powers wanted any domination over
the other nations. He wanted to "blast this thing hard and quick,"
and went to Hull's apartment to get a statement. In conversation
with Assistant War Secretary John J. McCloy, Stettinius was even
more blunt, saying that Dewey's statement was "blowing our security conference all to pieces. It was just a damn dumb thing." To
his brother-in-law Juan Trippe, Stettinius characterized Dewey's
statement as "playing cheap politics." It was "just rotten the way

52 *Washington Post*, Aug. 17, 1944.
53. Stettinius-Wagner and Stettinius-McCloy, memoranda of phone conversations, Aug. 16, 1944, and Stettinius, calendar notes, Aug. 22, 1944, SP.

they [Republicans] were taking this Dumbarton thing apart down here, which they were turning into tricky political maneuvering."[54]

After consulting Hull it was decided to rebut the Republican statement yet to hold the door open for reviving bipartisan cooperation. Hull's reply on August 17 called the fears Dewey had voiced "utterly and completely unfounded"; and Hull said he would gladly talk with Dewey to clarify any misunderstandings. Dewey accepted this offer and named Wall Street lawyer John Foster Dulles as his representative in conversations with the State Department.[55]

The secretary told Stettinius that he feared a situation similar to that preceding the election of 1920, in which the League of Nations issue had wrecked Democratic hopes. In an effort to avoid this, Stettinius met with Hull and other top State Department experts on August 20. It was decided that Hull should seek Dewey's pledge to keep the issue out of politics. Dumbarton Oaks should be treated on a nonpartisan basis. If Dulles promised such treatment, Hull would provide Dewey with a copy of the tentative American plan, and the department would try to act on his criticisms by modifying it.[56]

The Hull-Dulles talks overlapped the start of the Dumbarton Oaks Conference and were conducted in a public atmosphere politically advantageous to the Republicans. Newspaper reactions showed the Republicans had scored a coup in championing the democracy issue in the UN policy. The *New York Mirror* editorially complained that Russian actions in eastern Europe justified Dewey's "timely warning" to the administration that the war "is being fought for the American principle of self-determining rights of small nations."[57] Republican historian Raymond L. Buell suggested to Dulles that Dewey should try to capitalize on the small-nation issue to win ethnic votes from Roosevelt, especially the five million Polish voters.[58]

54. U.S., Department of State, *Bulletin*, 11 (Aug. 20, 1944): 173; Hull, *Memoirs*, 2: 1689.

55. Stettinius-Hull, transcript of phone conversation, Aug. 20, 1944; and Stettinius, calendar notes, Aug. 21, 1944, *SP*.

56. *New York Mirror*, Aug. 23, 1944.

57. Buell to Dulles, Aug. 19, 1944, The John Foster Dulles Papers, Firestone Library, Princeton, New Jersey.

58. Dulles to Sen. Henrik Shipstead, Sept. 8, 1944, Dulles Papers.

Whatever Dulles's intentions, he found Hull a shrewd political bargainer. The secretary tried every way possible to extract an ironclad commitment from the Republicans to keep the UN question entirely out of the campaign. After a two-day stalemate they agreed that the UN policy would not be a partisan matter. In return Hull provided a copy of the American plan and pledged to keep Dewey abreast of developments during the Dumbarton Oaks Conference.[59]

The statements of Dulles and other Republicans, during and after the discussions with Hull, made clear that the GOP was not abandoning foreign policy as a campaign issue. Even the UN matter was a possible target unless the administration allowed full and open public airing of the question. When Hull's concluding statement to the press indicated the UN policy was removed from partisan debate, Dulles quickly replied to reporters that this in no way precluded thorough discussion of the policy. The public needed, he had indicated earlier, fuller information than it had yet received.

Dulles's emphasis on full information signaled a switch in Republican efforts. The issue of the small powers' rights, while appealing to the American sense of fair play, carried far less impact than the theme of secret diplomacy. This became the GOP's chief target until the election. Only three days after Dulles returned to New York, Senator Bridges condemned the American plan; by then the press had shown that the American plan would lead directly to domination by the Big Four. The American people were being hoodwinked by the Democrats, he claimed, and he condemned the secret diplomacy surrounding the Dumbarton Oaks proceedings.[60]

The epithet "secret diplomacy" was very effective in arousing American suspicions and was the subject of extensive comment over the next two months. While Hull had gained an important victory in the bipartisan approach to the UN, his achievement was less significant than some believed. Over the long run, the secrecy issue raised by the GOP was important in making the American

59. John Foster Dulles, *War or Peace*, pp. 124–125; Hull, *Memoirs*, 2: 1690–1693; *New York Times*, Aug. 26, 1944.
60. U.S., Congress, Senate, *Congressional Record*, 78th Cong. 2d Sess., pt. 6: 7334–7336.

people more suspicious than they had been earlier. This was later reflected in December in the rapid upsurge of isolationism in the country when Russian and British actions seemed to show that indeed the Republicans had put their finger on the pulse of great-power plotting.

In reality, the Republicans and Democrats had sparred on basic issues. Roosevelt and Hull had been so fearful of stirring American opposition by a full and frank public airing that they wrapped the UN policy in shrouds of ambiguity. Earlier, Clark Eichelberger, a prominent Republican internationalist, had warned the administration that by soft-pedaling the UN plans it risked an isolationist backlash. This is what lay ahead as the Dumbarton Oaks negotiations opened.[61]

61. Eichelberger to Jonathan Daniels, Apr. 8, 1944, Hull Papers.

2

Dumbarton Oaks
The Search for Allied Unity

THE STATELY GEORGIAN MANSION, NESTLED AMID TALL shade trees, afforded a welcome respite from the relentless August heat. The motto *Quod severis metes* greeted all who entered, a fitting reminder that as the negotiators sowed, so indeed would they reap. The building was made available by Harvard University for the conference. Ordinarily it served as a center of Byzantine studies, and rare art objects provided a spectacular setting as Cordell Hull opened the first plenary session on August 21. Here, for the next seven weeks, Big Four representatives pursued the holy grail of unity on international organization. The Chinese, at Russian insistence, were kept waiting in the wings, and their role in the last two weeks was largely confined to discussion of what had already been decided.

The Dumbarton Oaks Conference occurred at a time when political issues among the Big Four were reaching serious magnitude, yet the conferees in Washington were so engrossed in the technical questions of international organization that political problems remained in the background. This created an aura of unreality about the proceedings. Especially in America, where newsmen kept the UN policy continuously before the people with all sorts of speculation about the conference, the impact was to distract the public from the realities of international tension among the Allies.

While the delegates deliberated in Washington, the Warsaw uprising ran its tragic course. It caused considerable alarm in the West about Stalin's intentions in eastern Europe, as did the surrender terms that Russia imposed on the governments of southeastern Europe.[1] But officials kept their doubts to themselves and publicly maintained an optimistic tone. Neither America nor Britain probed Russia too closely out of fear that ensuing difficulties over liberated Europe might upset the fragile balance at Dumbarton Oaks.

The American government, in particular, was more firmly committed than ever to achieving agreement for its postwar UN policy before examining current wartime political dilemmas. The eagerness to have the UN policy accepted was given urgency by the expectation in Washington and London that German defeat was imminent. The "best" military information he had, Roosevelt told Stettinius in late August, was that Germany would collapse by Christmas.[2]

The conviction that the conference was of historic importance was best stated by James Reston, whose shrewd coverage of the conference for the *New York Times* won him a Pulitzer Prize. Reston compared Dumbarton Oaks to the Louisiana Purchase, the Monroe Doctrine, gaining of a Pacific empire, and rejection of the League, as one of the nation's major decisions. Would the United States agree to participate in a really effective international organization or would the UN be a replay of the ineffective League? The specter of missile warfare showed the urgency of the matter, he contended. Clearly future aggression would be swift. An organization was needed to forestall this danger.[3]

Leadership of the American effort was entrusted by Hull to Stettinius. With Hull's energies lessened by age and his voice affected by a throat ailment, the undersecretary was a natural choice.

1. Feis, *Churchill, Roosevelt, and Stalin,* pp. 410–411; Rozek, *Allied Wartime Diplomacy: Pattern for Poland,* pp. 249–264; George Kennan, *Russia and the West Under Lenin and Stalin,* p. 365.
2. Stettinius, calendar notes, Sept. 6, 1944, SP.
3. *New York Times,* Aug. 27, 1944.

Insofar as Stettinius had proven that he could work harmoniously with Hull, the selection was wise. Stettinus had demonstrated his ability to make men work effectively through the difficult and wearing process of committee decisions; he was gifted in cutting through wrangling to get at the heart of issues. His performance during the Dumbarton Oaks negotiations showed that Stettinius was quite competent in defending the American position, and he displayed personal charm in working with Ambassador Andrei Gromyko, the chief Russian delegate. This was important in holding the conference together during its many difficult moments. Stettinius's main role at Dumbarton Oaks was to coordinate decisions on the UN policy within the American government. He had insisted to Hull, when accepting the assignment, that his authority must be commensurate with his responsibilities. He insisted that he be boss and that no American officials consult with Roosevelt or Hull until after they had informed him.[4]

One of the major challenges Stettinius faced was the public demand for information. Ironically, he encountered great personal frustration in contending with this problem. The State Department had tried to maintain a careful balance in its public relations, releasing enough information to build public support for the UN policy and to counter political attacks, but not revealing its full plans for fear of jeopardizing discussions with the Allies.

This approach worked satisfactorily at the outset. The Dumbarton Oaks discussions opened in an aura of good will from the press, which evidently expected the same full access that had been granted to the recently concluded Bretton Woods negotiations on postwar economic policy. But after the flurry of publicity attending the opening session, a clamp on information was put into effect at Dumbarton Oaks. Then on August 23 James Reston of the *New York Times* published a detailed analysis that purported to reveal the substance of the position of each nation.

Reston's scoop, which had come through leaks from the Chinese delegation, set off a howl of protest from other reporters.[5] Stettinius was infuriated but felt his hands were tied by the decision by the

4. Stimson Diary, July 21, 1944, The Henry L. Stimson Papers, Sterling Library, New Haven, Connecticut; Stettinius-Hull, transcript of phone conversation, May 24, 1944 and Stettinius, calendar notes, June 21, 1944, *SP*.

5. *New York Times*, Aug. 23, 1944; Divine, *Second Chance*, p. 221.

Dumbarton Oaks steering committee that no separate press statements would be made. He conferred with Sir Alexander Cadogan, British Undersecretary of State and head of the British delegation, and Gromyko about meeting with a small group of reporters who would voice the complaints of the entire press corps. The meeting occurred on August 24. The papers that day were full of charges that the State Department was using secrecy to cover a plot of the Big Four powers to rule the postwar world. The meeting with the sixteen press representatives went badly. They demanded an end to the "vacuum of ignorance," while asking for daily summaries of the conversations. The three delegation chairmen emphasized that, because of the preliminary nature of the conversations, it was imperative that the talks be free from the public spotlight. The session ended in this atmosphere of stalemate.[6]

Over the next five days papers across America blasted the secrecy of the negotiations and raised questions about the sinister secrets the powers must be hiding. Numerous editorials pointed out the danger that this policy would turn public opinion against the UN and pointedly suggested that the same fate which had befallen Woodrow Wilson might be repeated. Marquis Childs, Washington correspondent for the *St. Louis Post-Dispatch*, wrote that the secrecy policy would only breed confusion and distrust.[7]

Stettinius meanwhile worked feverishly to prepare a justification of the press policy. He strongly believed that full disclosure could undermine chances for reaching agreement on the issues with Britain and Russia, a position which President Roosevelt fully endorsed. On August 29 Stettinius, Cadogan, and Gromyko met with the full press corps of almost 200 reporters. Stettinius read a statement that emphasized the tentative nature of the conference. He pledged that full press coverage would be accorded the big UN conference that would include all the Allied nations. He outlined the powers sought, stressing their democratic features, and pledged there would be no binding commitments without prior op-

6. The three chairmen thought that the Reston story was "quite unreliable and misleading." But this was an overstatement of the actual facts, made in the heat of their anger. See Dumbarton Oaks Steering Committee, minutes, Aug. 24, 1944, *SP*; Stettinius, Dumbarton Oaks Diary, Aug. 24, 1944, *SP* [hereinafter cited as *DO Diary*].

7. *Chicago Daily Tribune*, Aug. 25, 1944; *Washington Post*, Aug. 24, 1944; *New York Herald-Tribune*, Aug. 27, 1944.

portunity for full public consideration.[8] He concluded by citing examples of past negotiations where secrecy was in force, such as the Constitutional Convention, and asked for patience on the part of the press and public.

This appeal had little effect in quieting the critics. The *Detroit Free Press* disparaged the value of Stettinius's remarks, "all of which could have been written on a postal card a year ago."[9] Charles Van Devander in the *New York Post* admitted the need for some secrecy but said that the press "certainly didn't expect a complete shutout." He called the news conference a "farce." Radio commentator Upton Close attacked the proceedings at "Dumb Oaks," claiming it repeated the pattern followed at the end of World War I.[10]

Stettinius made another attempt to win press support in a meeting with reporters on September 4, but his effort proved disastrous. His approach was ingratiating and patronizing; his habit of using reporters' first names fell flat. At times he spoke in a half apologetic manner, and he experienced difficulty in framing answers. The conference lasted more than an hour and Stettinius left the meeting feeling as if he had revealed too much in his "gruesome experience." He asked aides to go over the transcript to spot "the things they got me in the corner on."[11] After this, there was practically no official contact with the press for over a week. Stettinius decided to avoid the large press conference and directed press aide Michael McDermott to meet with small groups of reporters on a daily basis. This arrangement was ineffectual in correcting the rumors that persisted throughout the entire conference, and the problem of press relations was never satisfactorily resolved.

Much of the problem was that the conference had been spotlighted by the government as a major step toward peace, and the public was anxious for news. Assistant Secretary Dean Acheson pointed this out for Stettinius, "We failed fundamentally in having a secret conference too highly played up." It had been, he added, a

8. U.S., Department of State, Press Release, No. 399, Aug. 29, 1944, *SP*; *Christian Science Monitor*, Aug. 29, 1944.

9. *Detroit Free Press*, Aug. 31, 1944.

10. *New York Post*, Sept. 2, 1944; *Congressional Record*, 78th Cong., 2d sess., pt. 11: Appendix A4002–A4003.

11. U.S., Department of State, press and radio news conference transcript, Sept. 5, 1944; Stettinius, calendar notes, Sept. 5, 1944, *SP*.

mistake to hold the meeting in the capital.[12] Undoubtedly Stettinius made matters worse by his inept handling of reporters. A nervous man when in the spotlight, he disliked press conferences and usually fared poorly at them. The caustic Drew Pearson wrote: "One of the saddest sights was to see Stettinius plodding along the rough roads of diplomacy like a youngster wearing his daddy's size 12 boots."[13] This picture was both cruel and misleading, for Stettinius was proving quite capable in the diplomatic encounters, but the people did not see this side of the undersecretary, and the visible actions were not impressive.

This was shown in his leadership of the American group. It comprised eighteen representatives, plus an ample staff. It was the largest delegation with the most sophisticated organization. This reflected the intricate planning by the State Department. Six of its members came from the army and navy. These military experts gave valuable advice on technical security questions. They also spoke freely on the basic concepts of the proposed organization. Hull provided further liaison with the military by means of weekly meetings with Stimson and army Chief of Staff General Marshall. There were no congressmen on the delegation, since the Dumbarton Oaks meetings were not considered as formal negotiations. William Fletcher, a prominent Republican lawyer, was a delegate and this lent a bipartisan flavor to the proceedings.

In the weeks before the conversations opened, the American group minutely examined the tentative proposals. For this purpose, the group divided into three sections: structure and establishment of the organization; pacific settlement of disputes; and security arrangements. Stettinius was chairman of the last section, but his chief influence was exerted through the steering committee of the delegation. Its members were: Stettinius; James C. Dunn, director of the Office of European Affairs; Edwin C. Wilson, director of the Office of Special Political Affairs; Pasvolsky; and Green Hackworth, legal adviser. These men came from the State Department. Admiral Russell Wilson and General George Strong represented the Joint Chiefs of Staff.[14]

12. Stettinius, calendar notes, Sept. 1, 1944, *SP;* Ruth Russell, *The UN Charter, The Role of the United States, 1941–1945,* p. 412.

13. *Washington Daily News,* Sept. 20, 1944.

14. Harley A. Notter, *Postwar Foreign Policy Preparation, 1939–1945,* pp. 302, 308–312.

The steering committee made the major decisions for the delegation during the conversations. Originally the Americans expected that the full delegation of each country would meet together, but Gromyko asked that the discussions be conducted on a more intimate level. Consequently, the chairmen of the delegations formed a joint steering committee, and this body handled the conversations. In practice, Stettinius made decisions after consulting with the American steering committee and then informed the other delegates about them. This procedure meant that those delegates not on the American steering committee were isolated from the mainstream of the proceedings. Because of the intricate nature of the conversations, changes in proposals were often misunderstood as they were relayed from one committee to another.[15] Stettinius wrote of these difficulties: "The meetings were the scenes of lengthy debate, hard under-pressure drafting, and planning. The heat and the pressure sometimes rubbed tempers raw but by and large these daily meetings, always fully attended during Washington summer heat, were a magnificent exhibition of devotion to an undertaking by a group of outstanding Americans there for the single purpose of serving country with the added desire of assisting in building a better world."[16]

Stettinius tried to minimize confusion by keeping people as closely informed as possible, so that they understood the changes, which often occurred by the hour. He did this also for Hull and Roosevelt. He prepared a daily summary outlining major developments. He then saw the president around five o'clock each day. Sometimes these meetings lasted only a few minutes; more frequently they involved long discussions of deadlocked issues. When Roosevelt attended the second Quebec Conference, Stettinius gave his reports to Hopkins. He also talked almost daily with the ailing Hull. Significantly, these many high-level exchanges practically never related the UN policy to current political problems among

15. American Group, minutes, Aug. 29, 1944, *SP*; Russell, *The UN Charter*, p. 446n.
16. Stettinius, *DO Diary*, Aug. 22, 1944, *SP*. This diary was compiled by assistants of the undersecretary sometime shortly after the end of the Dumbarton Oaks conversations. It was composed from notes that Stettinius dictated each day; thus the thoughts are clearly his own although the wording varies occasionally from the original calendar notes. For further comment on his compiling the diary, see *FRUS, 1944*, 1: 730n.

the Big Four governments. The discussions always pointed to the future, underlining McNeill's point that American leaders ". . . tended to think of the establishment of an international organization as a sort of talisman which would possess a powerful virtue to heal disputes among the nations."[17] Had Stettinius been more of a student of international relations or appreciated the functioning of power politics, he might, in his important liaison role, have provided the president a much needed bridge between war and postwar political issues. Roosevelt made little effort himself in this direction—separating examination of policy for Germany totally from the UN policy, at this time, by means of a hastily assembled ad hoc committee which deliberated entirely apart from the work of the American delegation at Dumbarton Oaks.

The American plan envisioned two broad purposes for an international organization: to preserve peace and security; and to promote international cooperation. The second goal involved all nations cooperating to eradicate economic and social ills, which the Americans regarded as the breeding grounds of war. Membership would be open to all peace-loving nations dedicated to the principle that "no nation shall be permitted to maintain or use armed force in international relations in any manner inconsistent with the purposes . . ." of the organization.[18]

The new organization should have five major functional divisions: an Executive Council, a General Assembly, an International Court, a Secretariat, and subsidiary agencies. This last category was made broad to allow for flexibility so that the organization could grow to meet future demands. Initially, however, the Americans suggested that two areas for which specialized agencies should be created were international economic cooperation and dependent territories.[19]

Since security functions were the main reasons for establishing a new organization, the American document spelled out in great detail measures which the organization should take to preserve the peace. Here the American plan differed radically from that of the old League of Nations. Under the old system both the

17. McNeill, *America, Britain, and Russia,* p. 501.
18. Notter, *Postwar Foreign Policy,* pp. 595–606 for the United States Tentative Proposals, Arts. I, II, VIII.
19. Tentative Proposals, Arts. II, VIII.

Assembly and the Council shared the police powers. Therefore lines of authority became blurred. This caused endless delay when a breach in world peace developed, and the League had often let precious time slip by. In the new organization security functions were clearly and solely vested in the Executive Council.[20]

Therefore, the structure of this Executive Council was of major importance. The American tentative proposals suggested eleven members. The Big Three Allies plus China and France would be permanently represented since they must shoulder the burden of any enforcement actions. The other six seats would rotate among the other members. This privileged place for the big powers was further buttressed by the voting arrangement. Any one permanent member could block action in matters regarding decisions to investigate disputes, negotiations and terms of settlement, the use of sanctions, or the employment of force. This gave a veto power to the great powers in each of the areas which comprised the Executive Council's activity: peaceful settlement and action to stop breaches of the peace. But subsequent negotiations showed wide areas of disagreement when the nations tried to spell out exactly how the veto power should be applied. One question caused more dispute than all of the others combined. Would a permanent power have its veto right when it was involved in a dispute? The tentative proposals reflected American indecision on this: "Provisions will need to be worked out with respect to the voting procedure in the event of a dispute in which one or more of the members of the council having continuing tenure are directly involved."[21]

The American planners had deleted the provision under the League of Nations Covenant which gave a veto power to all members of its Council, for too often this had meant that no action could be taken.[22] The American modifications represented a frank recognition of the dominant status of the great states. It was hoped that this would secure their full support.

The central organ of the international organization was the General Assembly. It was to receive reports, make recommendations, and coordinate the policies of all other league agencies, including the Executive Council. Each member would have a seat

20. Tentative Proposals, Arts. III, VI; Russell, *UN Charter*, pp. 208–212.
21. Tentative Proposals, Art. III, sec. C, para. 5.
22. Russell, *UN Charter*, pp. 208–212.

in the Assembly and one vote, regardless of the nation's size or importance. But with the security power solely in the hands of the Executive Council, the projected Assembly would not have the measure of power enjoyed by its counterpart in the League of Nations.[23]

To foster cooperation between nations, the proposals recommended "additional organs" whose function would be to make recommendations about social and economic problems. The Americans had in mind an economic and social council. Such a body would initiate studies and work with particular governments, "with a view to promoting the fullest and most effective use of the world's economic resources."[24] This concept was one of the major American contributions to the United Nations. Neither Russia nor Britain included such provisions in their plans. It reflected the American belief that the new organization should be more broadly conceived than solely as a security organization.

A separate American statute dealt at length with the proposed international court. Its machinery and procedures were so complex and technical that study on this statute had been carried on somewhat apart from the general preparation of the tentative proposals. The court's powers were to be similar to those of the existing Permanent Court of International Justice. The Americans hoped the court would have a large voice in broadening the influence of international law, but it was not to have any compulsory powers in effecting settlements. One clause, however, did provide that two nations might jointly agree to give this compulsory power to the court in affairs relating to disputes between those two powers.[25]

A director general was to oversee the administration of the new organization. His functions would include reporting on the activities of all agencies. He would also make appointments to administrative posts. His most important role would be to act as a liaison agent between the Executive Council and the General Assembly.[26]

At the outset the major problem was the scope of the UN.

23. Tentative Proposals, Art. II, secs. B and C.
24. Tentative Proposals, Art. VIII.
25. Notter, *Postwar Foreign Policy*, pp. 666–677, for the United States Draft Statute of the Permanent Court of International Justice with the proposed revisions.
26. Tentative Proposals, Art. X.

Cadogan initiated it on August 25 by stating that the British agreed with the American view that the UN should have a broader role than that of policing the peace. The Economic and Social Council should be included. To ignore such problems, he warned, would allow economic and social injustice to continue and lead to wars.

The slow-speaking Gromyko replied by pointing out that Soviet experts had analyzed the proceedings of the League of Nations and determined that 77 percent of the questions before it had dealt with subjects of the "secondary" nature. He emphasized in his precise English, "The Soviet view is that the primary and indeed the only task of the international organization should be the maintenance of peace and security."[27]

The reasoning which Gromyko used to support the Russian position had already appeared in print in July in a Leningrad periodical, *Zvezda*. State Department officials thought it had possibly been written by former Soviet Foreign Minister Maxim Litvinov, for he had pointed it out very carefully to American officials as "worth attention." The burden of the argument was that the League of Nations failed for two reasons. It had required unanimity among the great and little powers before taking action. Secondly, it had ignored Russia for fifteen years. This was very grave; for peace depended upon the cooperation of all the great nations, since they were equipped to deter aggression.

The way to rectify the League of Nations' weaknesses was to cement the union of the big powers. The new organization must recognize their special position. These powers should join in a "directive body," empowered to make "urgent" decisions without having to worry about the opinion of the General Assembly. The executive body would be governed in voting by a requirement of unanimous agreement before acting. It should be empowered to enact economic and diplomatic sanctions, and to use force. So that the organization could act swiftly, the *Zvezda* article proposed placing an international air force at the disposal of the executive body.

The Russians did not expect that all nations would immediately become models of virtuous behavior. This had been the mis-

27. Gromyko did not indicate how much time the 23 percent of questions devoted to security matters had consumed. Neither Cadogan nor Stettinius challenged this convenient statistic. *DO* Steering Committee, minutes, Aug. 25, 1944, *FRUS, 1944*, I: 735.

take at Versailles. Now an organization was needed with sufficient force to act quickly against aggression. Therefore, the new organization should deal solely with security. One of the problems of the old League of Nations had been its involvement in: " . . . functions having no relationship to its direct task, the safeguarding of security and peace. . . . It will be much easier to observe the success or failure of an organization for security if it is not burdened with an endless number of superfluous functions."[28]

Stettinius minimized the issue. Gromyko's point had "impressed" him, he said, but he did not believe the difference in positions was very broad. The United States simply wanted to put all international relations under "one tent." America did not deny that security functions were the most important issue. But surely it would be easy to make provision for the Assembly to create whatever subsidiary bodies it thought proper. The United States had an open mind. It only wanted such a provision included in the Charter.

Pasvolsky forcefully buttressed this argument. Both the Americans and Soviets wanted an Executive Council which would have primary responsibility in handling security matters. The Assembly was to be largely concerned with promoting peace and working on problems to improve international stability. The Economic and Social Council would be part of this Assembly work, entirely separate from the Executive Council. Its activities would not prevent the great powers from moving swiftly to curb aggression.

Although the Americans and British stressed the positive force which an economic and social council could exert, the Russians remained unconvinced. Gromyko's close adviser, Arkadei Sobolev, criticized the Council's recommendatory powers. Suppose its suggestions were ignored. The UN could not guarantee universal prosperity. To promise it and fail to achieve it would discredit the organization. They had better limit the UN to security problems—an area in which they could reasonably hope for success.[29]

Beyond this dispute over the scope of the organization, the

28. N. Malinin, "Regarding International Security Organization," Zvezda, No. 4, 1944 (English translation made by United States embassy in Moscow); see U.S. Embassy, Moscow, to Department of State, telegram, July 25, 1944, SP.

29. DO Steering Committee, minutes, Aug. 25, 1944, SP. In a number of instances the set of minutes in the Stettinius Papers is more detailed than the edited material in Foreign Relations.

three Allies agreed on the main functions for the Executive Council and the General Assembly. The Council must give the permanent powers a primary role. The smaller powers would have a less powerful position on this Council than they had enjoyed under the League of Nations, especially in that they would have no veto power. It was agreed that the permanent powers should have this veto power, but its details were yet to be worked out.[30]

The Russian document proposed that the General Assembly be allowed to discuss issues relating to peace and security in their more theoretical aspects, such as disarmament. The American idea was to keep the Assembly out of the problems concerning security, leaving these entirely up to the Executive Council. In the American view the Assembly would concentrate on the positive side of international cooperation. But it was quickly seen during these initial exchanges that plans could be worked out to have the Assembly handle questions, or at least to discuss them, that related to both security and international cooperation.[31]

On the crucial matter of determining what enforcement powers the organization should have, the chief dilemma was the Soviet proposal for establishing an international air force. General Wilson of the American delegation reported that a military committee was examining this suggestion and noted that it was the only point on which there had been much controversy. On all other military problems he reported that there was close agreement between the British, Russian, and American experts.[32]

The voting issue absorbed much time and effort on the part of the Americans. The plan submitted to the president in December, 1943, proposed that "in no decision of the Executive Council should the vote of a party directly involved in a dispute and represented on the Council be counted."[33] This position was maintained in subsequent drafts until late April, 1944, when a major shift oc-

30. *DO* Steering Committee, minutes, Aug. 22, 1944, *SP*.
31. Check List of Essential Differences Between the United States, the British, and the Soviet Proposals, memorandum, Aug. 19, 1944, *SP*; Stettinius to Roosevelt, Progress Report on Dumbarton Oaks Conversations—Third Day, memorandum, Aug. 23, 1944, *SP*.
32. Dumbarton Oaks, American Group, minutes, Aug. 25, 1944, *SP* [Hereinafter cited as American Group].
33. Notter, *Postwar Foreign Policy*, pp. 576–581, for Plan for the Establishment of an International Organization for the Maintenance of International Peace and Security, Dec. 23, 1944.

curred. The draft that Hull provided to the senators omitted all reference to the voting rights of powers involved in disputes. It simply stated that each permanent member of the Council would have a veto on substantive matters.[34] Hull wanted to avoid such an explosive topic until he gained the senators' support of American participation in a security organization.[35]

When the American delegation was organized in July, it spent many hours considering a formula to cover voting by Executive Council members in cases when they were parties to a dispute. The realities of power politics seemed to demand complete unanimity among the permanent Council members. It would be impossible, in any event, to enforce a decision against the will of a nation such as the United States or Russia. To insist on modifying the veto power would create a serious rift among the major Allies and might well kill the organization before it was formed. Proponents of the complete veto argued that the permanent powers would abstain in minor matters. In more important disputes, the standard channels of diplomacy would have to be utilized. Since Hull had given the senators the impression that the United States would have a veto, it was argued that to modify this stand would lessen chances of obtaining senate approval of the organization.

Those Americans who favored having no veto on this issue also had convincing arguments. If a major power could veto its own case, the organization would be no more effective than the League of Nations in preventing war. Past experience indicated that self-imposed restraints rarely worked. Furthermore, with an all-embracing veto the organization would be open to the charge that it was more a big power alliance than a genuine world organization. It would be difficult, if not impossible, to gain the support of the small nations. Besides, as no effective action could be taken against the wishes of the United States, it had nothing to lose by yielding in this point.[36]

Unable to decide, the American group presented the alterna-

34. Voting Procedure on the Executive Council in the Event of a Dispute to which a Member of the Executive Council is a Party, memo, pt. I, Sept. 21, 1944, SP; Notter, Postwar Foreign Policy, p. 585, Possible Plan for a General International Organization, Art. III, sec. C, para. 2.

35. Hull, Memoirs, II: 1653, 1662–1663; Vandenberg (ed.), Private Papers, p. 106; Russell, United Nations Charter, p. 274.

36. American Group, Aug. 10, 1944, SP.

tives to Hull on August 19. The secretary decided that America would support the British stand that a permanent power should not have a veto when it was involved in a case before the Executive Council. Hull and Stettinius discussed their recommendation with Roosevelt on August 24, and Roosevelt agreed that the position was sound. Hull next secured the agreement of the committee of eight senators.[37] This brought the issue back to the interpretation it had held in American drafts up to late April.

The next morning Stettinius presented the American proposal. He told the joint steering committee that the United States had been studying the matter of voting by a permanent power when it was party to a dispute and had decided to support the British position. Pasvolsky explained the American decision:

> The American group had come to the conclusion that it could not devise a satisfactory special procedure to meet this situation. He said that the American group feels so confident that this country will not wish to use force on a unilateral basis that it is willing to recommend that the United States should put itself on the same plane as all other nations of the world in regard to the settling of disputes. He said that the American group had felt that if the United States were ever to conclude that it was not willing to listen to the Council in the event of a dispute in which it might be involved such a conclusion would be practically tantamount to a decision that the United States was ready to go to war with the rest of the world. He said that the American group could not imagine such a development taking place and it therefore believes that any risks involved in its proposal are outweighed by the advantage of strengthening the Organization by a provision that in this respect all countries be placed on the same footing.[38]

This caught Gromyko completely by surprise, for it struck at

37. Hull, *Memoirs*, II: 1676–1677; *FRUS, 1944*, I: 731; Hull-Vandenberg, Connally, et al., memorandum of conversation, Aug. 25, 1944, Hull Papers. Although there is no specific mention of the veto in this memorandum, it was undoubtedly discussed since Hull met with the senators to brief them on changes in the American position. Further, several of these senators were familiar with the change in position on the veto even before the meeting was called. See American Group, Aug. 25, 1944, SP; Breckinridge Long, Diary, Aug. 30, 1944, Breckinridge Long Papers, Library of Congress, Washington, D.C.

38. *FRUS, 1944*, I: 738–743.

the heart of Russian insistence on complete Big Four unanimity as the key to the UN. Protesting that the Americans had violated the basic principle of unanimity among the great powers, he said that he would reply on this topic later.[39]

Gromyko then dropped a bombshell of his own by announcing that Russia wanted all sixteen Soviet republics included as charter members of the UN. This left Stettinius and Cadogan practically speechless.[40] The reason for this surprise is not clear, for in February, 1944, the Soviet government had indicated that it might make this request when negotiations began. At that time Roosevelt had told Stettinius that it must be perfectly clear there would be just one representative for each nation "and there will be no sixteen Russian votes." The Russian government had not pressed its point and the subject remained dormant until August.[41]

When Stettinius told Roosevelt of the day's ominous events, the president's reaction on the sixteen votes was almost apoplectic. "My God . . . tell the Ambassador that this might ruin the chance of getting an international organization accepted publicly in this country." The president immediately insisted that a curtain of absolute secrecy be thrown around the subject. Stettinius described the American method of handling the crisis: "This was to become a rather explosive topic for the balance of the conversations and we made every effort to keep the matter secret, only two or three of our group knowing of it. We always referred to it as the X matter and kept it out of the regular minutes which were circulated, keeping a special file of a secondary set of minutes with references to it carefully guarded in my safe."[42]

When Stettinius disclosed the president's rejection of the extra seats request to Gromyko the next morning, he was prepared for stiff resistance, but Gromyko seemed unperturbed. He told Stettinius that there was no urgency on the Russian request. It could be raised at a more opportune time. Instead Gromyko was much more disturbed over the American view on the veto. To Stettinius it seemed that the usually calm ambassador now verged on despair. The Russians, he argued, had already indicated willingness to view

39. Ibid.
40. Stettinius, *DO Diary,* Aug. 28, 1944, *SP.*
41. Stettinius, calendar notes, Feb. 11, 1944, *SP;* Russell, *UN Charter,* p. 359.
42. Stettinius, *DO Diary,* Aug. 28, 1944, *SP.*

the UN in the broader terms wanted by the Americans when they believed in a strictly security-oriented organization. To concede what the West now asked would threaten the entire Russian concept. Gromyko was also aware that the West looked with disfavor on the Russian proposal for a UN air force which would be in constant readiness to strike at aggressors on short notice. Both England and America had stated a preference for military contingents coming from national forces, rather than a standing UN force. Gromyko could only tell Stettinius that it appeared that the veto might be a point of "actual disagreement."[43]

Thus, as the Dumbarton Oaks negotiations entered September, from the Russian perspective there was cause for grave doubts about Western intentions. The West seemed bent on supporting the pretensions of the London Poles and had strongly supported Polish Prime Minister Mikolajczyk in his August talks with Stalin. The Warsaw uprising was seen by Moscow as an effort to claim the Polish capital for the anti-Russian elements. Western policy in general appeared designed to undermine Russia's security interests in Poland.[44] The knowledge that Roosevelt and Churchill were preparing to meet soon at Quebec must also have been disturbing to the Russians. What secret plans would the West concoct there? Finally the reports from Gromyko on Anglo-American behavior at Dumbarton Oaks must certainly have raised questions in the Kremlin about the motives of the democracies. Could it be that the West wanted an organization stacked against Russia, the sole communist nation?

The American UN policy in fact did envision postwar relations from a noncommunist viewpoint. The liberated nations should be left alone to build their own political future, the assumption being that, free to choose, the choice would be democracy. The policy was not intentionally anticommunist, but it would make difficult, if not impossible, Russia's political hegemony in eastern Europe.

What the Russians took as American obduracy actually arose

43. Stettinius, *DO Diary*, Aug. 29, 1944, *SP*; *FRUS, 1944*, I: 748.
44. Gen. O. T. Bor-Komarowski, *The Secret Army*, pp. 201–205, 339–360; Winston S. Churchill, *Triumph and Tragedy* (vol. 5 of *The Second World War*), chap. 9; Alexander Werth, *Russia at War*, chap. 8; Ministry of Foreign Affairs of the U.S.S.R., *Stalin's Correspondence with Churchill, Attlee, Roosevelt, and Truman, 1941-1945*, I: 249, 254.

from concern that too powerful an organization would be created (not, as Kolko inaccurately asserts, from American attempts to pack the UN against Russia[45]). The American dilemma was well illustrated when Gromyko proposed an international air force. Russia wanted the Allies to contribute units to an international air force which would be under jurisdiction of the Executive Council, ready to use at a moment's notice. Smaller nations, which could not contribute airpower, could aid international security by placing bases at the organization's disposal. This would give the UN a system of worldwide bases to use in conducting military operations.[46]

The air force proposal posed a peculiar difficulty for the Americans. Under the Constitution the power to declare war rested with Congress. Thus there were serious doubts about whether the executive branch could order its agent on the council to commit American forces to military action by the organization. The State Department had earlier sought the advice of prominent legal authorities. University of Virginia Law Dean Frederick Ribble had suggested that nations had the right to establish organizations, that they had the right to enforce their decisions, and such enforcement "is not normally considered war in a legal sense." Disputes among member nations could be considered civil conflicts; therefore a declaration of war would not be necessary. Congress could, as it had done in the American Civil War, confirm action taken by the president. Ribble admitted that a treaty specifying the right of the president to act rested on uncertain legal grounds, and he concluded that it would be sounder for Congress to pass a joint resolution that vested in the executive branch the power to direct the American delegate's vote on force.[47] Despite loopholes that might be employed, such as relying on the president's war-making powers, there was no argument that could mean anything less than asking the Congress to surrender a large measure of one of its vital responsibilities. Hull shrank from such a confrontation.

The American military experts explained the problem to the Russians. The Americans, they said, favored each nation providing

---

45. Kolko, *Politics of War*, pp. 273–275.

46. *FRUS, 1944*, I: 710–711, 748–749.

47. Chronological Notes of the Second Meeting of the Group of Military Representatives of the Delegations, Aug. 30, 1944, *SP*; *FRUS, 1944*, I: 748–749.

a contingent of air power, but it would remain for the governments to grant permission before the Council could use such forces. Gromyko argued that the Soviet idea would enable the Executive Council to take faster action, but he said Russia might compromise on an air force composed of national units rather than an independent, international entity. There seemed to be room for some mutual agreement in this.[48]

As finally agreed, the Dumbarton Oaks Proposals reflected Russian accession to American sensitivities: "In order that all members . . . should contribute to the maintenance of international peace and security, they should . . . make available to the Security Council, on its call and in accordance with a special agreement concluded among themselves, armed forces, facilities, and assistance necessary for . . . maintaining . . . peace and security."[49] The proposals called for members to have in readiness "national air force contingents," but these were to be in the hands of the contributing nation. The other military paragraphs did not elaborate specific steps such as Russia had wanted.[50]

This outcome particularly pleased the State Department because it was flexible enough for the Americans to claim that the war-making power of Congress was still protected. Prior to this solution, there had been lively debate among the Americans on the issue, and the newspapers discussed it freely despite Stettinius's pleas for reticence until the conversations were finished. This caused some concern among the more influential senators, especially among top Republican leaders such as Joe White of Maine and Vandenberg. Hull feared the Republicans might make protection of congressional prerogatives a campaign issue.[51]

Vandenberg raised the question in a letter to Hull. He argued that when the American delegate to the Executive Council voted for force it was a "clear commitment" by the United States and ". . . tantamount to a Declaration of War. I believe our Constitution clearly lodges the exclusive power to declare war in the Congress.

48. Frederick G. Ribble, memorandum, ca. Apr. 20, 1944, Pasvolsky Papers.

49. *FRUS, 1944*, I: 896.

50. Ibid., pp. 896–897.

51. *Washington Post*, Aug. 30, 1944; *Washington Times-Herald*, Aug. 30, 1944; *Christian Science Monitor*, Aug. 30, 1944; Long Diary, Aug. 30, 1944, Long Papers.

Frankly, I do *not* believe the American people will ever agree to lodge this power anywhere else."[52]

Vandenberg said that he raised this question now to avoid future collision and to suggest a possible solution. At numerous times in American history the president, as Commander-in-Chief, had committed troops without prior congressional approval. Perhaps the Senate would agree to delimit the area of the world in which the president could act without first getting the permission of Congress: "We might accept North and South America (under the 'Monroe Doctrine') as our *primary* responsibility in respect to the use of military force (just as we have always done); and allow the President and his Delegate to act for us, without Congressional reference, in this *primary* field. But if the dispute discloses an aggressor who cannot be curbed on a regional basis—if it takes another world-wide war to deal with him—I do not see how we can escape the necessity for Congressional consent."[53]

Basically, Vandenberg was showing a willingness to cooperate; it was part of his gradual shift from isolationism toward belief in a world organization. Hull reacted with more suspicion than warranted and continued to work through the Committee of Eight.[54] The problem was made less urgent when the conference agreed that each member nation should make a separate arrangement with the UN governing its commitment of military forces.

Although Stettinius talked with Hull about this problem several times, the credit for avoiding a rift with Congress belongs to the secretary. Stettinius concentrated on finding a basis for agreement on the veto crisis and moving the negotiations to a rapid close. Despite the decision to talk as long as was necessary to force Russia to yield her position, Stettinius looked for some dramatic way to gain a breakthrough.

The overall progress of the conversations was reviewed in a lengthy meeting between Roosevelt, Hull, and Stettinius on September 6. The president stated that his best military advice estimated the war in Europe would last " 'for another five or six weeks.' " This appeared to Stettinius all the more reason to wind up the initial discussions at Dumbarton Oaks. He wanted a full-

52. Senator Arthur S. Vandenberg to Cordell Hull, Aug. 29, 1944, *SP*.
53. Ibid.
54. Long Diary, Aug. 30, 1944, Long Papers.

scale United Nations conference "in the latter part of October." Roosevelt doubted the wisdom of this course. Isolationist senators would be sure to attack the whole project; it might be better to wait until after the election.[55]

No major idea emerged from this review. The veto deadlock continued, as Stettinius reported to the American group on September 7. "The American and British chairmen stated strongly that under no circumstances could their countries agree to a document that left out a statement to the effect that a party to a dispute would not be able to vote on the question of the use of force in settlement of that dispute. He [Stettinius] said that apparently Ambassador Gromyko felt that we would collapse with regard to this subject and was ready once he had won this point to agree to the removal of all other brackets in the paper."[56] Russia, it appeared, was applying its own variety of pressure—tying up the entire conference until it broke British and American resistance on the veto issue.

With this problem in mind, Stettinius tried his first major gambit: "I came to the apartment at 4:00 p.m. and mulled the matter over in my mind. I came to the conclusion that we would have to call out our last remaining big guns as we were going over three weeks of discussion. The success or failure of this thing depended on winning this point. I telephoned Mr. Hull at 4:30 and reported to him in detail on today's developments and told him of this one remaining open subject and that I felt some bold action was now required."[57] Stettinius suggested four alternative steps: Hull might call Russian Foreign Minister Molotov; Roosevelt might wire Stalin; Ambassador Harriman could talk with Molotov; or Roosevelt could send for Gromyko and discuss the issue with him directly. Hull thought that the last idea was the best, but he cautioned that it should not appear that the president was sending for Gromyko. With this course chosen, Stettinius phoned Hopkins to arrange a meeting between Roosevelt and Gromyko. Hopkins suggested that the president should also send a wire to Stalin.

Moving rapidly, Stettinius checked with Roosevelt on the plan.

55. *FRUS, 1944*, I: 772–776.

56. American Group, Sept. 7, 1944, *SP*.

57. Stettinius, calendar notes, Sept. 7, 1944, *SP*; in a slightly different form, *FRUS, 1944*, I: 780.

Based on recent conversations with Gromyko, Stettinius was convinced that agreement could be reached on the Economic and Social Council and the international air force question, if the veto deadlock were broken. If they acted decisively and quickly, Stettinius thought solutions on other questions would be reached "with flying colors in a few hours time." The president liked the plan of a conference with Gromyko, but he was soon to leave for the second Quebec Conference with Churchill. Could Stettinius bring Gromyko to the White House the next morning at 9:30? Roosevelt would see them in his bedroom. Stettinius escorted Gromyko into the White House the next morning.

After a general exchange on the military progress in Europe, Roosevelt changed the conversation to the topic of voting on the Executive Council by way of an analogy. "The President told a beautiful story," Stettinius wrote, "tracing the development of this American concept of fair play back to the days of our founding fathers." He cited the example of husbands and wives who had difficulties. They could present their arguments to a court but were never allowed a voice in determining their own cases. Gromyko listened closely and "accepted the remarks gracefully."

The president then asked when they thought the conversations would be finished. Stettinius and Gromyko agreed that they might conclude within four or five days. Then the second phase of the talks involving China would open. Russia, which was not officially an ally of China, would not take part in this part of the conference. Roosevelt directed them to move quickly to complete the Chinese phase by the time he returned from Quebec.[58]

Stettinius left the White House doubly pleased. The meeting had gone well, and he learned from Gromyko that Russia would accept the Americans' position on an Economic and Social Council. He phoned Hull: "I feel more encouraged than at any time and the Russians have formally accepted the Economic and Social Council matter. We are settling satisfactorily the matter of the international air force. The one remaining thing open is the question of the voting procedure, but I am sure we are softening them, and Gromyko said this whole thing could be settled by Monday."[59]

58. *FRUS, 1944*, I: 784–786.
59. Stettinius-Hull, transcript of phone conversation, Sept. 8, 1944, *SP*.

Hull's confidence was supported by a State Department report on the progress at Dumbarton Oaks, which concluded that the Dumbarton Proposals would embody "all of the essential points in our 'Tentative Proposals' of July 18."[60] Stettinius allowed these hopeful signs to dull his diplomatic caution, for on September 13 he was taken back when the Soviet ambassador stated that the Russian position on voting remained "unchanged." Stettinius wrathfully warned of the adverse effect this news would have on American public opinion and on the opinions of the small nations of the world. It was "a great disappointment and a great blow" to hopes for the UN. It meant in all probability that the United States could never agree to hold a United Nations conference. The American government "simply cannot understand how any country could take the position that if it became involved in a dispute that dispute could not be brought before the Organization." Without agreement on this point, Stettinius thought it would be useless for them to issue any document at the end of the Dumbarton conversations.

Cadogan reiterated these points on behalf of Britain, but Gromyko did not flinch. He launched a detailed justification of the Russian position, adding that there "was no possibility of any change." Complete unity among the major Allies was essential. Gromyko thought the small powers accepted this, "that in fact it has been taken for granted by everyone." It was "incorrect" to assume that the great powers would have disputes. When quizzed by Stettinius on how Russia thought its view of the veto would be accepted by small nations, Gromyko replied that " . . . he did not believe that the other nations are interested in being able to vote; they are chiefly interested in peace and in an effective organization designed to preserve peace."

Stettinius again stressed the care with which the American position had been formulated. It had been approved by the president, Secretary of State, and Joint Chiefs of Staff and "is unalterable regardless of future developments. He [Stettinius] said he wanted Ambassador Gromyko to understand this quite thoroughly; that he did not want the ambassador to think that there is any chance of the American position being altered." The meeting adjourned on

60. "Results to Date of the Dumbarton Oaks Discussion," memorandum, Sept. 11, 1944, SP.

this note of finality. The only mutual agreement reached was that "no whisper" of the deadlock must reach the public.[61]

Immediately following this session, Stettinius went to the State Department to confer with the secretary. Hull suggested that Stettinius call the American Group together and review the entire principle of voting on the Security Council. Stettinius opposed this idea. The American position was "final"; they could not switch horses in midstream, but Hull directed that an effort be made.

Stettinius decided that the small Formulations Committee might come up with a fresh approach. He told Gromyko, "We have nothing new but feel we should explore each other's minds a lot further to find our way out of this thing to everybody's satisfaction."[62] Gromyko thought the idea worthwhile. Pasvolsky represented the United States on the Formulations Committee; Gladweyn Jebb represented Britain, and Sobolev represented Russia. They met for several hours late in the afternoon of September 13 and worked out a compromise on the veto issue, which, essentially, was the formula later written into the United Nations Charter. It gave to any permanent member an unqualified veto over any matter pertaining to the use of force even if the member was a party to a dispute under consideration by the Council. There would be no veto for a permanent power party to a dispute with respect to all decisions which came under the heading of "Pacific Settlement of Disputes," (Section VIII-A of the Dumbarton Oaks Proposals).[63]

It was a compromise from the Russian view because Sobolev was saying, in effect, that now we will narrow our demand for unanimity. No longer will the veto apply to every substantive decision. On matters under the peaceful settlement paragraphs Russia will give up the veto when it is involved in a dispute. The British and Americans were yielding also. They could say they had maintained all along at Dumbarton Oaks that a permanent member must not vote on any decisions bearing on a dispute in which it is involved, whether the decision concerned peaceful settlement or enforcement measures. Now Britain and America will yield to

61. *FRUS, 1944*, I: 798–804.

62. Stettinius-Gromyko, transcript of phone conversation, Sept. 13, 1944, SP.

63. *FRUS, 1944*, I: 805–806.

Russia by agreeing that when enforcement comes into the picture, the permanent members once again have the right of veto even though they are parties to the dispute.

Despite his earlier statement to Gromyko that America could not change her position on the veto issue, Stettinius apparently accepted the compromise readily. It was not a totally new idea, since the American Group had considered this very formula in mid-August.[64]

Stettinius called Hull and described the compromise. The secretary thought the plan feasible but reserved his judgment until the complete papers from the committee session were in hand. Later Hull wrote of the compromise, "I regarded this formula as a substantial concession to the Soviet point of view and the absolute minimum of what we could accept."[65] Stettinius rapidly sounded out Cadogan and Gromyko for their reaction. Both men were noncommittal simply stating that they would refer the matter to their respective governments. Hopkins thought that Stettinius should cable the compromise immediately to Roosevelt in Quebec, since it was such a major development.[66] Of all the men involved, Stettinius was the most hopeful of a breakthrough.

The day after sending the compromise to the president, Stettinius motored to Horseshoe for a day's rest. It was a respite he never got, for when he arrived he was greeted with a phone call from his aide, Hayden Raynor, saying that Roosevelt and Churchill had just cabled their rejection of the compromise proposal. Stettinius turned around and sped back to Washington, where he found the president's message awaiting him.[67] The cable indicated that Roosevelt favored submitting the veto deadlock to the UN Charter conference. Churchill was dubious. According to Roosevelt, the Prime Minister " . . . is afraid that this procedure will be unacceptable to the Russians, as they would know that they would be overwhelmingly defeated in a United Nations meeting and that they

64. American Group, Aug. 17, 1944, SP.
65. Stettinius-Hull, transcript of phone conversation, Hull, *Memoirs*, II: 1701.
66. Stettinius-Gromyko, transcript of phone conversation, Sept. 14, 1944; Stettinius-Cadogan, transcript of phone conversation, Sept. 14, 1944, SP; Stettinius-Hopkins, transcript of phone conversation, Sept. 14, 1944, SP.
67. Stettinius, *DO Diary*, Sept. 15, 1944, SP.

would get sore and try to take it out on all of us on some other point."[68]

Roosevelt suggested a solution to Stettinius. "I think we should keep on trying but if we cannot agree on this or any other point, I am inclined to favor either not mentioning disagreement or putting disagreements under a general statement that certain points have not been agreed on."[69]

Roosevelt and Churchill were more concerned at this moment with coordinating policies for the final push on Germany and in deciding what to do with Germany after the war, and in this situation the less urgent problem of the international organization took a back seat. The news discouraged Stettinius and angered Hull. The secretary resented the offhand manner in which the two Allied leaders had rejected the compromise. He thought they had been too engrossed in military problems and had simply brushed it aside.[70]

But Roosevelt and Churchill might well have been influenced by a message which Stalin sent to the president at the same time the State Department sent the compromise proposal to Quebec. The Russian Premier was replying to the appeal that Roosevelt had made on the veto, after the bedroom conference with Gromyko on September 8. Stalin's message was unusually courteous. He thought the international organization question was of great importance and that it could "play a prominent part in furthering cooperation between our countries . . . " but the voting procedure was a vital cornerstone of that organization. He hoped that Roosevelt would accept the Russian view: "Otherwise the agreement we reached at the Tehran Conference, where we were guided by the desire to ensure above all the four-power unity of action so vital to preventing future aggression, will be reduced to nought."[71] Roosevelt, with this message in mind, thought it best to avoid a showdown over the veto.

Important strategic factors prompted this decision. The British were worried about facing a Europe dominated by Russia after the war. Churchill and Roosevelt had achieved scant cooperation from

68. *FRUS, 1944,* I: 814–815.
69. Ibid.
70. Hull, *Memoirs,* II: 1701.
71. Stalin to Roosevelt, cable, Sept. 14, 1944, quoted in *Stalin's Correspondence,* II: 160.

Stalin on sending relief supplies to Warsaw, and the Russians largely discounted the West in handling the surrenders of Rumania and Bulgaria. By the time of the Quebec Conference, Harriman and Kennan were providing Roosevelt with reports that pessimistically predicted difficulties in future political relations with the Allies.[72] Churchill was soon to try a direct appeal to Stalin to work out a sphere of influence agreement with Stalin, but Roosevelt was unwilling to risk American involvement in areas of direct interest to Russia. He was directed in his thinking by awareness of America's need for Russian support in the great assault on Japan. Neither western Ally was prepared to alienate Russia.

With the voting crisis no nearer settlement, the American leaders at Dumbarton Oaks considered how Allied conflicts in Europe were affecting their deliberations. Stettinius and his aides discussed this problem on the night of September 16. They felt that a basic Anglo-Soviet antagonism over the future of Europe might underlie the veto deadlock: "This led into a discussion of the vital importance to us of maintaining our position, keeping our friendship with the Soviet Union, and not being led into what might be a possible issue against them [Russia] on the part of the smaller nations."[73] Stettinius suggested that Russia might be deliberately delaying agreement on the UN until the end of the war, when she could better gauge her strategic advantages in Europe and the Far East.

At this point in the Dumbarton conversations, the Americans were in a tight spot. Russia had compromised her original stand on numerous points. It could easily be argued that the Americans were acting unreasonably in trying to win their way on everything. Stettinius discussed his thoughts with the president the next day, and Roosevelt agreed that there might be more to Soviet resistance on the veto than met the eye. They both thought that to adjourn the conversations and bare the controversy to public scrutiny would be "the worst possible course." They decided the only alternative was to end the work at Dumbarton Oaks "in some grace-

72. FRUS, 1945, IV: 223; Feis, Churchill, Roosevelt and Stalin, pp. 410–411; Rozek, Allied Wartime Diplomacy, pp. 249–264; George Kennan, Russia and the West Under Lenin and Stalin, p. 365.

73. Stettinius, DO Diary, meeting with Pasvolsky, et al. in Stettinius's apartment, Sept. 16, 1944, SP.

ful way as promptly as possible."[74] But neither man suggested how this was to be accomplished.

While Stettinius worked on this problem the American Group labored on the veto. The failure of the compromise proposal created serious strain among the members of the American Group and resulted in the development of a group which favored further concessions to the Russians. Assistant Secretary of State Breckinridge Long vociferously argued this view, and he was supported by most of the military members. Long argued that no international organization could work without the complete solidarity of the major Allies.[75] Admiral Hepburn presented the opinion of the military delegates: "It seems to me that realities are being thoroughly fogged by theory. Either we must be prepared to waive our principle of not voting when we are parties to a dispute and face the consequences, or we must ditch collective security which practically can be effective only if the three great powers hang together."[76]

On September 18, military representatives presented a lengthy memorandum to their colleagues and Secretary Hull. It clearly reflected the fears which haunted military leaders regarding Soviet-American relations. A volatile situation now existed at Dumbarton Oaks. Without agreement on the veto, they pointed out: " . . . no matter how it is dressed up, this country and the world will realize that the meeting has been a failure. If this conference fails to reach an agreement on this vital point, there will be the most serious, if not fatal consequences."[77] Without Russian participation the UN policy would crash to the ground: "The military consequences for the immediate future will be very grave so far as the United States is concerned, particularly in the Far East. In that area, we shall have to understand that a break on this matter with Russia is likely to mean that the entry of Russia into the war against Japan [will] be delayed."

With no security organization, international channels of com-

74. "Conversation by phone with the President," Stettinius to Hull, memorandum, Sept. 17, 1944, SP.

75. Long Diary, Sept. 14 and 19, 1944, Long Papers.

76. American Group, Discussion of Voting Provisions, memorandum, Sept. 14, 1944, SP.

77. Draft memorandum by Long-military group, Sept. 18, 1944, SP. This was essentially the same as the memorandum presented to Hull, but since it was the actual basis of discussion in the American meeting, it is used here.

munication would be weakened. Russia was certain to be the dominant European power after Germany's collapse, and the West would have to assume a heavy burden of arms production to counterbalance this power.

The military advisers proposed three alternatives: First, the president should appeal to Stalin to accept the provisions of the compromise proposal of September 13. Second, if Stalin rejected this compromise, the Long group suggested agreeing that a permanent member of the Security Council could veto any matter. A permanent member could abstain from voting when involved in a dispute. This would absolve that member from charges of unjust voting. If the permanent power chose to vote in its own case, its opponent in the dispute could sit on the Council and also vote. The third alternative, should Russia refuse all compromise, was to accept the Russian view of a veto on all matters. Assistant Secretary Long inaccurately argued this meant "a return to the American position . . . stated in every paper on the subject for more than two years prior to the Dumbarton Oaks Conference and which is in substance the same as the Russians."[78]

The volatile Long vehemently sided with the military proposals.[79] But he erred when he claimed that Hull and the State Department had favored an unqualified veto power for all decisions by the Security Council. This mistake irritated the secretary when Stettinius reported it. Hull claimed that Long's statement to the American group " . . . was completely erroneous. . . . The secretary stressed that he had never made up his mind on this point . . . powers voting when parties to disputes [and] that at one time in his discussions with Congressional groups he had told them that he was in favor of a country *not* voting in a dispute in which it was involved and that the group thought his position was correct."[80] Hull refused to accept the argument of the Long military group and killed their proposals.

Leo Pasvolsky had been a leading architect of this compromise and now worked earnestly to combat Long's attacks. He presented a memorandum to Hull on September 18 in which he argued,

78. Ibid.
79. Long, Diary, Sept. 19, 1944, Long Papers.
80. Stettinius, *DO Diary*, meeting with Hull, Pasvolsky, and Dunn, Sept. 19, 1944, *SP*.

first, that the September 13 compromise preserved the democratic principle that, in pacific decisions, parties to disputes could not judge their own cases. Second, he insisted that a compromise would be more palatable to Congress than the earlier American position because it gave the United States a veto over the use of force in all decisions. Third, it was the compromise position which the American group had strongly favored just before the Dumbarton conversations began. Fourth, the compromise was realistic for it did not set up a theoretical power which could be defeated by any great nation, should that nation decide on the use of unilateral force.[81]

The secretary was gloomy about the prospects,[82] but Stettinius believed a solution could be found: "My own view is that our American Group has gotten a little bit hysterical. We could publish the draft of the document so far with the voting thing as yet to be determined, and adjourn for a month or two and we might get by without any disastrous effects either militarywise or have any domestic reaction from the isolationists. . . . I think the admirals and generals and some of our political advisers have lost their grip and are not thinking straight about this thing at all. I am not discouraged. This thing, while it is not 100 percent a victory, is well around 75 percent a victory, and there is no reason to think this is [as] bad as some of our people are making out."[83]

Stettinius had already concluded that further negotiations on the veto issue must wait personal attention by the Big Three. All other provisions of the Dumbarton Oaks Proposals had now been drafted and Stettinius was eager to conclude the Soviet phase of the talks. He seized on the president's suggestion that the conferees cloak the voting disagreement in covering language, with the understanding that the problem would be studied and renegotiated.[84] He enlisted Cadogan's aid in persuading Gromyko to accept this formula. Cadogan emphasized the broad Allied agreement on a num-

81. Points in Favor of the Compromise Proposal, memorandum, Sept. 18, 1944, SP.

82. Stettinius-Hull, transcript of phone conversation, Sept. 18, 1944; Stettinius, DO Diary, meeting with Hull and Pasvolsky, Sept. 19, 1944, SP.

83. Stettinius, calendar notes, Sept., 1944, SP.

84. Memorandum for the Secretary of State, on the Dumbarton Oaks Situation, Sept. 18, 1944, SP.

ber of vital issues regarding a peace organization.[85] Gromyko delayed his answer until September 27:

> During the course of the meeting Ambassador Gromyko said that he wanted to make it clear that the agreement of his government to participate in a general United Nations conference on world security at a later date is contingent on the British and American governments meeting the Soviet proposals as to voting in the council and on the X matter. On the voting question he said his government wished to reaffirm that it considers the principle of unanimity of the four great powers must be carried out unconditionally.[86]

The next day Stettinius watched the delegates enter the great drawing room at Dumbarton Oaks. Despite its ample size, the room was full as Stettinius rapped for order with a gavel hewn of wood from the old navy ship, *Constitution*. The last meeting of the Soviet phase of the conversations had an unreal atmosphere, for the work had been done in numerous small committees or in impromptu conversations.[87]

The Russians left Dumbarton Oaks, but the Americans and British remained for the Chinese portion of the conversations, which lasted less than a week. One reason for the briefness of the Chinese conversations was that China's Foreign Minister, Wellington Koo, had been in Washington since late August and knew everything that had transpired in the Russian phase of the talks. Stettinius had assigned Assistant Secretary Joseph Grew the job of briefing the Chinese.[88] The Chinese phase consisted largely of confirming decisions already made. China had come to Dumbarton Oaks resigned to accepting the ideas agreed upon by the United States, Britain, and Russia. Koo had explained this to his close friend, Breckinridge Long: "Koo said he had no disposition to quibble about any details; that the most important thing was to agree to *something*; that practically any provisions we should want would be approached by

85. Dumbarton Oaks Joint Steering Committee, minutes, Sept. 27, 1944, *SP*.

86. Ibid.

87. Stettinius, *DO Diary*, Sept. 28, 1944, *SP*.

88. Stettinius, *DO Diary*, Aug. 25, 1944, *SP*.

them in the belief that any United States serious proposal would be fair and without selfish intent."[89]

The Dumbarton Oaks Proposals were released in early October. The world then had its first solid evidence of the determination of the major Allied powers to build a new order for lasting world peace. A remarkable degree of agreement had been achieved on the structure and powers of the proposed international organization. The basic question of regionalism, which had been discussed by the press so prominently during the summer, had caused no serious problem. It was agreed that regional bodies would be subject to the power of the new international organization in the vital area of enforcement. This question, however, was to erupt with great fury in the full-dress United Nations conference the following May.

89. Long, Diary, Aug. 20, 1944, Long Papers.

3

The Specter of Isolationism

POPULAR DISMAY OVER RIFTS IN ALLIED UNITY SOON replaced the happy welcome accorded the Dumbarton Oaks Proposals. By focusing on its postwar UN policy the American government had ignored the pressing political issues that demanded agreement before the UN could function. The Dumbarton Oaks Conference had created a blueprint for the postwar world by which the American public could judge all relations among the Big Four Powers. The American government, now irrevocably committed to the UN policy, found itself forced to push acceptance of the Dumbarton Oaks proposals during a time when events in Europe plainly indicated that Britain and Russia were preparing for a postwar power struggle. This discrepancy brought forth a renewal of American isolationism, the public mood being to reject postwar involvement with Allies who were acting in imperialistic ways. The ultimate result of this American disillusionment later manifested itself in America's quest for security through unilateral power. Under President Truman, this was evident when the U.S. relied first on the atomic bomb and, when that failed, on an anticommunist Western bloc.

This direction of policy, contrary to the views expressed in

Kolko's *Politics of War,* was not one of conscious design for building America as a "free world colossus." The administration after Dumbarton Oaks was divided as to how quickly it should proceed on calling a full meeting of the Allies to write the UN charter, but it agreed that the UN policy itself was perfectly valid. Undersecretary Stettinius, now unofficially Acting Secretary because of Hull's illness, advised Roosevelt to move rapidly on creating the UN. Stettinius argued that by establishing the UN machinery now, it could be used in reconciling the difficult political problems associated with the end of the war. Roosevelt, who had much less faith in the usefulness of the UN for this purpose than either Hull or Stettinius, rejected this advice. He told Stettinius that he preferred to wait until after the elections and wanted to have a meeting with Churchill and Stalin before proceeding on the UN.[1]

By deciding to put off the UN meeting Roosevelt gave up the initiative that he had heretofore enjoyed in diplomacy. The American government's entire postwar planning was bound up in the UN policy of getting Britain and Russia committed to an international democratic community. In convening the great powers at Dumbarton Oaks, the Americans had focused wartime relations on this goal, despite the difficulties occurring at the conference. Then having the lead, the Americans should have pushed on to get the UN organized and operating. Roosevelt's decision to delay was further evidence of his faulty handling of the politics of wartime diplomacy.

The initiative was now seized by the British government. Churchill, whose faith in international organization was a wan flicker compared to the fiery defense he could muster on behalf of the Empire, moved toward a direct deal with Stalin regarding postwar Europe. He had chafed under American pursuit of its UN policy, which he regarded as a diplomatic will-o'-the-wisp, but British ambitions, Churchill fully knew, were limited by American economic power. It was only when the American government showed itself committed fully to the UN policy, via its heavy emphasis on the Dumbarton Oaks negotiations, that Churchill risked the displeasure of Washington by going to Moscow. Thus, the

1. Stettinius to Hull, memorandum, Sept. 26, 1944; Stettinius, calendar notes, Sept. 27, 1944, *SP.*

timing of the events at Dumbarton Oaks and Churchill's mission to Russia were closely related.

The Prime Minister had watched the military success of the Red army with rising alarm. To him the menace of communism "raised its head behind the thundering Russian battle front."[2] After observing the trend of American policy at Dumbarton Oaks, he acted swiftly in early October. Without informing Roosevelt, he cabled Stalin on October 1 and asked to come to Moscow to discuss European questions. Within a week Churchill and Eden were in the Kremlin. Over the next ten days, Churchill and Stalin discussed many European questions, but Churchill raised his paramount concern at the outset. His objective was to secure a pledge from Stalin that Russia would not attempt to move into a politically dominant position in any country bordering the Mediterranean. To this end he offered Stalin a blank check to deal with Rumania and Bulgaria as he wished, if Stalin would grant Greece to the British sphere. Yugoslavia, where Churchill feared communization by Tito, was more of a question mark, and he was satisfied to gain Stalin's assent to a fifty-fifty division of influence between East and West.

This proposal met with rapid assent from Stalin. It achieved part of what Russia had sought throughout the war, British acceptance of Russian territorial gains. It suited Stalin well to have evidence that the two Western democracies were not working in perfect harmony, for he was well aware of American opposition to wartime political decisions. It must have amused Stalin when Churchill, in a moment of conscience, suggested they burn the paper with the jottings of the percentages agreement. Churchill thought the world might think it "cynical if it seemed we had disposed of these issues, so fateful to millions of people, in such an offhand manner. Let us burn the paper." Stalin insisted that Churchill keep his handiwork.[3]

These proceedings had been observed by American Ambassador Averill Harriman, at Roosevelt's suggestion. The president had been angered by Churchill's Moscow trip, and the percentages agreement increased his irritation. Because these events came at the height of his preoccupation with the election campaign, Roosevelt contented himself with informing Stalin that any agreements

2. Churchill, *Triumph and Tragedy*, p. 181.
3. Ibid., pp. 196–197.

would not be binding on the Americans.[4] The chief result was to widen the breach of confidence that was growing between Roosevelt and Churchill.

These events occurred while the State Department was organizing its campaign to promote public support for the Dumbarton Oaks Proposals. Although the American press and public were unaware of the percentages agreement, much of the comment on the UN policy now focused on territorial questions. Could the permanent powers on the Security Council be trusted to keep the peace unselfishly? Or would they cloak expansionist ambitions behind the facade of the UN, using the veto to prevent action unfriendly to their designs? Realizing it was impossible to fathom the answer, most analysts concluded that unanimity among the permanent powers was "realistic." It was argued that no power would thwart the will of the entire world.[5]

Public opinion polls supported the optimism of the professional commentators. The State Department, which utilized private polling groups for elaborate studies on all phases of public opinion, found that 90 percent of the people favored United States participation in a postwar international organization. The American public preferred a limited veto. In response to a question which asked if a great power should have a veto power to "block action of the Council when it itself is accused of aggression," 71 percent of those polled thought a permanent member of the Council should not have this right and 63 percent would be willing for the United States to join the organization even if the peace terms were not fully satisfactory. On the difficult issue of allowing the United States representative on the Security Council the power to commit troops without prior congressional approval, there was a balanced division of opinion.[6] This poll, conducted for the department by the office of opinion research of Princeton University the week before the Dumbarton Oaks Proposals were published, marked a high tide in public optimism during the war years. Erosion of public confidence became evident in the face of adverse developments in the winter of 1944–1945.

4. *Stalin's Correspondence*, 2: 162–164.
5. *Washington Post*, Oct. 10, 1944.
6. Stettinius to Roosevelt, "Public Opinion on International Organization," memorandum, Oct. 19, 1944, Official File 5557, Roosevelt Papers.

Stettinius, whose forte in industry had been public relations, avidly studied polling results in the belief that they were valid indicators of public opinion. He turned energetically to selling the Dumbarton Oaks Proposals to the American people. Stettinius took personal command of the publicity campaign, aided effectively by John S. Dickey, chief of the department's public liaison division. They ordered American participants in the Dumbarton Oaks Conference to devote their efforts to the "highly important" public information program. By the time Stettinius issued this directive on November 4, thousands of pamphlets promoting the proposals were coming off the presses and department experts had already participated in eleven informational meetings.[7]

Stettinius concentrated his effort on lining up private organizations to assist the department in a mammoth campaign to sell the Proposals to America. He went first to private internationalist groups, for their attitude was vital in molding general public opinion. The oldest and most prestigious of these groups was the League of Nations Association (founded in 1924) and the Commission to Study the Organization of Peace (established in 1939). The older group endorsed the Dumbarton Oaks Proposals a day after their publication, and the Commission acted favorably after a review of several weeks.[8] The newer internationalist groups expressed greater dissatisfaction. Americans United for World Organization, which had been organized in the summer of 1944, remained silent until mid-November, then refused to give outright endorsement. Instead a press release, issued by its president, Dr. Ernest M. Hopkins, president of Dartmouth College, called the proposals "a first long step." The two-year-old Non-Partisan Council did not comment until December 27; then it stated that the proposals could be considered only as a basis of discussion and that many changes were essential.[9]

Many internationalists feared that the Dumbarton Oaks Proposals pointed toward a concert of powers, but they realized the dangers if they turned their backs on the administration. This was

7. Stettinius to Members of the American Delegation at Dumbarton Oaks, memorandum, Nov. 4, 1944, SP.

8. Divine, Second Chance, pp. 31–33, 53–54, 164–165, and 232.

9. Americans United Press Release, Nov. 21, 1944; Non-Partisan Council Press Release, Dec. 27, 1944, Carnegie Endowment Archives 64055, Columbia University Library, New York. [Hereinafter cited as CEA.]

precisely what had occurred in 1919 when the liberals, in a fit of pique, deserted Wilson because he failed to achieve all his announced goals. Now liberal editors warned that by expecting perfection they would provide ammunition for an isolationist resurgence. Stettinius sought to bind all groups together in a huge meeting held on October 16. It included representatives of ninety-five private organizations of all types. Patriotic groups such as the American Legion and the Daughters of the American Revolution sent delegates and subsequently backed passage of the United Nations Charter. In later years, however, these organizations preferred to forget their role as advocates of the UN policy. There were religious, union, educational, and farm groups represented—indeed all interest groups in the country were present through some organization.[10]

In his greeting, Stettinius described the Dumbarton Oaks Proposals as a "synthesis" of the major powers' views and claimed that "the wide area of agreement" they had achieved demonstrated the "broad harmony of purpose and intention which united the four principal United Nations." Stettinius pointed out the tentative nature of the proposals and called for "wide, intelligent, and maturing consideration" by the American people as the process of writing the charter moved forward: "Only as there develops in this country a substantial and informed body of public opinion can the government go forward successfully in the task of participation in the further steps needed for the establishment of an international organization. Only against the background of such a body of public opinion can the organization itself function effectively, for no institution, however perfect, can live and fulfill its purposes unless it is continuously animated and supported by strong public will and determination."[11]

At this and ensuing meetings the State Department found a receptive audience, with the participants ready to ask questions and express opinions. Even the lack of precision in the replies of

10. Selig Adler, *The Isolationist Impulse. Its Twentieth Century Reaction,* chap. 3; *Nation,* 159 (Oct. 21, 1944): 451; *New Republic,* 111 (Oct. 2, 1944): 429; ibid. (Oct. 23, 1944): 510–511; Stettinius to Hopkins, Sept. 15, 1944, *SP;* U.S., Department of State, *Bulletin,* 11 (Oct. 22, 1944): 450–451, cites the figure of ninety-five organizations; but Divine, *Second Chance,* p. 245, places it at "more than a hundred."

11. U.S., Department of State, *Bulletin,* 11 (Oct. 22, 1944): 452.

State Department officials failed to dampen the enthusiasm. After the meeting Hopkins told Stettinius that appreciation of the State Department's efforts "is going to be repeated to thousands of their associates all over the areas east of the Rocky Mountains." An official of Americans United best summed up the reaction: "I don't know how you people in the State Department feel about it, but we think this has been a red-letter day in the history of the State Department. It seems revolutionary for the Department to call in representatives of the public and discuss matters."[12]

While moving ahead with this massive publicity campaign, on the assumption that Roosevelt would win reelection, high State Department officials watched for signs that the Republicans might break the tenuous bipartisan agreement on the UN policy. Hull received a gloomy forecast from White House aide Josephus Daniels. The GOP, he warned, " . . . has not changed its colors since Lodge and Harding sabotaged the League of Nations. . . . If we are to win, we must pull every string."[13] Hull feared that Vandenberg might inject the war power of Congress into the campaign. To avoid this, he assiduously courted Dulles and played on the eastern Republicans' fear of Vandenberg's isolationist supporters and stressed the need for a united stand to keep Vandenberg in line.[14]

As for outright opposition to the Dumbarton Oaks Proposals, there was little in the campaign. Hull had provided Dewey with an advance text of the Proposals and elicited the Republican nominee's criticisms. Dulles, in his role as foreign policy adviser to Dewey, had responded with a memorandum which suggested actually enlarging the power of the international organization in the field of domestic jurisdiction. Citing vast armies, propaganda, persecution of minorities, and misrule of colonial peoples as causes for wars, Dulles called for omitting the domestic jurisdiction clause. "The best hope of future peace lies in recognition of the fact that any national action which in fact has disturbing external repercussions is not just a domestic matter but a matter of general concern."[15]

12. "Reaction to the Discussion Meeting of October 16 with Leaders of National Organizations," memorandum, n.d., SP.
13. Josephus Daniels to Hull, Sept. 12, 1944, Hull Papers.
14. Stettinius, DO Diary, Sept. 17, 1944, SP.
15. Republican diplomat Hugh R. Wilson acted as the on-the-scenes man for the GOP during the Dumbarton Oaks Conference. His work was so confidential that only Hull and Assistant Secretary James C. Dunn knew of his

Shortly after the Proposals were released, Dewey issued a statement endorsing them. It was not that the New York governor would not have welcomed a reason to attack Roosevelt on foreign policy questions. Neither he nor Dulles wanted to do anything to undermine the president's position in matters where both parties had taken a bipartisan position.[16]

The Democrats benefited most directly from a split within the Republican party. When Wendell Willkie fell ill in late September, Senator Joseph Ball (R-Minnesota) stepped into the role of chief GOP spokesman for internationalism. He doubted Dewey's sincerity on the UN and dramatically announced on September 29 that he could no longer back the nominee. Coming from a man who had seconded Dewey's nomination, this was a body blow to the governor's hopes. Dewey seemed caught by surprise, and his replies to Ball's challenges about his UN views were ambiguous, especially on the question of committing American forces to UN action by executive authority.[17]

Roosevelt quickly took advantage of the GOP division. Addressing the Foreign Policy Association in New York on October 21, he linked the Republicans to isolationism. Then he told his large audience that the Security Council of the United Nations must " . . . have the power to act quickly to keep the peace by force, if necessary." Turning to his favorite oratorical device of the homely analogy, Roosevelt asked whether anyone would expect the police to call a town meeting to obtain authorization before stopping a burglary. "So to my simple mind," he deduced, "it is clear that, if the world organization is to have any reality at all, our American representative must be endowed in advance by the peo-

---

role. Hugh R. Wilson to Dulles, Oct. 4, 1944, Dulles Papers; Dulles to Hull, memorandum, Oct. 3, 1944, SP.

16. Herbert Brownell Interview, 2–7, Dulles Oral History Project, Dulles Papers.

17. Overcautiousness explains, I believe, much of the uncertainty that marked Dewey's campaign at this point. Dewey relied heavily on Dulles; and Dulles's correspondence shows that he was undecided on crucial questions such as the powers of the American representative on the Security Council, Dulles to Vandenberg, Sept. 9 and 11, 1944; Vandenberg to Dulles, Sept. 6 and 11, 1944; Dulles to Severs Mallet-Prevost, Sept. 13, 1944; Dulles to Dr. Kenneth Thompson, Nov. 21, 1944, Dulles Papers; Divine, Second Chance, pp. 237–240.

ple themselves, by constitutional means through their representatives in the Congress, with authority to act."[18]

Within two days Roosevelt garnered the fruits of his thrust at Republican isolationism when Senator Ball declared he would support Roosevelt for reelection. Though Dewey had given the Dumbarton Oaks Proposals a clear endorsement, he had failed to win the backing of the internationalists. After mid-October, internationalist journals seemed convinced that Roosevelt represented the best hope of liberal world organization. The *New Republic* thought that Ball's stand had done much to harm the GOP, while the *New York Times*, which had opposed Roosevelt in 1940, praised Ball's courage and announced its support for Roosevelt's reelection. *Times* publisher Arthur H. Sulzberger told Undersecretary Stettinius that his paper's officials had decided to support the Democrats because Dewey projected an inadequate image in world affairs. Sulzberger explained that, while the *Times* believed FDR was undesirable on grounds of domestic policy, Roosevelt's views on foreign problems were less likely to result in a new war than those of the Republicans. Walter Lippmann told Stettinius that Dewey had been a disappointment as a candidate, and he followed this up in his column by asserting that Dewey was still too green in the vital area of international relations and " . . . cannot be trusted now with responsibility in foreign affairs." Malcolm H. Davis, who represented the Carnegie Endowment Fund in administering funds allocated to support the work of private internationalist organizations, expressed the relief felt in these groups. Writing to Edgar A. Mowrer of the Non-Partisan Council, Davis said that by his New York statement Roosevelt "has pretty well cleared the decks" with regard to his position on the powers of the United States delegate.[19]

Thus Roosevelt was able to capture the initiative in the campaign regarding foreign affairs even though the central question of international organization was supposedly sacrosanct. Fears in some Democratic quarters, expressed by Breckinridge Long in a memorandum to Hull, were that the Republicans were trying to twist the proceedings at Dumbarton Oaks and make it appear to the

18. Samuel Rosenman, ed., *The Public Papers and Addresses of Franklin D. Roosevelt* (13 vols.), 13: 344–350.

19. *New Republic,* 111 (Oct. 23, 1944): 520; *New York Times,* Oct. 23, 1944; Stettinius, calendar notes, Oct. 18, 1944, *SP*; Malcolm Davis to Edgar A. Mowrer, Oct. 24, 1944, *CEA* 64039.

people that Dewey had been the moving force in the progress toward world organization. To Long it had seemed that the bipartisan approach on foreign policy was in "real danger." It was the president who had found an opening in the bipartisan agreement and had violated the spirit of the understanding. As Robert Divine has observed, "Dewey provided the opportunity when he failed to answer Ball's third question promptly, and Roosevelt adroitly exploited this lapse to capture the internationalist vote."[20]

Roosevelt's electoral margin was a huge 432 to 99, but the popular vote was closer, the president winning 53.7 percent of the ballots. The Democratic victory was interpreted as definitive evidence that the United States had repudiated the experience of 1919. There would be no turning away from world organization after this war. The *New York Times* saw the election as atonement for America's betrayal of Wilson. "The election returns have announced to the world that 1944 is not 1920!" the *Nation* proudly proclaimed. Certainly the congressional elections demonstrated the shift toward electing leaders with a broad world view. All over the nation isolationist senators had lost in primaries; and those who won in the primaries, such as Gerald Nye (R-North Dakota), went down to defeat on November 7. New senators like Wayne Morse, William Fulbright, and Leverett Saltonstall were avowed internationalists.[21]

Whether Roosevelt's victory was fortunate for the nation is debatable. At the time it was hailed as assuring fulfillment of the UN policy. The unfortunate fact was that Roosevelt's grip on policy matters was slipping seriously. At the crux of the problem, even more than the president's health, was the general disarray in coordinating foreign policy. Cordell Hull was ill and embittered by the shabby treatment he believed Roosevelt had accorded him during the recent Quebec Conference. After solemnly promising to summon Hull if political questions arose at Quebec, Roosevelt sent for Treasury Secretary Morgenthau and accepted his plan for postwar Germany, which undercut months of planning by the State Department. Although Roosevelt soon abandoned the Morgenthau Plan, Hull decided that it was time to resign.

20. Long to Hull, memorandum, Oct. 19, 1944, Long Papers; Divine, *Second Chance*, p. 241; Burns, *Roosevelt: The Soldier of Freedom*, p. 526.
21. Divine, *Second Chance*, p. 241.

Before entering the hospital Hull went to the White House for a showdown, but Roosevelt persuaded him not to quit immediately, as this action might throw the election to Dewey. After Roosevelt's victory Stettinius became the liaison man in the secret struggle between Roosevelt and Hull. The president's attempts to keep Hull in office frustrated Stettinius. He felt the State Department was crippled at a decisive moment of the war, and he bluntly expressed his fears to Roosevelt " . . . that regardless of the Secretary's situation . . . things in the Department had to be straightened out, that if we didn't move fast there would be all sorts of criticism from the newspapers and columnists and the Congress—that we had these gigantic world situations ahead of us, the International Organization, and I told the president frankly we just didn't have competent people in the Department. . . . we had to straighten it out ourselves. The president agreed and said 'You're dead right.' I mentioned to the President that I was getting the work done all right, but if I was going to carry on I had to have help. Mr. Hull had been away for two months, I was Acting Secretary, my place as Undersecretary was vacant, Long had been away for a month, Berle was in Chicago, Shaw had been away for a week, Jimmy Dunn was on a holiday, Norman Armour was not well and didn't like his work, and I was practically, with the exception of Acheson, running the whole works alone. I said, 'Mr. President, we will have to move in a bold sweeping manner to save this situation and to strengthen it [the Department] in order to be equipped to carry the load. . . . We have to revitalize the Department.'"[22]

Roosevelt proved receptive and, seizing on the idea of revitalization, said, " 'That's a good word and applies exactly.' " The two men talked about prospective changes, and Stettinius drew out of his pocket a memorandum he had written in longhand, gave

22. Fred L. Israel, ed., *Long Diary*, p. 387. Long has interesting coverage of Hull's resignation, but he mistakenly thought he was the only person who knew what was on Hull's mind. For illustration of Hull's irritation over Roosevelt's policy on Germany and Lend-Lease, see Stimson, Diary, Sept. 9–12 and Oct. 19, 1944, Stimson Papers; Hull, *Memoirs*, 2: 1715–1718; Stettinius, calendar notes, Nov. 20, 1944; Stettinius-Roosevelt memorandum of conversation, Nov. 21, 1944; Stettinius calendar notes on meeting with Roosevelt, Nov. 21, 1944; on Hull's resignation, see Stettinius, calendar notes on visit with Hull, Nov. 20, 1944; memorandum of conversations with Roosevelt, Nov. 21, 1944; calendar notes, on conversation with Mrs. Hull, Nov. 21, 1944; and calendar notes, Nov. 26, 1944, SP.

it to Roosevelt and stated, "Now here are the kind of people and the names we ought to have as a start." The extensive discussion which followed clearly indicates that Stettinius expected to be chosen as Hull's successor. They covered changes among top State Department posts as well as shifts in ambassadorial posts. With only one exception, the men whom Stettinius suggested were the ones Roosevelt nominated to Congress in December.[23]

The White House announcement of Hull's resignation on November 26 brought little surprise. Hull's entry into the hospital weeks earlier, the hurried going to and fro of Stettinius, and even the president himself had stirred speculation. The hottest talk around the capital centered around a successor. Editors and radio commentators focused on Hull the statesman, his liberal trade policies, and his dreams of fulfilling the Wilsonian tradition. The doubts voiced were given to how a successor could carry out the vital work of establishing the international peace organization.

Roosevelt chose Undersecretary Stettinius to succeed Hull as Secretary of State. The news met with enthusiastic public approval. White House mail ran heavily in favor of the selection. Stettinius was well-known. A poll conducted by the American Institute of Public Opinion, headed by George Gallup, showed that 58 percent of those asked had heard of Stettinius, a percentage that Gallup called "high" for a man relatively new to political life. Most important, among those who knew him, 92 percent approved his appointment as secretary of state. Gallup commented, "Probably few men appointed to any cabinet have started with such a high vote of personal approval from the rank and file of the nation."[24]

Stettinius's youth was commented on widely, and his lack of diplomatic experience was questioned. Yet editorials emphasized his successful handling of wartime assignments and brilliant record in business. Many editors seemed to believe that achievement in the business world would guarantee success in diplomacy.[25] The

23. Ibid.

24. For reaction to the Stettinius nomination, File Box 23, Official File, Roosevelt Papers; Richard L. Walker, *Edward Stettinius,* vol. 14 in Ferrell, ed., *American Secretaries,* pp. 9–13 for a good appraisal of Stettinius's appointment.

25. *Knoxville Journal,* Nov. 29, 1944, was one of the few papers criticizing Stettinius as inexperienced in diplomacy. Far more typical were those praising his attainments in industry and achievements in wartime service. See, *Boston*

general belief was that Roosevelt had selected Stettinius because he commanded wide respect on Capitol Hill, which would be an important asset in pushing the UN Charter through the Senate.

Some observers saw Stettinius as a younger Cordell Hull. Stettinius had succeeded in winning the job, it was said, because he had worked closely and harmoniously with Hull. This was a favorite point brought out by cartoonists—Hull with his hands on Stettinius's shoulders, or turning over the helm to Stettinius, or Hull's robe of leadership now worn by Stettinius. The distinct feeling imparted was that Stettinius had inherited the Hull legacy and would simply continue until Hull's goals were fulfilled. A second assumption was that Roosevelt intended to continue as his own secretary of state. Most observers found it acceptable that Roosevelt should direct affairs both in the White House and at the State Department. The *Albany Knickerbocker*, in assessing Stettinius as an indecisive man, said, "If Mr. Roosevelt is to control foreign affairs completely, it might be better for unity if his Secretary is not a dominant personality." Or as *Time* magazine expressed it, "Few doubted that under [Stettinius's] regime the real Secretary of State would continue to be Franklin Roosevelt."[26]

No commentators knew the inside story of Hull's resignation or how Roosevelt had virtually selected Stettinius before accepting Hull's decision. The popular image of Stettinius as a front man entered the record and was perpetuated by historians. The history of these events thus missed an important facet of American diplomacy in the late war years, namely, the efficiency that Stettinius brought to the State Department's operations.

Stettinius set out immediately in December to correct the disarray in communications between the State Department and the White House. Stettinius made two major innovations to improve communications. He appointed Charles E. Bohlen to work in the White House as a special expediter and liaison between the White

---

Herald, New York World Telegram, Brooklyn Citizen, Minneapolis Star-Journal, all Nov. 28, 1944.

26. Stettinius, scrapbook number 50, contains a number of such cartoons, and there are others among the unfiled memorabilia in the Stettinius Papers; Albany (N.Y.) *Knickerbocker News*, Nov. 28, 1944; *Time*, 44 (Dec. 4, 1944): 11; similar views were contained in *Seattle Times*, Dec. 1, 1944; *New York World* and *New York Herald-Tribune*, both Nov. 28, 1944; *Philadelphia Inquirer*, Dec. 1, 1944.

House and the Department of State. Stettinius also created a top-level State-War-Navy coordinating committee. On December 19 Stettinius and Navy Secretary Forrestal met with War Secretary Stimson. They discussed "the present chaotic situation" hampering relations among their departments. Stettinius said that important diplomatic information coming into the State Department often had not reached Stimson and Forrestal whereas the State Department might miss information coming through military channels that would be of benefit to the Secretary of State. It was decided to arrange for Assistant Secretary James Dunn, acting as chairman, to meet weekly with Artemus Gates of the Navy and John J. McCloy of the War Department for the purpose of exchanging information and discussing mutual problems. That same day the three men met and agreed that State Department communications should go to the Joint Chiefs of Staff through the War and Navy Departments. This corrected a practice that had constantly upset Stimson: Hull had often dealt directly with the JCS, leaving Stimson and Forrestal uninformed.[27]

These changes in external communications were matched by similar efforts to streamline top-level communications within the Department of State. Foremost among these changes was the creation of the Secretary's Staff Committee, consisting of Stettinius, Grew, the Assistant Secretaries, and Pasvolsky and Hackworth. These men met each morning and achieved a regular means of keeping abreast of current problems to a degree unknown in the Hull administration.[28]

All these efforts brought enthusiastic approval from Stimson, Marshall, and Grew. Stimson had felt for months that Roosevelt and Hull were slipping in their control of decision-making. Com-

27. FRUS, 1944, Vol. 1, General, pp. 1466–1470; Stimson Diary, Sept. 11, Dec. 19, 1944, Stimson Papers.

28. Walter Lawes and Francis O. Wilcox, "The State Department Continues Its Reorganization," American Political Science Review, 39 (Apr., 1945): 309–317; Walter Johnson, "Edward R. Stettinius, Jr.," in Norman Graebner, ed., Uncertain Tradition, American Secretaries of State and Their Diplomacy in the Twentieth Century, p. 214; Undersecretary Grew, who served forty years in the Department of State, observed of Stettinius's reforms, ". . . the old Department had never in all its history . . . been so effectively organized as under the Stettinius regime. He understood teamwork better than any chief I have ever served under." Joseph C. Grew to Robert J. Lynch, Sept. 28, 1945, in Joseph C. Grew, Turbulent Era, A Diplomatic Record of Forty Years, 1904–1945, ed. Walter Johnson (2 vols), 2: 1524.

menting on Stettinius's performance at the first State-War-Navy committee meeting, Stimson wrote, "The whole meeting was full of pep and energy. My only fear is that they might in some respects be going a little too fast and run up against some of the usual snags that I found my course blocked by in the past. But I am very glad that they should be so forward-minded and energetic about it."[29] After his next meeting with Stettinius and Forrestal, Stimson commented that Stettinius's approach was "a real refresher." Stettinius had presented an "organized program" of information from his Department which he thought would be useful to Navy and War. Stimson thought the new system contrasted favorably with the "decadence" that marked Hull's contacts with himself and Forrestal. It would also help to regulate the three departments' relations with the president: "It served as a pattern for other meetings and it showed how we could be drawn together and the necessary spade work done to clear the track and, being in that position, we were less likely to get overruled by some fantasy of the President's."[30] Marshall commented to Stimson that he was "greatly pleased" with Stettinius's efforts and thought that the new committees "would be a great source of assistance and regularization of the work of the Joint Chiefs of Staff."[31]

The significance of Stettinius's effort was that it brought diplomatic and military decision-making into a closer relationship at the very time when many men in the State, War, and Navy Departments, as well as the Joint Chiefs, were seeking ways to focus their rising doubts about communism. So long as Roosevelt remained president his policy of cooperation with Russia was followed by the American government. With Roosevelt's death in April, 1945, Truman found Stettinius, Stimson, and Forrestal anxious for a stiffer approach in dealing with the Russians. By bringing the military and civilian leaders into a close liaison from December, 1944, on, Stettinius greatly contributed to this shift in approach.

Stettinius's new directions for the State Department could not bear immediate fruit. Much to his displeasure, he found himself hamstrung during his first month in office by problems in getting

29. Stimson Diary, Sept. 16, 17, and Dec. 19, 1944, Stimson Papers.
30. Ibid., Dec. 27, 1944.
31. Stimson paraphrasing Marshall, Stimson Diary, Dec. 19, 1944, Stimson Papers.

the Senate Foreign Relations Committee to act on the nominations Roosevelt had submitted for assistant secretaries. The hearings of the Foreign Relations Committee were not significant except as an indication of the slow working of the Senate machinery, and they brought out no important debate on fundamental issues in foreign policy. They came, however, at a time of severe testing of the administration's UN policy arising out of divergent Allied policies. Entangled in the hearings, the State Department was less effective at a moment of crisis than it might have been.[32]

This dilemma in Allied relations arose out of Churchill's attempts to capitalize on his percentage deal with Stalin. Believing that he could move forcefully in the Mediterranean politics because he had neutralized the Russians, Churchill stepped into a crisis of government in Italy in early December. The Cabinet of Premier Ivanhoe Bonomi was reorganized to include left-wing elements through the appointment of Count Carlo Sforza as Foreign Minister. Churchill regarded Sforza as pro-communist and announced that Britain would not support any Italian government which included him in the cabinet.

Reports reaching the State Department from London expressed the conviction of Ambassador John G. Winant and other United States observers that the British were acting in a high-handed manner. It was argued that Sforza's presence in a government did not portend a communist takeover, that Churchill was acting out of personal pique, and that no vital British interests would be threatened if Sforza did become Foreign Minister. The real culprit was Churchill, who wanted an Italian government completely subject to his will.[33]

The U.S. press adopted a highly critical position, accusing the British of sacrificing the Atlantic Charter on the altar of power

32. *Congressional Record*, 78th Cong., 2nd sess., 1944, pt. 7: 8901–8908; Allen Drury, *Senate Journal*, pp. 306–307; Minutes of Meeting in Room 285, Dec. 11, 1944, SP; U.S., Congress, Senate, *Hearings Before the Committee on Foreign Relations, United States Senate, 78th Cong., on the Nominations of Joseph C. Grew et al.*, Dec. 12 and 13, 1944 (Washington, 1944), pp. 74, 79–85; Stettinius-Byrd, transcripts of phone conversations, Dec. 16 and 18, 1944; Stettinius, calendar notes, Dec. 9 and 18, 1944; Stettinius to Roosevelt, telegram, Dec. 18, 1944, SP.

33. Anthony Eden, *The Reckoning*, pp. 574–582; Stettinius, Record, vol. 1, pp. 7–10, SP, an account of his service as Secretary of State, compiled from official sources; *FRUS, 1945, Conferences at Yalta and Malta*, p. 429.

politics.[34] Within a few days of Churchill's statement reporters besieged the State Department about the American position on the Italian question. Without taking time to consult the British Ambassador, Stettinius authorized preparation of a statement. Then he read it in person to reporters on December 5. Stettinius declared American policy to be that Italy and other European nations should work out their own political destinies: "The position of this Government has been consistently that the composition of the Italian Government is purely an Italian affair. . . . This Government has not in any way intimated to the Italian Government that there would be any opposition on its part to Count Sforza. . . . We have reaffirmed to both the British and Italian Governments that we expect the Italians to work out their problems of government along democratic lines without influence from the outside. This policy would apply to an even more pronounced degree with regards to governments of the United Nations in their liberated territories."[35] The afternoon papers carried an account of the Stettinius statement, and by the morning of December 6 the news of an Anglo-American split was being read by millions. Much of the editorial comment was favorable. At last the United States was taking a positive stand and telling Churchill that Washington would not tolerate a return to British imperialism.

News from Greece compounded the Anglo-American crisis. A civil war erupted in Athens in early December in which British-backed royalist forces were pitted against the communist guerrilla National Liberation Front (EAM). Coverage in the American news media was sympathetic toward the EAM and painted the British as imperialists. Throughout December, British military units participated in the effort to suppress the communist uprising, and Churchill and Eden paid a visit to Athens at the height of the fighting.[36]

To most Americans British moves in the Mediterranean were seen simply as a return to imperialism. Much of the irritation with Britain represented a deep-seated distrust of British motives, harkening back to World War I and earlier, a feeling that the British

34. *Washington Times-Herald*, Dec. 7, 1944; *New Republic*, 111 (Dec. 11, 1944): 783–784.

35. U.S., Department of State, *Bulletin*, 11 (Dec. 10, 1944): 722.

36. *FRUS, 1944*, vol. 5, *The Near East, South Asia, Africa, the Far East*, pp. 141–161; Eden, *The Reckoning*, pp. 574–582.

had always tried to use the Americans to preserve their empire. A considerable amount of this Anglophobia was an expression of the isolationism rooted deep in the American spirit. Assessing the impact of the Stettinius statement, *Time* magazine warned, "Between U.S. meddling and abstention, Europeans found ground for revival of their worst fear: that at war's end the U.S. would refuse, as it had 24 years ago, to accept its share of responsibility for the peace."[37]

Statements of righteous indignation came from the Congress where Senator Allen Ellender (D-Louisiana) castigated Britain for "taking the lead in causing disunity among the Allies." He expressed his conviction that the British hoped to expand their already vast empire by forming power blocs of nations "here and there all over the world."[38] Stettinius reported to the president in Warm Springs that the members of the Senate Foreign Relations Committee were "considerably aroused" over the British actions in the Mediterranean. The committee wanted, he said, a clear American expression of democratic freedoms for the people of Europe. There was growing concern that the United States might become entangled in the British action, particularly in Greece, where there were many American relief officials in the midst of the fighting. The president maintained silence on the Mediterranean crisis, leaving Stettinius to bear the brunt of the public furor.[39]

Criticisms from the *Washington Daily News*, the *Chicago Tribune*, and Ellender, echoed the post-World War I attitude that the governments of Europe could never be trusted to break from their old habits of military alliances and balance of power politics —evil devices from which the United States must stay aloof. The internationalists also blasted the British, charging that British actions threatened the delicate framework of postwar cooperation which had been achieved during the Dumbarton Oaks conversations. The *New Republic* accused Churchill of trying to establish a "pro-Mussolini conservative and capitalist state" by supporting the right-wing elements. Americans United for World Organization sent a statement of endorsement to Stettinius noting that previously

37. *Time*, 44 (Dec. 18, 1944): 17.
38. U.S., Congress, Senate, *Congressional Record*, 78th Cong., 2d sess., 1944, pt. 7: 8975–8976.
39. Stettinius to Roosevelt, telegram, Dec. 14, 1944, *SP*.

there had been no clear statement of Anglo-American policy. The new secretary was hailed for accepting the slogan of Americans United: "nail to the American masthead . . . the phrase 'We will not have truck with fascism.'" The Stettinius policy was also associated with the struggle for a new international organization. "The strongest peace enforcement machinery will not suffice to enforce a peace which is not based upon justice and the worldwide establishment of human freedom."[40] From his New York headquarters where he was directing a major campaign to acquaint the American people with the Dumbarton Oaks Proposals, Clark Eichelberger wrote to Stettinius that his statement "will certainly serve both the ideals and the self-interest of the United States to be the inspiration of the small states in the United Nations Organization."[41]

If he received praise and support from various spokesmen for American opinion, Stettinius drew a wrathful reaction from the British. The day after his press statement Stettinius received a call from Michael Wright, counsellor in the British embassy. Wright informed the secretary that a cable had arrived from Eden expressing deep British resentment. Churchill and Eden had been extremely embarrassed and faced a serious challenge in the House of Commons. The United States statement had exacerbated a difficult political situation. Wright regretted that he could not provide Stettinius a copy of Eden's message but it was "too personal," and "too unpleasant" in tone. He described the prime minister as angered that the American government had placed him "on a hot spot." Then, expressing the real intent of his call, Wright asked the secretary to help undo the damage. The British suggestion was that at a news conference the secretary could arrange for a question on the American view of the Greek situation. In reply Stettinius might say that he had noted Churchill's statement on the floor of Parliament expressing faith in the importance of democratic institutions. Stettinius might say that the United States and Britain saw eye to eye on this matter. This would be of great help to Churchill in answering his critics.

Stettinius was only partially moved by Wright's appeal. He had acted correctly, he believed, in replying to the American popular

40. *New Republic*, 111 (Dec. 11, 1944): 783–784; *Congressional Record*, 78th Cong., 2d sess., 1944, pt. 11: Appendix, A4656–A4657.
41. Eichelberger to Stettinius, Dec. 6, 1944, *SP*.

demand that the State Department express clearly the goals of United States foreign policy. He called Wright's attention to the favorable expressions of congressional and press support. He also criticized Churchill for failing to give the American government advance notice. Had the State Department been properly advised, the split might never have developed. Stettinius insisted "that all we have done is to reiterate the policy agreed upon between your government and this government at Moscow." Nonetheless, he promised an effort to heal the breach.[42]

The next day, December 7, Stettinius told reporters that he was pleased with Prime Minister Churchill's assurance to Parliament that the choice of the government in Athens was entirely a matter for Greeks to decide. The United States was in "full agreement" with this approach and hoped that the British and Greeks could work together effectively in rebuilding Greece.[43] This provided Churchill some ammunition in fighting a Labour Party censure motion, but it did little to rehabilitate the British image in the minds of the American people. In fact, Stettinius, who thought he had been essentially correct in his original pronouncement, so filled his second statement with references to self-determination that his new statement was interpreted as reinforcing the first one.[44]

These events convinced Stettinius by mid-December that America's UN policy faced catastrophe unless Roosevelt moved to restore public confidence. But the president's next action only made matters worse. No sooner had Roosevelt returned to the capital from Warm Springs than he startled reporters with a casual remark that neither he nor Churchill had ever signed the Atlantic Charter. This was widely interpreted as a move to downgrade the charter's significance. Roosevelt spoke up in defense of the charter's principles at his December 22 news conference, but it was too late. Public confidence in the administration was seriously shaken.[45]

To State Department officials, the most disturbing impact of the crisis in Allied relations was the damage to the people's faith in the Dumbarton Oaks Proposals. The energetic campaign by the

42. Stettinius, calendar notes, Dec. 6, 1944, SP.

43. U.S., Department of State, Bulletin, 11 (Dec. 10, 1944): 722.

44. Time, 44 (Dec. 18, 1944): 17; New Republic, 111 (Dec. 18, 1944): 815–816.

45. New York Times, Dec. 20, 1944, and Dec. 23, 1944.

Department and private internationalist groups to sell the proposals to the public had created national discussion, and there had
been hundreds of suggestions for modifications. All of which events
were healthy enough until the analysis of the Dumbarton Oaks
agreements got entangled in the disillusionment with events in
Europe. Reports coming across Stettinius's desk by December 21
plainly showed that dangerous development.

A State Department survey of leading midwestern newspaper
editors indicated that, while they supported the idea of a postwar
organization, recent developments in eastern Europe and the Balkans had forced them to conclude that a substantial reappraisal
of the Dumbarton Oaks Proposals was necessary. Stettinius warned
the president that unless Britain and Russia altered their policies
in the liberated areas, "favorable action on the world security organization may be jeopardized," and the United States might retreat into isolationism. Despite efforts to publicize the proposals,
opinion polls indicated widespread ignorance of the structure and
functions of the projected organization. Under these circumstances,
a turn to isolationism could easily occur.[46]

Stettinius pressed Roosevelt to issue a vigorous statement of
American foreign policy. At the first meeting of his staff committee
Stettinius dwelt on this need, and MacLeish added that there was
real danger that the presidential silence on foreign policy might in-
duce anger over apparent attempts to keep the public in ignorance.
Stettinius directed MacLeish to work with presidential speech
writer Sam Rosenman to include in the upcoming state of the
Union message a positive, forthright declaration of American goals.
When the Secretary of State met with Roosevelt on December 30,
however, he found that the president thought the State Department recommendations "went a bit far at this time." He preferred
to confine the State of the Union message to generalities, "that he
should primarily say we had gone to war because we had been attacked by aggressors and that it was our desire to end the war and
bring our troops home as soon as possible." Stettinius was distressed
at the president's failure to assert strong leadership in Allied rela-

46. Stettinius to Roosevelt, memorandum with enclosed "Observations
from the Midwest," Dec. 21, 1944; U.S., Department of State, Fortnightly
Surveys of American Opinion on International Affairs, December: Last Half,
No. 18, Jan. 6, 1945, SP.

tions. He pressed his point by showing Roosevelt public opinion polls, gathered by the State Department, which reflected increasing discontent among the people. He also noted privately of the president, "He did not show in his discussion with me the keen grasp I had hoped he would get from the memorandum we had sent to him." But Stettinius had no alternative except to direct a rewriting of the foreign policy section of the state of the Union message.[47]

It was indeed as Bruce Bliven observed in the *New Republic*, "Not a Merry Christmas." The carols, the flickering candles in windows, the tinny sounding little bells of Salvation Army workers, all seemed a little more forlorn that Christmas season of 1944. Hope of early victory was crushed by the German counteroffensive in the Ardennes forest, and the vision of postwar international cooperation was clouded by the resurgence of old fears of power politics, so common to Europe, so detested by the still innocent Americans. As Bliven lamented:

> This is no merry Christmas. War abroad, victory delayed and inter-Allied dissension; and at home, a grim choice between the lofty principles of the Atlantic Charter and our Allies. But since we cannot abandon our Allies without abandoning our sons at the front, there is really no choice at all. A scaling down of the Atlantic Charter, willy nilly seems the inevitable consequence of recent developments in Greece and Poland. . . . That is the real choice which internationalists will have to make, like it or not—and it is not an agreeable one. Are they prepared to reconcile themselves, under protest, to Anglo-Soviet spheres of influence in Europe so far as they have gone, and fight to salvage the world-security organization? Or are they to be provoked into the perfection which certainly kills the treaty?[48]

The president seemed determined to do as little as possible to allay public fears. He even abandoned his usual practice of delivering the state of the Union message personally and sent it to be read by the Clerk of the House. It was an uninspiring statement

47. Secretary's Staff Committee, minutes, Dec. 20, 1944; Stettinius, calendar notes, Dec. 30, 1945, *SP*.
48. *New Republic*, 111 (Dec. 25, 1944): 866.

which warned that "perfectionism, no less than isolationism or imperialism or power politics, may obstruct the paths to international peace." He promised that his administration would secure "so far as is humanly possible" the goals of the Atlantic Charter, but added, "I do not wish to give the impression that all mistakes can be avoided and that many disappointments are not inevitable in the making of the peace." The great hope of lasting peace, he stressed, was to move forward with "vigor and resolution" to create a realistic international organization which would provide security and foster economic and social progress: "Most important of all—1945 can and must see the substantial beginning of the organization of world peace. This organization must be the fulfillment of the promise for which the men have fought and died in this war."[49]

Congress had returned in as rebellious a mood as it was in when it adjourned in December; Republican internationalist Senators Ball and Hatch were threatening a full debate on foreign policy. Only a long briefing by Roosevelt had temporarily swayed their resolve. Senator Connally informed Stettinius that his ability to forestall a debate was slipping but agreed to try to keep the lid on until the Big Three meeting. This was made difficult by the disappointing State of the Union message. Connally warned Roosevelt that many senators favored a "country-by-country" floor debate. From the House came a request by Estes Kefauver (D-Tennessee) asking that Cabinet officials and other key administration figures appear on the House floor periodically for "a report and question period." Roosevelt asked Stettinius's reaction and received a negative answer. The secretary stated that he would be willing to see Connally on a regular weekly basis and also meet with the full Senate Foreign Relations Committee whenever necessary. He said that there were "certain risks" even in this plan, but added that he would initiate it if Roosevelt approved. The president, hoping to take the edge out of Kefauver's proposal, which could have represented a dangerous erosion of presidential control over foreign policy, gave quick assent to Stettinius's alternate idea.[50]

49. U.S., Congress, Senate, *Congressional Record*, 79th Cong., 1st sess., 1945, pt. 1: 65–70.

50. Divine, *Second Chance*, 261; Stettinius, calendar notes, Jan. 5, 1945, *SP*; Tom Connally and Alfred Steinberg, *My Name is Tom Connally*, p. 271; Kefauver to Roosevelt, Jan. 6, 1945, *SP*; Stettinius to Roosevelt, Jan. 6, 1945, Official File 20, Roosevelt Papers.

Administration spokesmen could not completely control the critics. On January 5, Senator Burton K. Wheeler (D-Montana) attacked on radio the administration's foreign policy, charging that United States policymakers had misled the people about the Dumbarton Oaks Proposals which were nothing but a "grim hoax" and that Britain and Russia were carving up the postwar world. Stettinius moved quickly to counter the harmful impact of Wheeler's attack. In a strong news release the secretary accused Wheeler of giving aid to the enemies of the U.S. by encouraging them to hope that if they held out long enough the Allies would become fragmented and unable to achieve victory. Wheeler speaks not for the American people, the Secretary continued, " . . . but for a discredited few whose views have been overwhelmingly rejected by their fellow citizens of every party."[51]

Wheeler was widely known as a bitter foe of international cooperation, so his words could be judged in that light. More serious was the disillusionment developing among moderate Republican leaders, including the powerful trio of Dewey, Dulles, and Vandenberg. These men had not been dissatisfied with the state of U.S. foreign affairs during the election campaign, but the events of December convinced them that their earlier faith had been wrong.[52] Local leaders in the party were expressing their disenchantment. Brooks Emeny, president of the Cleveland Council on World Affairs, wrote to Dulles: "One of the most alarming features of the New Deal leadership in recent months has been the complete silence of the Administration on most of the difficult and disagreeable problems of our foreign relations. The American public has been fed largely on vague general principles in the form of Dumbarton Oaks, but no spokesman for the Administration has as yet had the courage to point out consistently to the American public the difficulties of our new world position nor the sacrifices which are necessarily involved in the administration of our new world order."[53]

Dulles spearheaded creation of a foreign policy clearing house

51. U.S., Congress, Senate, *Congressional Record*, 79th Cong., 1st sess., 1945, pt. 1: 85; Stettinius-Grew, memorandum of phone conversation, Jan. 6, 1945, Grew Papers; State Department Press Release No. 22, Jan. 6, 1945, *SP*.

52. Herbert Brownell, interview, 7, Dulles Oral History Project.

53. Brooks Emeny to Dulles, Dec. 22, 1944, Dulles Papers.

at GOP National Committee headquarters in Washington under Hugh Wilson's direction. Dulles hoped it would enable Republicans to offer sharper criticisms of administration actions, but he found most party leaders apathetic.[54] An exception was Vandenberg. Vandenberg believed that the events of December pointed to a resumption of power politics by Britain and Russia. He determined that his voice must be raised to assert the legitimate national interests of America. His new image became that of a nationalist. As he wrote to a friend: "I too fear that we are once more headed for tragic disillusionment. I too wish that the high spokesmen for our own America would always be as loyal to our own indispensable self-interest as Mr. Churchill is to Britain's and as Mr. Stalin is to Russia's."[55]

The administration had allowed matters to drift. The time was at hand for action, a golden opportunity for Vandenberg to speak for the nation, for his conscience, and for his political future. Fully aware of the significance of his speech, he worked long hours and consulted with numerous friends, particularly the newsmen close to him in the capital. Among the latter, James Reston was particularly helpful in the decision to call for a treaty against the Axis among the major Allied powers. After rewriting his material twelve times, Vandenberg headed for the Senate floor.[56]

With customary frankness, Vandenberg hurled a direct chal-

54. Sen. Wallace H. White, Jr., to Herbert Brownell, Jan. 16, 1945, Dulles to Brooks Emeny, Feb. 1, 1945, Dulles Papers.

55. Vandenberg to Dr. Henry Hatfield, Dec. 29, 1944, Vandenberg Papers.

56. Vandenberg, *Private Papers*, citing Vandenberg to James H. Sheppard, Jan. 2, 1945, pp. 128–129. The full text is in the Vandenberg Papers, Clement Library; Vandenberg to Thaddeus M. Machrowica, Dec. 30, 1944, Vandenberg Papers; author's interview with James Reston, June 12, 1962; Vandenberg, *Private Papers*, chaps. 1, 3, 6, and 7 provide glimpses of the development of the senator's thinking up to the time of the Jan. 10 speech, but the picture is less comprehensive than one would desire. The senator left little direct evidence of the influences that shaped his speech. Interviewers of the Dulles Oral History Collection attempted to elucidate a possible Dulles role in the speech. While a number of people speculated that Dulles did exert a significant influence, they offered no firm proof. Neither the Vandenberg nor the Dulles papers contain any evidence that Dulles had any direct part in writing the speech, but the rapidly developing friendship between the two men—in which Vandenberg tapped Dulles's knowledge of international law—suggests that Vandenberg utilized Dulles as a catalyst to mature his thinking on international relations.

lenge to the president. At this critical moment in the nation's life, we must "call for the straightest, the plainest, and the most courageous thinking of which we are capable." Instead "a great American illusion seems to have been built up—wittingly or otherwise—that we in the United States dare not publicly discuss these subjects lest we contribute to international dissension." There certainly was no such compunction in London or Moscow, he asserted, when British or Soviet national interests were at stake. Yet our government has kept silent: "It cannot be denied that citizens, in increasing numbers are crying: 'What are we fighting for?' It cannot be denied that our silence . . . has multiplied confusion at home and abroad. It cannot be denied that this confusion threatens our unity —yes, Mr. President, and already hangs like a cloud over Dumbarton Oaks." Vandenberg called on the administration to adopt "a new rule of honest candor" as a substitute for generalities. The administration must cling to the tenets of the Atlantic Charter: "These basic pledges cannot now be dismissed as mere nautical nimbus. They march with our armies. They sail with our fleets. They fly with our eagles. They sleep with our martyred dead. The first requisite of honest candor, Mr. President, I respectfully suggest, is to relight this torch."

To make sure of achieving these goals, Vandenberg proposed "a hard and fast treaty between the major Allies" aimed at preventing any Axis resurgence. The alternative was for each nation to go its own way. The example of Russia building a zone of buffer states against Germany was "affronting the opinions of mankind." While Vandenberg seemingly reaffirmed his support of the UN policy, he really undermined the administration's internationalist approach to security through the UN. Plainly, Vandenberg the nationalist was speaking, and his message was clear: America should seek a great-power alliance, but if this were not forthcoming, America might have to adopt a unilateral defense posture. There was small space for a powerful UN between these alternatives.[57]

Vandenberg's shrewd timing was proven by the burst of enthusiasm which greeted his speech. *Time*, usually more reserved, said flatly that "it might well prove to be the most important

57. U.S., Congress, Senate, *Congressional Record*, 79th Cong., 1st sess., 1945, pt. 1: 164–167; Adler, *Isolationist Impulse*, pp. 316–318, contains an excellent sketch on Vandenberg's speech.

speech made by an American in World War II," and the *New Republic* agreed, calling the speech "a turning point in world affairs." It pointed out that the Michigan senator had always been considered an isolationist. With his support of collective security, "it is a reasonable supposition that at least sixty-four members of the Senate will do likewise." In early February a *New York Times* survey indicated sufficient Senate support to carry a treaty such as suggested by Senator Vandenberg. It seemed doubtful, however, that the American people were prepared to agree that the president could use American forces to enforce such a treaty without congressional approval. In a survey conducted by the American Institute of Public Opinion at the end of January, while 92 percent thought the Axis should be kept "permanently disarmed," only 41 percent believed the president should have "the right to order the use of American armed force immediately." The poll did indicate that 57 percent favored treaty negotiation before the war ended. The administration probably could have counted on the backing of more than half the people had it been willing to negotiate a treaty preserving the traditional power of Congress to declare war.[58]

A number of prominent leaders supported Vandenberg's treaty proposal. Dewey called it the "clearest call for constructive action" since the recent elections, and Dulles said it was a "notable contribution" to foreign policy. The Republican National Committee accepted the plan as party policy, and talk mounted about Vandenberg as the GOP candidate for 1948.[59] Vandenberg's challenge also struck a sympathetic note within the administration among men who favored a nationalistic approach to postwar American security rather than the UN policy. Stimson, in a memorandum to Stettinius just before the secretary departed for Yalta, strongly commended the Vandenberg idea. And from his New York home, Bernard Baruch, who was a staunch advocate of permanently debilitating Germany and Japan, wrote warmly to Vandenberg how, "on

58. *Time*, 45 (Jan. 22, 1945): 15–16; *New Republic*, 112 (Jan. 22, 1945): 103–104; *New York Times*, Feb. 4, 1945; Adler, *Isolationist Impulse*, p. 315–316; both Democratic and Republican voters showed the same percentage on disarming the Axis and making a treaty prior to the end of the war. Fifty-four percent of Democrats favored allowing the President to commit troops before Congress declared war, but only 31 percent of Republican voters agreed to this, "The Quarter's Polls," *The Public Opinion Quarterly*, 60 (Spring, 1945): 71–81.

59. Divine, *Second Chance*, p. 263, cites the quotations used here.

every side I hear superlative expressions concerning your recent speech." It was "a landmark along the road to peace."[60]

Roosevelt and Stettinius took the opposite view of Vandenberg's speech. Stettinius had been advised by Vandenberg that he was about to make a speech. Stettinius and the president feared the treaty proposal would become a rallying point for an alternative security system to challenge the UN policy. Stettinius thought Vandenberg might sabotage the bipartisan approach to foreign policy and lined up "some of our friends" in the Senate to answer Vandenberg if need arose.[61] After assessing initial public reaction, the secretary recommended that the administration should cold-shoulder the Vandenberg plan.

In an effort to undercut Senate backing of Vandenberg, the administration arranged for members of the Senate Foreign Relations Committee to discuss foreign policy problems with the president. This meeting was held on January 11. The senators found Roosevelt in an unusually candid mood. The president was bitter about recent British actions. He had refused to cooperate with Churchill in a military campaign in the Balkans, FDR said, because he had foreseen the political troubles this would entail. He had foreseen the explosion in Greece, "if one knew the contentious qualities of the Greeks." The president, in fact, was prepared to write off most of eastern Europe to the Russians. It was a matter of matching military and political power Roosevelt told the senators: " . . . because the occupying forces [the Red Army] had the power in the areas where their arms were present and each knew that the others could not force things to an issue. He said that the Russians had the power in eastern Europe, that it was obviously impossible to have a break with them and that, therefore, the only practicable course was to use what influence we had to ameliorate the situation."[62]

Germany's Ardennes offensive, which had seriously delayed

60. Stimson to Stettinius, memorandum for the Secretary of State, Jan. 23, 1945, *FRUS, Malta and Yalta,* pp. 78–81; Baruch to Vandenberg, Jan. 16, 1945, Vandenberg Papers.

61. Stettinius to Roosevelt, Memorandum for the President on Congress and Foreign Policy, Jan. 10, 1945, *SP.*

62. Report on Meeting between the President and Senators Connally, Barkley, White, Austin, Vandenberg, and Thomas, memorandum for the Secretary of State, Jan. 11, 1945, *SP.*

the progress of the Western armies, weighed on Roosevelt's mind. Hopes of victory in Europe before the end of 1944 had turned to fear that America could not sustain the effort needed to win in Europe and simultaneously increase power in the Pacific for the onslaught against the Japanese home islands. On December 27 Stimson had reported to the cabinet on shortages in Europe of both men and supplies, and General Marshall had warned that should the Germans win the Battle of the Bulge, " . . . we should have to take a defensive position on the Germany boundary . . . and then have the people of the United States decide whether they wanted to go on with the war enough to raise the new armies which would be necessary to do it."[63] Though the Germans were contained by mid-January, the strain on American resources was critical and underscored the desire of the Joint Chiefs of Staff that the Soviet Union enter the war against Japan as soon as possible.[64] These military realities alone dictated the caution with which Roosevelt weighed Russian actions in Eastern Europe.

Roosevelt wanted to make certain the senators appreciated the intimate relationship between American policy in eastern Europe and the Far East. In the Pacific war, where Japan was such a formidable foe and Russian help was so needed, the Americans faced a precarious political situation. China offered the only hope for a democratic alternative in the Far East, but Roosevelt found Churchill always belittling American policy. FDR told the senators that British policy in the Far East was outmoded; one day China would become a world power of consequence, and he underlined "the importance of turning the Chinese away from an antiwhite race attitude which could easily develop."[65]

What Roosevelt wanted was a cooperative Russia and a stable China which would enable America to reduce its armed forces quickly after the war. The UN policy would provide the means of achieving Roosevelt's goal—maximum American security at the min-

63. Stettinius, calendar notes on Cabinet meeting, Dec. 22, 1944, SP; Stimson Diary, Dec. 27, 1944, Stimson Papers.

64. U.S., Department of Defense, "The Entry of the Soviet Union into the War Against Japan: Military Plans, 1941–1945" (Washington, D.C., 1955), mimeographed, pp. 36–40. [Hereinafter cited as "Soviet Entry into the War Against Japan."]

65. Report on Meeting between the President and Senate Leaders, Jan. 11, 1945, SP.

imum national cost. The president viewed this policy as a realistic one because he believed the American people would demand a reorienting of the economy away from war. Americans traditionally opposed large standing military forces.

The president's assessment of the public temper was buttressed by the extensive analyses of public opinion the State Department provided to the White House. These covered all aspects of public attitudes toward foreign policy questions. Stettinius often discussed the findings directly with Roosevelt. The most striking quality of the American mind revealed by these reports was the volatile nature of opinion on international relations. This was undoubtedly affected by the intense interaction of global military and political events. The confusion of the public mind was reinforced by the diversity of reporting and wide speculation among columnists who built stories on bits and pieces of information.[66] A memorandum from the Division of Public Liaison to Stettinius on January 3 pinpointed the problem: "In view of the *volatile* character of American opinion—its excessive sensibility to specific events frequently oversimplified and inadequately understood—a heavy responsibility devolves on those who can, in their day-to-day writings, do much to establish a valid *frame of reference* for the public judgment."[67]

Reports reaching the White House warned the president that the people had developed a disturbing ambivalence toward major problems. Dissatisfaction with Allied cooperation had risen from 28 percent in early December, 1944, to 44 percent by the end of the month. Confidence in the reliability of Britain and the Soviet Union had reached its lowest point of the war. These reports re-

66. One example of the confusion the public media faced was the War Department's handling of the ammunition shortage during the German offensive in December, 1944. The chairman of the Blue Radio Network vigorously protested that the War Department had issued contradictory statements and confused the public. See Chester La Roche to Robert Patterson, Dec. 12, 1944, Patterson Papers. Oversimplification of the war was a chronic problem as shown in Sydney Weinberg, "What to Tell America: The Writers' Quarrel in the Office of War Information," *The Journal of American History,* 55 (June, 1968): 73–89; Burns, *Roosevelt: The Soldier of Freedom,* p. 607, sees Roosevelt as "unduly sensitive to both congressional and public opinion; he used public opinion polls much more systematically than was realized at the time."

67. U.S., Department of State, Division of Public Liaison, The Present Climate of Opinion in the U.S. on International Developments, memorandum for the Secretary of State, Jan. 3, 1945, *SP.*

flected a strong rise of isolationism in America. Evidence indicated that the American people supported the Atlantic Charter and deplored imperialism,[68] but opposed direct American involvement in sorting out Europe's political problems. Only one person in three thought America should have taken a stronger stand on the recent Italian crisis. On Poland, Americans strongly supported the administration's continued recognition of the exiled Polish regime, but they sensed America's helplessness to force Russia to adopt a satisfactory policy toward Poland.

The department noted a "marked deterioration" in public confidence in future international relations which it attributed to distaste for British and Russian actions in Europe, dissension among the major Allies, and doubts over the effectiveness of U. S. diplomacy. The polls showed, however, that the American people, by a margin of 90 percent, continued to believe that the United States should join an international organization, and 60 percent of them favored membership even if the peace settlement were not "completely satisfactory" to the United States.[69]

One significant aspect of public attitudes was that while support for American entry into the UN continued at a high percentage, surveys sponsored by the State Department showed that only 30 percent of the public had any concept of the contents of the Dumbarton Oaks Proposals. An additional 42 percent had never heard of the proposals.[70] Yet Roosevelt preferred to take refuge in

68. The term *imperialism* was used loosely during this time to indicate national actions that thwarted popular aspirations and imposed a system of spheres of influence and power politics on a region.

69. U.S., Department of State, Division of Public Liaison, The Present Climate of Public Opinion . . . , memorandum for the Secretary of State, Jan. 3, 1945; Latest Opinions in the United States, memorandum for the President, Jan. 6 and 12, 1945; G. Haydon Raynor, American Opinion on Selected Questions, memorandum for the President, Jan. 16, 1945. Of 4300 pieces of mail dealing with the Greek and Italian problems, "an unusually large" 40 percent gave specific approval to Stettinius's statements of December 5 and 7, 1944. But af.er Roosevelt's remarks on December 19 suggesting the lessened status of the Atlantic Charter, letters to the Department of State became increasingly disillusioned and isolationist. See U.S., Department of State, Division of Public Liaison, Public Comment Mail for Month of December Growing Out of the Greek and Italian Situation, memorandum for Assistant Secretary MacLeish, Jan. 15, 1945, SP.

70. Secretary's Staff Committee, minutes, Jan. 3, 1945; The Present Climate of Opinion . . . , memorandum for the Secretary of State, Jan. 3, 1945; Raynor, American Opinion . . . , Jan. 16, 1945, SP; MacLeish subsequently de-

the UN policy rather than accept Vandenberg's approach. He told the Senate Foreign Relations Committee on January 11 that the ultimate answer to all the vexing political issues dividing the Allies lay in pressing for acceptance of the Dumbarton Oaks Proposals and creating the UN.[71]

In effect the American government and people were engaged in building a masquerade peace. The people were confused and resented the actions of Britain and Russia. Yet they opposed any role increasing American responsibility in Europe. The U.S. public had little faith in future harmony among the Big Four powers and was ignorant of how the UN would operate. Yet there persisted in America a childlike faith that America must join the UN to preserve future peace. American support of the UN policy was irrational and suggests that in large measure the motivation was atonement for the sin of having failed the world in Wilson's time. The Roosevelt administration preferred to nourish this public support, seeing it as the easiest way of avoiding the kind of immediate political decision involved in the Vandenberg treaty proposal. For the government and the people, the UN policy before Yalta was becoming an escape from reality.[72]

Roosevelt was trapped. He could have warned the American people candidly about the aims of Russia in eastern Europe and the fears that communism might emerge as a greater menace than fascism, but he knew the American people were war-weary and little inclined to postwar sacrifices. The UN policy seemed the only available means of holding everything together. As tenuous as this hope was, Roosevelt clutched at it with increasing desperation in the last two months of his life.[73]

---

manded that the Staff Committee face up to the Department's being "seriously" behind in its educational efforts on the Dumbarton Oaks Proposals, but he failed to get the power he wanted to correct the information lag. He blamed red tape in the Department for delaying the publicity effort: Secretary's Staff Committee, minutes, Jan. 19, 1945, SP.

71. Report on Meeting between the President and Senate Leaders, Jan. 11, 1945, SP.

72. This theme was expressed constantly in government and Congressional statements as well as in editorials and columns.

73. Burns, *Roosevelt: The Soldier of Freedom*, pp. 548–552, contains a provocative analysis of the dichotomies between the pragmatic and idealistic elements in Roosevelt's personality as they affected his strategy.

4

The UN Policy at Yalta

JUDGED BY THE YARDSTICK OF FOREIGN POLICY OB-
jectives that Roosevelt laid down in his private discussions with
Senate leaders three weeks before the Yalta Conference, American
diplomacy won a stunning victory at the Big Three meeting. Roosevelt left the conference with his two allies firmly committed to the
UN policy, largely on American terms. He put the spotlight on
Russian activities in eastern Europe by obtaining a public Soviet
pledge to observe democratic political processes throughout Eastern
Europe. On the difficult Polish question, the Russians promised to
reconstitute their Lublin government to include democratic elements. This meant that the Russians were risking either having
their control over Poland substantially weakened or facing world
censure for violating their word—something the Kremlin leadership did not like to do in public. America had also gained a firm
commitment for Russia's entry into the Pacific war and a clear
pledge that Russia would support the Nationalist government of
China and leave the Chinese communists to their fate.

In return America agreed that Russia should regain Far Eastern
territories that she had held prior to the Russo-Japanese War of
1904–1905, plus acquiring the Kurile Islands from Japan. This con-

stituted simply a realistic acceptance of Russia's renewed role as a Far Eastern power, a fact which Japan's defeat ensured with or without American help. If Roosevelt were guilty of agreeing to Russian demands in the Far East without first gaining China's approval, the fact was that Roosevelt was participating in power politics because to do so suited America's interests.[1]

Most historians who see America as having been duped by Russia at Yalta are indulging in post hoc wisdom. They overlook the background or fail to see the importance America attached to its UN policy. Only by understanding the UN's central place in American thinking can U.S. actions at Yalta be appreciated. Another dimension should be mentioned: for years after Yalta, large segments of world opinion viewed Russia with deep suspicion for the ways in which it (supposedly) callously betrayed its Yalta commitments. Indeed, the whole traditional view that the onus of the Cold War rests on the Russians because of their violation of the Yalta agreements testifies to the success of American diplomacy. For it was U.S. policy to tie Russia publicly to promises it subsequently found embarrassing to default on. Although such outcomes were not intended by Roosevelt at the time, this was the common result.

Yalta must also be viewed as part of Roosevelt's continuing diplomacy, not as the final act of his life. He went to Yalta with certain limited objectives in view and a willingness to compromise on European political questions that Russia regarded as vital to itself. Much like Wilson, who expected the League to modify weaknesses in the Treaty of Versailles, Roosevelt counted on the UN to arbitrate differences arising out of the Yalta agreements.

Roosevelt took pains, before leaving for Yalta, to mend the rift between America and Britain by dispatching Harry Hopkins to see Churchill. After a week of discussions Hopkins flew to Naples, where he reported his findings on January 31 to Stettinius, who had stopped there enroute to the Crimea. Hopkins described Churchill's mood as "volcanic." The prime minister thought the Americans had deserted him at a critical moment.[2]

---

1. See Divine, *Roosevelt and World War II*, chap. 3, for interesting analysis of Roosevelt's *Realpolitik*.
2. Sherwood, *Roosevelt and Hopkins*, p. 847; Edward R. Stettinius, *Roosevelt and the Russians*, pp. 48–49.

Much of Stettinius's conversation with Hopkins centered around the British interpretation of the United Nations organization. This was of particular concern to the secretary because the British had changed their position several times on the voting question since the conclusion of the Dumbarton Oaks meeting. Within two weeks after leaving that conference, the British had altered their stand so that it coincided with the Russian view that permanent members of the council should have a veto in all matters. By early January word came that Britain had reversed this position. Now she would stick with the American compromise, in which permanent members would have no veto in cases of pacific settlement of disputes in which they were involved.[3]

Hopkins threw some light on these baffling shifts in British thinking. He told Stettinius that Churchill feared that he could not carry his Cabinet and Parliament if Britain accepted the American compromise. In fact, one Cabinet member, Sir Stafford Cripps, argued strongly that the Russian position was in Britain's best interests. Hopkins had later learned that the Foreign Office disagreed strongly with the prime minister in assessing British political reaction to the veto. Eden thought that the British public would protest angrily if the Russian formula were accepted at Yalta. Hopkins concluded by observing that Churchill was still wavering between these opposing views.[4]

This news discomfited Stettinius as he flew toward Malta for an Anglo-American discussion prior to the Yalta Conference. Hopkins's report confirmed the American suspicion that the British were half-hearted in supporting the UN policy. The State Department believed that Britain's policy had shifted since the summer and now favored the construction of a Western bloc against Russia. This view was supported by an analysis of British motivation prepared by Hamilton Fish Armstrong, who had served in London on leave from his regular job as editor of *Foreign Affairs*. His report reached Stettinius just before the secretary departed for Europe.

3. Draft Memorandum to the President on Following up the Dumbarton Oaks Conversations, Oct. 24, 1944; Stettinius to Roosevelt, memorandum on Voting in the Security Council, Jan. 17, 1945, SP.

4. Notes on discussion between the Secretary of State and Mr. Hopkins, morning of Jan. 31, 1945, at the Villa Laura in Naples [no author given, but either Bohlen or Matthews], SP.

The British, he found, had concluded that Russia would pursue its security interests apart from any cooperation with Britain and America. Furthermore British leaders expected America to withdraw from world affairs as she had after 1919. Thus Britain was moving to build her own security—hence her actions in the Mediterranean.[5]

In light of the caustic criticism Churchill had heaped on the State Department's role in the Italian and Greek episodes, Stettinius was uncertain about the reception which awaited him. He feared this would compound the task of reconciling the British to American views on the UN policy. His question was soon answered. On the very evening of his arrival in Malta, the secretary dined with Churchill and Eden. He found Churchill "rather outspoken to me regarding Greece and Italy." Stettinius later recalled that Churchill was magnificent in defending the British position. "There was nothing he loved more dearly than to hurl himself into the fray."[6]

The following morning, February 1, Stettinius and Eden discussed recent Anglo-American difficulties. Eden's mood was gloomy. He told Stettinius that Churchill was worried about holding the government together against a Laborite challenge. He believed that Churchill and Roosevelt had bungled the coordination of policy, and he was "very discouraged with the world situation." Although he knew that Eden would welcome suggestions of a firm Western entente, Stettinius carefully avoided encouraging this hope. Instead he concentrated on cementing British support for the American view of the veto problem in the UN. Eden conceded that the American compromise plan, which had been sent to Stalin in early December, "was virtually essential to the creation of the World Organization."[7]

Stettinius was less successful in persuading Eden of the importance of a State Department plan to establish an Emergency High Commission for Liberated Europe. It would provide the Allies

5. Hamilton Fish Armstrong, memorandum for the Secretary, Jan. 20, 1945, SP. Armstrong served as a special consultant to the Department of State at Stettinius's request.

6. Stettinius, Record, sec. 1, 7–11; Stettinius, calendar notes, Jan. 31, 1945, SP; Stettinius, Roosevelt and the Russians, pp. 60–61.

7. Stettinius, calendar notes, Feb. 1, 1945, SP; Eden, The Reckoning, p. 591; FRUS, Malta and Yalta, pp. 498–507.

with control machinery and a clearing house for managing affairs
in Europe during the transition from war to peace and operate as
an interim body until the UN was functioning. Hopkins had told
Stettinius, in their Naples talks, that the British agreed with this
plan; but the secretary found Eden doubtful. He thought it would
be difficult to get Russia's agreement to the Commission because
of the necessity for Moscow to maintain tight control on any representative who might be appointed to such a body. This was
hardly a consistent argument since Soviet diplomats operated this
way on the European Advisory Commission and certainly would
work the same way in the United Nations. Eden stated that Britain
favored a plan for quarterly meetings of the foreign ministers of
the great powers; he feared that the European High Commission
would undercut this plan.

Nonetheless, the two men left Malta in agreement that the
European High Commission idea should be explored at Yalta. Stettinius did not press the High Commission concept more forcefully
since Roosevelt had earlier expressed skepticism about the plan because it would detract from "the World Organization which Roosevelt saw as the question of paramount importance." Thus there was
no commitment beyond the State Department's backing.[8]

The Malta discussions revealed confusion on yet other aspects
of the UN. Stettinius discovered that neither Churchill nor Roosevelt had a firm picture of the Dumbarton Oaks Proposals. He first
observed this on the evening of February 1 at dinner with the
prime minister. Churchill was particularly talkative, and the atmosphere was warm and intimate. But he was despondent over
Europe's desperate economic and social condition, as noted:
"Churchill was very depressed on the outlook of the world. He said
that there were probably more units of suffering among humanity
of the world as of this hour when we sat down to dinner, than at
any [other] time during the history of the world . . . and as he
looked out on the world it was one of sorrow and bloodshed." He
spoke longingly about world peace, but his ideas on world organization were hazy, as Stettinius noted: "The Prime Minister did
not seem to understand the international organization or the voting
procedure in the Council. He made a great feature of the new organization doing nothing other than keeping the peace and not

8. *FRUS, Malta and Yalta,* pp. 498–507.

getting into social or economic things. Eden and I talked with him about this and I told him we would be disappointed if the social and economic council would not have an important place."[9]

Stettinius soon learned that Roosevelt's grasp was no clearer. Roosevelt arrived at Malta the morning of February 2. People had been assembling for hours around the Grand Harbor of Valetta, atop buildings and leaning out windows, straining to catch a glimpse of the leader of the greatest of the wartime nations. Spitfires droned back and forth across the warm sky. Binoculars trained on the harbor entrance. Eden later recalled the drama: "While the bands played and amid so much that reeked of war, on the bridge, just discernible to the naked eye, sat one civilian figure. In his sensitive hands lay much of the world's fate. All heads were turned his way and a sudden quietness fell. It was one of those moments when all seems to stand still and one is conscious of a mark in history."[10]

As soon as Stettinius talked to the president, he learned that Roosevelt had developed a new idea about Security Council voting. At luncheon with Churchill and Eden, Roosevelt confided to Stettinius "that he had been giving the voting procedure in the Council much thought and that he had worked out a new plan during the voyage which he had not discussed with anybody yet, but wished to discuss with me at the first possible moment."[11] Actually the president's idea was neither his own nor new. It originated with Benjamin V. Cohen, a White House aide who had been on the American delegation at Dumbarton Oaks. He had fought hard for the view that permanent members of the Security Council should not vote on cases involving themselves either in pacific settlement or enforcement decisions. Cohen had converted James Byrnes to his view, and during the long ocean voyage to Malta Byrnes had won the president to Cohen's idea. As he outlined it to Stettinius, Roosevelt proposed that "in order to avoid inability to act because of the unanimity principle, there ought to be provision for action to be taken by four of the Great Powers."[12]

9. Stettinius, calendar notes, Dinner with Churchill and Eden, Feb. 1, 1945, SP.

10. Eden, The Reckoning, p. 592.

11. Stettinius, calendar notes, Welcoming Roosevelt, Luncheon aboard the U.S.S. Quincy, Feb. 2, 1945, SP.

12. Notes by Walter Johnson on letter from Alger Hiss to Johnson, Nov.

This proposal would have virtually scrapped the veto power and certainly have brought a quick rejection from the Russians. Very likely it would have aroused strong protests in the Senate, whose leaders had been assured of a veto clause. That the president would consider such a proposal—one which he and State Department officials had rejected earlier—indicates his superficial knowledge about the operation of the international organization.

Does Roosevelt's vagueness on the veto signal the illness which fatally struck the president two months later? While it has become standard for historians to write of Roosevelt as a "dying man" at Yalta, his driving pace and sustained performance during the Crimean negotiations attest to his capacity. One of the few qualified medical observers of the president at Yalta, however, was Lord Moran, personal physician to Churchill. Moran wrote: "The president looked old and thin and drawn; he had a cape over his shoulders and appeared shrunken; he sat looking straight ahead with his mouth open, as if he were not taking things in. Everyone was shocked by his appearance and gabbled about it afterwards."[13] Certainly the strains of war leadership showed on the president, but to think of him as so incapacitated that he could not make clear decisions is unsound.

After these few exchanges on the UN policy, a somber Stettinius departed for the Crimea. How consistent would American policy be at the forthcoming conference?

On February 4, the three delegations entered a week of the most intensive, wearing, and exciting negotiations of the war. Many of the major decisions regarding the world organization were forged in the first four days of the conference. The process was rough from the outset. In his first extensive review with Roosevelt, Stettinius learned of the president's disappointing decision to abandon the European High Commission for Liberated Europe. Stettinius had outlined the Department's thinking for the president and explained that the Commission would bridge the gap between the end of the war and the establishment of the UN. Roosevelt objected to "another organization." Pointing to the European Advisory Commis-

14, 1948, *SP;* Russell, *UN Charter,* p. 519n; Stettinius, *Roosevelt and the Russians,* p. 87.
13. Moran, *Churchill,* p. 234.

sion, he claimed it had only worsened relations among the Allies in its tortuous quest for a common policy toward Germany. Roosevelt thought that periodic meetings of the foreign ministers could achieve the Allied liaison that the State Department wanted. Stettinius tried to dissuade the president. A foreign minister was confined largely to his capital. The State Department wanted a means of constant Allied supervision for Europe in the period before the international organization began full operation. Periodic meetings of foreign ministers were inadequate. The president remained unmoved, so the proposal died without having reached a plenary session.[14]

Although Stettinius did not confide his personal reaction to his diary, given the significance the State Department attached to the commission, he must have been greatly disappointed that Roosevelt rejected it. In retrospect, the president's decision assumes considerable importance. Had he forcefully urged the commission on Churchill and Stalin, an avenue would have existed for ironing out European problems during the gray months between war and peace. Instead, there was never any common machinery to handle overall European problems. Such a coordinated body might have enabled the Allies to avoid the misunderstandings that arose after Yalta.

Stettinius next focused on the presentation of the voting formula to the plenary session. This crucial occasion came two days later on February 6.

From his chair on the president's right, Stettinius read the U.S. voting proposal. He was most anxious that the three leaders see precisely how the veto would apply. Actions that would always require complete concurrence among the permanent powers were (1) recommendations to the General Assembly on the admission of new members, the suspension of a member, the expulsion of a member, the election of the Secretary General; (2) restoration of the rights and privileges of a suspended member; (3) removal of threats to the peace and suppression of breaches of peace, including the questions whether failure on the part of the parties to a dispute to settle it by means of their own choice or in accordance

14. Stettinius, calendar notes, Meeting of the President with his Advisers, Feb. 4, 1945, SP; FRUS, Malta and Yalta, p. 564–567.

with the recommendations of the Security Council in fact constitutes a threat to the peace, whether any other actions on the part
of any country constitutes a threat to the peace or a breach of the
peace, what measures should be taken by the Council to maintain
or restore the peace and the manner in which such measures should
be carried out, whether a regional agency should be authorized to
undertake measures of enforcement; (4) approval of special agreement or agreements for the provision of armed forces and facilities; (5) formulation of plans for a general system of regulation of
armaments and submission of such plans to the member states; and
(6) determination of whether the nature and activities of a regional agency or arrangement for the maintenance of peace and
security are consistent with the purposes of the general organization.[15]

Stettinius next moved to the section of the proposal where "in
decisions relating to peaceful settlement of disputes," unanimity
would be required among the five permanent members as a general rule, "except that a member of the Council could not cast its
vote in any such decisions that concern disputes to which it is a
party." These would include (1) whether a dispute or a situation
brought to the Council's attention is of such a nature that its con-
tinuation is likely to threaten the peace; (2) whether the Council
should call on the parties to settle or adjust the dispute or situation
by means of their own choice; (3) whether the Council should
make a recommendation to the parties as to methods and procedures of settlement; (4) whether, if there exists a regional agency
for peaceful settlement of local disputes, such an agency should be
asked to concern itself with the controversy.[16]

Stettinius noted the progress made at Dumbarton Oaks and
said that the voting question had subsequently received "intensive
study." The United States recognized the need for unanimity where
economic and military measures must be taken. Yet the great
powers had to admit "that the peaceful adjustment of any controversy which may arise is a matter of general world interest in
which any sovereign state involved should have a right to present
its case." Unless freedom of discussion were preserved, the estab-

15. *FRUS, Malta and Yalta,* pp. 660–671.
16. Ibid.

lishment of a world organization would be "seriously jeopardized."[17]

Much to Stettinius's relief, Churchill strongly backed the United States. Churchill explained that at one time he thought the British and American position might impair the collaboration of the great nations, but, after careful consideration, he was satisfied that harmony could be preserved. Churchill now supported the compromise voting formula and said that the entire British Commonwealth would concur.[18] He added: "In the last resort peace depended on the friendship and cooperation of the three great powers but the British Government would consider that they were committing an injustice if provision were not made for small countries to frankly state their grievances. If this were not done it would appear as if the three great powers were trying to rule the world, whereas their desire was to save the world from a repetition of the horrors of this war."[19]

Stalin took exception. The powers did not need to make any "proud submission" on this question. It was much more important to assure complete unanimity among the Big Three Allies at all levels in the world organization. This was the absolute foundation for future peace. To weaken this unity might provoke arguments among the great states and jeopardize their cooperation. This unanimity should be a primary objective of the forthcoming UN conference. Stalin feared that the United States formula and British support of it would open the way for dissension and threaten to collapse the entire movement for a security organization.[20] Yet Stalin stopped short of outright rejection, stating that he had not had adequate opportunity to study the Dumbarton Oaks Proposals.

This Russian argument was weak. It is unlikely that the Soviet government entered the Crimea negotiations so inadequately prepared. There had been ample time and opportunity to consider the proposals. Stettinius had encouraged a full exchange of views between Washington and Moscow, and to ensure this, Leo Pasvolsky had conducted a thorough discussion of the open issues with Ambassador Gromyko, particularly on the veto question. These talks

17. Ibid.
18. Churchill was being too optimistic, for the major members of the British Commonwealth bitterly opposed the veto power during the San Francisco conference.
19. Stettinius, calendar notes, Plenary session, Feb. 6, 1945, *SP*.
20. Ibid.

took place just before Gromyko departed from Washington for a full review in Moscow. Pasvolsky had the distinct impression that Gromyko understood the U. S. thinking about the veto question.[21] It is likely that the strong stand that Stalin took reflected the Russian reluctance to participate in an organization in which capitalist powers so greatly outnumbered communist ones. Further, the Russians placed a high priority on the great powers working out the postwar picture among themselves, leaving the other nations a relatively minor role. Unanimity was a legitimate part of this approach. Or possibly Stalin wanted to derive the maximum impact that a Soviet concession on voting would have in order to obtain leverage for extracting concessions from Roosevelt and Churchill on other matters.

The secretary soon learned that his presentation had made a good impression on the prime minister. At an intermission in the plenary session, Stettinius served drinks to Churchill and Eden in his apartment in Livadia Palace. There, Stettinius said, "Churchill told me I had done a magnificent job in presenting our position on the voting procedure and that not only Stalin but now he, the Prime Minister . . . really understood it for the first time."[22] Stettinius took this as a hopeful omen, but the Americans waited anxiously for the Russian reaction.

At a meeting the next morning, Hopkins and Byrnes agreed with Stettinius that to secure agreement on the points left open at Dumbarton Oaks "was of greater importance than anything else," and that European questions could wait until this was settled.[23] Their suspense was soon relieved. As the plenary meeting started that day, Stalin soon raised the UN issue and turned the floor over to Foreign Minister Molotov. He explained that Stettinius's report and Churchill's remarks had "clarified" the subject. The Russian government now believed that these voting proposals "fully guaranteed the unity of the Great Powers in the matter of the preservation of peace."[24]

This was welcome news, but Molotov quickly moved on to an-

21. Secretary's Staff Committee, minutes, Jan. 12, 1945, SP.
22. Stettinius, calendar notes, Feb. 6, 1945, SP.
23. Stettinius, calendar notes, Meeting with Hopkins and Byrnes, Feb. 7, 1945, SP.
24. FRUS, Malta and Yalta, pp. 709–718.

other topic which dampened British and American enthusiasm. They would recall, Molotov said, that Russia had raised the question of initial membership in the organization at Dumbarton Oaks. At that time, Russia had asked seats for each one of her sixteen constituent republics; but now she would not insist that all of them be initial members of the world organization. It would suffice if the Big Three agreed to admit three "or at least two" Soviet republics as charter members. Molotov proposed membership for the Ukraine, White Russia, and Lithuania since these were the republics that had suffered the most during the war. He hoped that Roosevelt and Churchill would think about these sacrifices and act favorably on the Russian request.[25]

The advantage on this issue lay clearly with Russia, for she had just yielded on the veto question. She also had taken a conciliatory stand on the initial membership dispute itself, since originally she had asked for sixteen seats. Now she asked for only two or three. There was a dramatic pause as Molotov waited for a response. Churchill looked to Roosevelt to answer. The British position was weak because of the Commonwealth arrangement, whose members would each be members of the international organization. Stalin could claim that Commonwealth nations had the same relationship to Britain as the member republics had to the overlying Soviet Union. Eden had pointed out this vulnerability to Stettinius during their Malta discussions, and he had explained that the United States must take the lead on it.[26]

Roosevelt had arrived at Yalta determined to oppose any Russian request along these lines. This was a position he had maintained consistently since Stettinius first told him of the Russian demand at Dumbarton Oaks. The president now resorted to delaying tactics in answering Molotov and suggested that the Russian proposal be studied by the foreign ministers. It seemed wiser to him to leave such questions to the future United Nations Conference.[27] Roosevelt got immediate support from Churchill on this point, although the British leader expressed his "great sympathy" for the Russian request.

At some point before the matter was discussed by the foreign

25. Ibid.
26. Russell, UN Charter, p. 520.
27. Stettinius, calendar notes, Fourth Plenary Session, Feb. 7, 1945, SP.

ministers, the president changed his mind and decided to accept Molotov's plea for seats for two Soviet republics. He informed Stettinius of this at their daily early morning review session: "It is definite that the president stated to me in the early morning that he thought it was all right to allow the Russian request and I repeated that I still think I should reserve the United States position at the meeting of the Foreign Ministers until he had an opportunity to give the matter more thorough thought."[28]

Roosevelt insisted, but Stettinius did not directly tell this to Eden and Molotov at their noon meeting, saying only that "it would probably be most satisfactory" to limit initial membership to those countries which had signed the United Nations Declaration of 1942 and declared war on Germany. This was a shrewd effort, for the Russians had used an identical argument at Dumbarton Oaks as the criterion for determining a nation's eligibility for membership in the world organization. If this test were adopted, it would automatically eliminate the sixteen Soviet republics since they had never signed the declaration.[29]

Molotov pressed hard and elicited from Eden the remark that Britain was "sympathetically inclined" toward Russia on this matter and would say so "at whatever was considered an appropriate moment." Eden even suggested that the foreign ministers put the subject on the agenda for that afternoon's plenary session. It now appeared that the United States might have the uncomfortable task of facing up alone to the Russian desire which seemed reasonable and came immediately after Stalin had made a major concession to the Americans. Stettinius was well aware of this and told Molotov that he would discuss the issue with the President "and hoped and expected that the United States would be able to give a favorable reply before the end of the day."[30]

Since Roosevelt had already indicated to Stettinius that he was inclined to allow the Russians the additional seats, the secretary was clearly trying to stall until he could discuss the entire matter at greater length with the president. Meanwhile an *ad hoc* committee of Alger Hiss, Gladwyn Jebb, and Andrei Gromyko was assigned the job of trying to reach agreement in wording a state-

28. Stettinius to Walter Johnson, memorandum, Dec. 2, 1948, SP.
29. FRUS, Malta and Yalta, pp. 735–738.
30. Ibid.

ment of common support for the Soviet position. They had made little headway, but Cadogan's report on the discussion made it appear as if the Americans were yielding. Alger Hiss, special assistant to the secretary, objected heatedly when he saw the document and went immediately to Eden to protest, but the British Foreign Secretary brushed off Hiss's objections with the cryptic remark, "something has taken place that you do not know."[31]

The "something" to which Eden referred occurred earlier in the afternoon, during the time of the subcommittee meeting. While the experts worked, Stettinius went to report to Roosevelt "some time after three o'clock." He told of British willingness to accept the Russian republics as initial members of the world organization, but before he could indicate that he had *not* promised United States approval, Premier Stalin entered the president's apartment and immediately asked whether the foreign ministers had agreed to the Soviet request on initial membership. Without waiting for Stettinius's answer, the president "waved his hand and told Stalin that agreement had been reached on everything."[32]

Since the Soviet Premier had arrived for a discussion on the Far East, Stettinius left without finishing his report. Roosevelt had seriously erred when he assumed that his secretary of state had agreed to admit the Russian republics as initial members. It is possible that Roosevelt decided to yield on this point because he was concerned with Far Eastern matters and wanted to have some added power in dealing with Stalin on Russia's entry into the Pacific war. Stettinius had certainly intended to delay action in the hope that the United States might devise some means of getting around the Russian position, but Roosevelt acted before he had fully discussed it with Stettinius. It was a decision he soon regretted.

Word of the president's action evidently reached the British independently of Hiss, and the foreign ministers' report was altered to reflect this. The plenary meeting of the 8th accepted this report. Britain and the United States agreed to vote in support of a

31. *FRUS, Malta and Yalta*, pp. 991–992; Notes by Walter Johnson on letter from Hiss to Johnson, Nov. 19, 1948, *SP*; Hiss's opposition to yielding to Russia on the issue of additional seats for Russian republics is clearly seen in memoranda he prepared for Stettinius, *FRUS, Malta and Yalta*, pp. 746–747.

32. Stettinius to Walter Johnson, Dec. 2, 1948; notes by Johnson on letter from Hiss to Johnson, Nov. 19, 1948, *SP*.

Russian request at the United Nations conference to have two of the Soviet republics admitted as original members of the international organization.[33] As news of this action spread among the United States advisers, a sharply critical reaction developed. Stettinius was not among these detractors, and he left no record of his inner reaction. That he thought this a mistake and was concerned about it was clearly shown in his attempt a month later to persuade the president to try to find some way to avoid keeping the agreement. Stettinius's action at Yalta in remaining quiet after Roosevelt's decision is revealing about how the secretary viewed the function of his office. He was quite willing to present and argue a position, but thereafter it was the president's duty to decide whether to accept the State Department's advice.

Other members of the American party at Yalta felt freer to press their "solutions." James F. Byrnes, who had accompanied the president as a White House adviser, was especially vocal. He told the president that the concession was "very unwise" and reminded him that when the Covenant of the League of Nations gave five votes to Britain because of the role of the Commonwealth, the isolationists in the United States had used this alleged British advantage to attack the whole League concept during the election of 1920. Byrnes suggested that Roosevelt tell Russia and Britain that the United States would also have to have extra seats. Further objection came from Admiral Leahy who predicted that the American people would reject the notion of one nation having more seats than another.[34] Adding weight to his argument was the secrecy involved in the entire affair. The president had insisted that it be kept a tightly guarded secret ever since the Russians first raised it at Dumbarton Oaks. To spring such a surprise on the American people now might provoke skepticism toward the entire UN policy.

With this consideration in mind, Roosevelt decided to write Churchill and Stalin about the peculiar difficulties he faced. The United States, he said, had agreed to back the admission of two Russian republics to the UN, "and I shall certainly carry it out," but this pledge might cause "political difficulties" in the United States: "It may be necessary for me, therefore, if I am to insure whole-

33. *FRUS, Malta and Yalta,* pp. 771–782.
34. James F. Byrnes, *Speaking Frankly,* pp. 40–41; William D. Leahy, *I Was There,* p. 310.

hearted acceptance by the Congress and people of the United States of our participation in the World Organization, to ask for additional votes in the Assembly in order to give parity to the United States."[35] Churchill and Stalin quickly agreed to support this request at the United Nations Conference.[36] There were no logical grounds for the United States to have additional votes except her control of the Philippines, Hawaii, Alaska, and Puerto Rico. Yet the Americans at Yalta did not argue in such terms. They wanted only to provide a cushion to absorb domestic political criticism.

The Americans had now weathered the two problems most critical to the UN policy, but other matters on which the Big Three must reach agreement remained. Most important was the criterion to be used in selecting charter members of the world organization. It was readily agreed that any country which had signed the 1942 United Nations Declaration should be eligible for membership. But was this to be a sine qua non for joining? The United States was anxious to invite all Latin American nations (except Argentina) to become initial members. A number of these countries had broken diplomatic relations with Germany but had not declared war. They had aided the Allied cause by providing strategic raw materials. Six prominent Latin American nations had this status.[37] Earlier in the war Roosevelt had promised them that their breaking diplomatic relations with Germany, would make them eligible to join any postwar international organization. But America could not deliver on this pledge unless Russia and Britain agreed. Stettinius had worked hard just prior to Yalta to persuade the Latin American countries to declare war on Germany. He had warned that discussions during the Dumbarton Oaks conversations indicated that unless a nation took this step, it might not be admitted as a charter member of the world organization.[38]

The United States had other reasons for wanting the six Latin American nations admitted as charter members. A major conference of the Western hemisphere nations was scheduled to convene shortly after the Crimea conference ended. One of Stettinius's

35. FRUS, Malta and Yalta, p. 966.
36. Ibid.
37. The six nations were Chile, Ecuador, Paraguay, Peru, Uruguay, and Venezuela.
38. Secretary's Staff Committee, minutes, Jan. 10, 1945, SP.

major tasks at that meeting would be to convince Latin American leaders that it was to their advantage to support the Dumbarton Oaks Proposals. It would be extremely embarrassing to Stettinius to have to inform some of these countries that they could not join the organization until after its charter had been written and it was in operation.

Roosevelt's desire to get membership for the six Latin American nations may have influenced him to agree to Stalin's demand for seats for White Russia and the Ukraine, for both of these matters came to a climax on the same day. No sooner had Roosevelt announced his willingness to accede to the Russian request than he asked Churchill and Stalin to agree that associated nations should be charter members of the peace organization.

Stalin balked. It seemed strange, he argued, that certain nations that had never recognized Soviet Russia now wished to join her in organizing the United Nations. How could Russia build "future world security" with such nations? The president replied evenly that he was certain that these nations wished to have diplomatic relations with Russia "but had just not gotten around to doing anything about it." He apologized for the United States having prematurely promised UN membership to these countries. He added that the United States was doing all it could to encourage them to declare war on Germany. Roosevelt then made a suggestion that, he said, "would save my life" if accepted. They could invite the associated countries to send delegates to the United Nations Conference, help write the Charter, and become initial members, on the condition that they sign the United Nations Declaration.

To his great relief, Stalin assented, and Churchill, who had remained silent throughout the discussion, agreed after dourly remarking about countries that "have played a poor part, waiting to see who would win." They agreed to allow the six Latin American nations until March 5 to sign the United Nations Declaration, the date set for issuing invitations to the United Nations Conference on International Organization.[39] Stettinius immediately sent directions to Acting Secretary Grew that he should increase the pressure on Latin American nations to declare war on Germany, calling quick action "absolutely essential."[40]

39. *FRUS, Malta and Yalta*, pp. 771–782.
40. Stettinius to Grew, cable, Feb. 9, 1945, *SP.*

Another question relating to initial membership involved the government of Poland. This was one of the major issues at the conference, the outcome of which was an agreement that the government in Warsaw (created by the Russians) would be reconstituted to include democratic leaders from both inside and outside Poland. A special commission, headed by Molotov, was to meet in Moscow to oversee this process. The restructured government presumably would include Poles from the exile London government, would then be recognized by all of the Allies, and would be invited to the United Nations Conference.[41]

A final matter related to international trusteeships. This sensitive subject, postponed in past meetings, now was explored among the Big Three for the first time. A major reason for the late start on this problem was the opposition of the United States Joint Chiefs of Staff. The secretaries of War and of the Navy wanted the United States free to establish its own system of security after the war. After months of patient work, the State Department had finally gained permission of military leaders for a general exploration of trusteeship matters at the Crimea conference.[42]

Trusteeships were raised at the foreign ministers' meeting on February 9, and that afternoon Stettinius addressed Roosevelt, Churchill, and Stalin on the topic: "It was agreed by the foreign ministers that the five Governments which will have permanent seats on the Security Council should consult each other prior to the United Nations Conference on providing machinery in the World Charter for dealing with territorial trusteeship and dependent areas."[43] At this moment, Churchill "blew up," interrupted Stettinius, and denounced the entire report on trusteeships. Never, he raged, would he countenance an international organization of forty-odd members "thrusting interfering fingers" into the business of the British Empire. "As long as he was Minister, he would never yield one scrap of [Britain's] heritage."[44]

Roosevelt finally was able to intercede to ask that Stettinius be allowed to finish. The secretary made the point that he was speaking about *enemy* dependent areas, not the British Empire. He

41. *FRUS, Malta and Yalta*, p. 793.
42. Russell, *UN Charter*, p. 573.
43. *FRUS, Malta and Yalta*, pp. 842–850.
44. Ibid.

concluded by recommending that the question be discussed at the forthcoming United Nations Conference. But Churchill was heard still muttering, "never, never, never."[45] During a short intermission Stettinius conferred privately with the prime minister. He showed Churchill a State Department memorandum which expressed United States opposition to placing any colony under a trust arrangement except by consent of the colonial power involved. This apparently mollified the prime minister, for he accepted the report when the plenary meeting resumed. The Big Three then agreed to hold special talks on trusteeships prior to the full UN conference.

The agreements reached on international organization at Yalta brought Britain and Russia firmly into line with America's UN policy and gained more time for the United States to convince its two main Allies that the UN could provide a satisfactory framework to ensure their security. In fact, most of the decisions at Yalta, dealing with liberated Europe, Germany, and the Far East, can best be understood when seen as part of America's drive to create the United Nations. Thus when Leahy disparaged the loopholes in the Polish agreement, Roosevelt immediately acknowledged his recognition of these defects. "I know, Bill—I know it but it's the best I can do for Poland at this time." What Roosevelt meant, of course, was that he recognized Russia's power to determine political events in Poland, but that future developments in Poland might be ameliorated. The mechanism of change would obviously be the United Nations.[46]

American policy neatly tried to cover the reality expressed in Leahy's remark by the Declaration on Liberated Europe. It pledged the great powers "to concert during the temporary period of instability in liberated Europe" their policies to help smaller nations "to solve by democratic means their pressing political and economic problems." This declaration promised that the liberated peoples would be free "to creat[e] democratic institutions of their own choice," and promised conditions of stability, to provide relief aid, to form democratic interim governments, and to facilitate free elections.[47] This declaration contained no measures for enforcement or

45. Stettinius, *Roosevelt and the Russians,* pp. 236–238.
46. Leahy, *I Was There,* pp. 315–316; Burns, *Roosevelt: The Soldier of Freedom,* pp. 569–572.
47. *FRUS, Malta and Yalta,* p. 972.

arbitrating disputes, such as would have been available by an interim UN.

Alperovitz claims that "before and during the conference that the president regarded the broadly phrased declaration primarily as a device to offset domestic criticism of the de facto spheres-of-influence understanding."[48] Unfortunately Alperovitz distorts his evidence. What the State Department referred to was the importance of its interim UN policy to offset domestic criticism and isolationism, not just to the Declaration alone. Roosevelt's rejecting the Emergency High Commission, while accepting the declaration, shows the president's own isolationist streak.[49]

When examined closely there was a tentative quality to most of the major agreements at Yalta, and the UN was Roosevelt's hope that difficulties might be adjusted in a spirit of understanding. Despite misgivings, many of which were voiced afterwards in memoirs, the American delegation left the Crimea in an optimistic mood. Even Harriman, who had been among the American analysts most suspicious of Russia's motives, wrote in a mood of anticipation to Stettinius: "I feel I must take this oportunity to tell you what a gratification it was to me to see at Yalta *the grasp which you have of our problems.* The careful preparation which you organized for the Conference and *the skill with which you handled the negotiations with Molotov and Eden laid the foundation for the ultimate decisions reached there* by the President with Marshal Stalin and the Prime Minister. Knowing Molotov and the other Soviet officials as well as I do, *I can say without qualification that your frankness and fairness in these discussions have,* in the brief period of the Conference, *materially improved our relations with the Soviet Foreign Office.* The historic suspicions of the Soviet Foreign Office have been much allayed. *I already sense the development of far franker relationships.* There is no doubt that we will have further difficulties. On the other hand I am satisfied that your discussions at Yalta have resulted in *a tremendous stride in the direction of greater mutual confidence* which will stand us in good stead in future negotiations. . . .

"The peace and tranquility of the world depends on the development of intimacy between the three great powers who are

48. Alperovitz, *Atomic Diplomacy,* pp. 135–136, 136n.
49. *FRUS, Malta and Yalta,* p. 98.

winning the war. This is the avowed Russian policy and I believe you have seen enough to accept its sincerity."[50]

This letter arrived just as Stettinius was beginning the Inter-American Conference on Problems of War and Peace in Mexico City. The letter reinforced his own beliefs. He spoke in glowing terms to Latin American statesmen about the achievements of the Crimea conference. Allied unity seemed to rest on firmer footing, and the questions left deadlocked at Dumbarton Oaks had been settled. Both Roosevelt and Stettinius were confident that Yalta had been the height of Allied wartime unity, and they looked forward to the conference in San Francisco which would funnel this unity into the postwar era. They were soon to realize how illusory this unity was and to see the breakdown of the Yalta agreements jeopardize the hope of establishing any international organization.

50. Harriman to Stettinius, Feb. 20, 1945, *SP;* italics in original.

5

Latin America and the UN Policy

WHEN AT LAST THE AMERICAN GOVERNMENT WON what it deemed a major victory at Yalta in the struggle for acceptance of the UN policy, it faced a stiff test of that policy from nations of the Western hemisphere. The occasion was the Inter-American Conference on Problems of War and Peace held in Mexico City from February 21 to March 5. Historians have virtually ignored the Mexico City Conference and thus have missed a vital turn in American foreign policy that began to emerge at this time, the challenge to the internationalist precepts that underlay the UN policy. The Latin American countries, because they feared postwar communist expansion, favored a purely regional approach to their security and challenged international alternatives. Both Britain and Russia were moving in the same direction. Significantly, for the first time American congressional and military spokesmen joined forces to support the regional approach. The Mexico City conference was the first one in which these two groups were jointly represented. Their influence steadily gained in force in the coming months as Allied cooperation disintegrated, and their views by the time of the San Francisco conference fundamentally altered the UN policy.

These developments still lay ahead as Secretary Stettinius stepped from his plane in Mexico City on February 20, waving his grey homburg and looking rested despite the strenuous pace of the past month. As he addressed the throng on American-Mexican friendship, Stettinius made an embarrassing slip which foreshadowed the difficulties of the next few weeks. He called Mexico "one of our own," whereas the text should have read "one of our friends."[1] Given the always sensitive Latin American spirit regarding U.S. intentions, this error might have caused a disagreeable stir; but the Mexican newspapers were polite enough to print the corrected version, which a State Department press officer hurriedly handed out. Thanks, however, to James Reston's sharp ear, the error reached the *New York Times* and other papers and was published as a great faux pas. Later Stettinius heatedly accused Reston of trying to sabotage the conference.[2]

Stettinius arrived in a good mood, buoyed by reports from Washington telling of the enthusiastic public reception given to the Yalta communique. Nelson Rockefeller, assistant secretary for Latin America, wrote: "You have no idea the impression it made in this country and the wave of confidence which has swept over the people. . . . Things are shaping up extremely well for the Conference in Mexico. There is a growing enthusiasm on all sides and I feel confident that the outcome will be of the utmost importance to the future of the country."[3]

Rockefeller's expectation of a smooth-running conference in Mexico City encouraged Stettinius. Time had not allowed him to prepare as thoroughly for Mexico City as he had for Yalta so he relied heavily on Rockefeller's analysis of Latin American affairs.

Stettinius and Rockefeller were the only official American delegates, but there were many military representatives plus five members of Congress: Senators Connally and Austin, and Representatives Bloom, Rogers, and Johnson.

The conference at Mexico City grew out of a request that Argentina had made to the Pan-American Union in November, 1944,

1. Stettinius, calendar notes, Arrival in Mexico City, Feb. 20, 1945, *SP*.
2. *El Universal* published the remarks as, "un firme defensor de las tradiciones democraticas de este hemisferio y un pais que estamos orgullosos de llamar nuestro amigo." Feb. 21, 1945; Reston interview with author, June 12, 1962.
3. Nelson Rockefeller to Stettinius, Feb. 15, 1945, *SP*.

asking the nations of the Western hemisphere to meet and review the heavily criticized Argentine policies.[4] This plea by the Farrell-Peron regime struck a sympathetic chord among the other Latin American nations. Many diplomats were eager to bring Argentina back into the hemisphere family of nations. As long as so important a country as Argentina remained an outcast, the Latin American nations could not speak with the authority that they might otherwise muster. The Argentine appeal was shrewdly timed, coming at a moment when Latin American leaders resented the Allied powers' failure to consult them before the Dumbarton Oaks Conference. They thought a hemisphere conference would enable them to restore Argentina to good grace and to work for amendments to the Dumbarton Oaks Proposals.[5]

The United States faced a delicate situation, for it had let inter-American relations drift during the war while preoccupied with its struggle against the Axis powers. The Latin American countries did contribute raw materials,[6] but Britain and America were the mainstays of this fight.

Latin American leaders patiently accepted this back-seat status, but the United States presumed too much when it worked out its UN policy without first considering the ideas of its hemispheric neighbors. The State Department belatedly attempted to correct this deficiency after Dumbarton Oaks by holding a series of briefings for ambassadors from Latin America in which Secretary Stettinius stressed "that the effect of [the Dumbarton Oaks Proposals] will be to enhance the position and responsibilities of the inter-American system." On Columbus Day Roosevelt had insisted that the Good Neighbor system would be enduring: "We have not labored so long and faithfully to build in this New World a system of international security and cooperation, merely to let it be dissipated in any period of postwar indifference."[7] Secretary Stettinius was confident that these official reassurances would mollify Latin

4. George Messersmith to Stettinius, Dec. 6, 1945, *SP*.

5. J. Lloyd Mecham, *The United States and Inter-American Security, 1889–1960*, pp. 255–256.

6. Michael Francis, "Attitudes of the United States Government toward Collective Security Arrangements with Latin America, 1945–1960" (University of Virginia, unpublished doctoral dissertation, 1963), p. 31.

7. *New York Times*, Oct. 13, 1944; Mecham, *Inter-American Security*, p. 256.

American grumbling, but he had misjudged the depth of the discontent. He was soon to learn, at Mexico City, the magnitude of his error.

The strains within the Good Neighbor family were readily apparent at Mexico City and showed that Rockefeller's optimism had been ill-founded. From the outset, the majority of the delegates favored a strong regional collective security system. When the conference steering committee met on February 21, Uruguay tried to put this topic on the conference agenda, but the United States successfully blocked this move. This victory was only temporary because proposals for a mutual security pact were soon presented to a committee of the conference that dealt with inter-American security.[8]

Three major resolutions came before this committee, all aimed at creating a strong, permanent inter-American security system. In the first and mildest proposal, Brazil called on hemisphere countries to reaffirm respect for each other's independence and to reiterate the importance of hemisphere solidarity against outside aggression. In case of an attack by one American state against another, the hemisphere nations should consult on measures to "lend proper help to the victim of aggression."[9] Uruguay's resolution elaborated on the Brazilian document by calling for a specific commitment on the part of each hemisphere government: "The High Contracting Parties bind themselves to uphold by all means, including force of arms, both collectively and individually, the territorial integrity and political independence of each and every one of them."[10]

Colombia submitted the most far-reaching plan for a security pact. It first reviewed the steps taken toward inter-American solidarity since 1890 and expressed a widely held Latin American belief that "the furtherance of these standards . . . constitutes an effective means of contributing to the general system of world

8. Inter-American Conference on Problems of War and Peace. [Hereinafter cited as Mexico City Conference], Developments of Feb. 21, Meeting of the Steering Committee, Summary, Feb. 21, 1945, SP.

9. Draft Resolution by Brazil, No. 37, as published in U.S., Department of State, *Report of the Delegation of the United States of America to the Inter-American Conference on Problems of War and Peace* (Washington, D.C., 1946), pp. 178–179. [Hereinafter cited as *U.S. Delegation Report.*]

10. Draft Resolution by Uruguay, No. 29, *U.S. Delegation Report,* pp. 155–156.

security and of facilitating the implementation of this system."[11] This goal could be achieved by a mutual guarantee of the "inviolability of the territory" and the "political independence" of every hemisphere nation, and Colombia suggested specific steps to take against an aggressor: "In any event, an invasion of the territory of a State by the armed forces of another, by crossing frontiers established by treaties in force, constitutes an act of aggression which makes mandatory immediate action against the aggressor by the signatory nations."[12] In deference to the UN, the Colombian regional system would carry out enforcement action "in harmony" with the UN.[13]

The movement represented by these resolutions was exactly what the Department of State had wanted to avoid at Mexico City, as it raised the problem of a regional concept versus an international concept of security. The department had had fair warning of this dilemma, for it had learned in January that Colombia's President Santos had sounded out Roosevelt about a regional security pact. Santos had told the president that such a treaty was needed because Lend-Lease aid had greatly increased the level of armaments in Latin America. The idea of a pact had been discussed by the secretary's staff committee, but no conclusion was reached except that by mid-February Rockefeller reported that Roosevelt had "said definitely" to Santos if Colombia proposed the pact at Mexico City, the United States would support it. Rockefeller also claimed that Colombian drafting of a treaty was "far advanced."[14]

This approval is further evidence that Roosevelt was a less enthusiastic supporter of UN dominance than Hull. It also shows the president acting in a way which helped to undermine the very policy vital to American postwar goals. By his agreement with Santos's proposal, Roosevelt set the stage for the upsurge in regionalism of the Mexico City Conference. The paradox was that by this time Roosevelt was relying more heavily than ever on fruition of the UN policy. The burden for undoing the presidential inconsistency rested on the State Department.

11. Draft Resolution by Colombia, No. 42, U.S. *Delegation Report*, pp. 185–187.

12. Ibid.

13. Ibid.

14. Secretary's Staff Committee, minutes, Jan. 10, 1945, and Feb. 12, 1945, *SP*.

Why had the department not acted earlier to squelch or post-pone this regional movement? Certainly a prime reason was the presidential blessing. Perhaps FDR did not fully grasp the difficulties which regionalism could cause, or he might have been trying to ride two horses at once, pacifying Latin American anxieties and winning support for the Dumbarton Oaks Proposals. But the most crucial factor in delaying State Department reaction to Santos's idea was that its highest officials were seriously split over the merits of regional security. Rockefeller favored having a strong regional system as the best way to protect the interests of the Western hemisphere.[15] He claimed that the department had to honor Roosevelt's promise to Santos, but Pasvolsky and Dunn vigorously dissented. This broad pact would open the floodgates at San Francisco, and every other nation would demand similar privileges in its area. It "would place a powerful weapon in the hands of the Russians who might ask that similar regional arrangements be applied to Eastern Europe." Rockefeller and Pasvolsky worked long hours seeking a solution, but they had no answer when the Mexico City conference opened.[16]

Once the problem was raised by the three resolutions in the conference committee, the same division that had hindered the secretary's staff committee appeared in the American delegation. Stettinius, who had been in Yalta during most of the discussion of the Santos idea, did not take an active role in these deliberations. From this moment on the full consequences of Roosevelt's appointing Stettinius Secretary of State became apparent. Hull would have moved quickly to squelch the regional movement, but Stettinius failed to comprehend its full significance. Consequently he let others take the initiative in the delegation deliberations. The representative of the Joint Chiefs of Staff, General Embick, told the delegation that American military leaders regarded the Colombian treaty proposal as "entirely satisfactory." Embick stressed the military value of inter-American solidarity. No one could foretell the success of the UN, and the Western hemisphere was essential

15. George Messersmith to Stettinius, Dec. 6, 1944, *SP*; Welles, *Where Are We Heading?*, p. 207.

16. Secretary's Staff Committee, minutes, Feb. 12, 1945; Charles W. Yost to Hayden Raynor, memorandum, Feb. 19, 1945, and U.S. Delegation, Committee on Inter-American Organization, minutes, Feb. 21, 1945, *SP*.

to American defense as a source of raw materials and for its strategic location.[17]

Pasvolsky had long favored the internationalist approach to world security, and he did not want to see the UN watered down by a series of regional pacts. In opposing the military views on the Colombian treaty, he cited the Moscow Declaration of 1943, which pledged the United States, Russia, and Britain not to "employ their military forces within the territories of other states except for the purposes envisaged in this declaration and after joint consultation."[18] He warned further of possible difficulties in securing Senate approval for a regional treaty.[19]

Embick was not to be put off so easily and he argued that there was nothing in the Moscow Declaration which prohibited a security treaty in the Western hemisphere. Here he had the best of the argument, for the United States was only obligated by the Declaration to consult with her Allies on using force in regional treaties; there was no requirement to get agreement. As for Pasvolsky's fear about Senate reaction, Embick declared his willingness to appear personally before the legislators to present his case, and two days later Congresswoman Edith Rogers supported his stand with the remark that "the establishment of an inter-American system would meet with the strong approval of Congress and the American people."[20]

General Embick presented the military position to Stettinius, and the secretary passed the information on to the State Department without comment. Stettinius was then in the midst of strenuous efforts to secure French approval of the Yalta agreements on international organization, so that he could announce the voting procedure to the Mexico City conference. He did not intervene actively to clarify American policy on the proposed inter-American treaty, and the initiative in this matter remained in the hands of the Latin American delegates.

17. Mexico City Conference, Report to the State Department, Developments from noon, Feb. 23, to 2 p.m., Feb. 24, 1945, and minutes of meeting in Hotel Reforma, Feb. 24, 1945, *SP*.

18. Ibid.; Moscow Declaration as quoted in Feis, *Churchill, Roosevelt, and Stalin*, pp. 208–209.

19. Minutes of meeting in Hotel Reforma, Feb. 24, 1945, *SP*.

20. U.S. Delegation, Committee 3, Inter-American Organization, minutes, Feb. 26, 1945, *SP*.

While the Americans discussed their differences, a conference subcommittee had been meeting to incorporate the Brazilian, Uruguayan, and Colombian resolutions into one draft treaty. By February 27 this work was done. The codified resolution reviewed the growth of inter-American cooperation and claimed that a Western hemisphere regional treaty would strengthen the international organization. It set forth provisions guaranteeing the political and territorial integrity of each Western hemisphere country and indicated the steps to be taken in the event of aggression by "any state" against a member republic. These ideas had all been contained in the earlier draft resolutions, but the subcommittee added a new paragraph that made the entire plan much more potent: "The signatory states undertake to defend by all means, including arms, the territorial integrity and political independence of each and every one of them, once it has thus been declared by the absolute majority of all the American states."[21]

The introduction of the new draft caught the American representatives on the committee of the conference by surprise, and the draft treaty was about to be passed by acclamation when Senator Austin drew on his skill as a parliamentarian to delay action. Would the delegates, he wondered, agree to postpone the vote? He noted that the only available copy of the resolution was in Spanish; he wished to study an English version. Further, Senator Connally had not arrived, and Austin wanted to do him the courtesy of consulting him before approving. The Latin American members of the committee had no choice but to agree to postpone the vote.[22]

When the American committee members caucused after this close call, Austin angrily denounced the unsuccessful railroading tactics that he had just witnessed. He called the draft treaty a "bombshell," which it was indeed; for the congressional leaders had not been told about the Roosevelt-Santos conversation on an inter-American security pact. The Department of State had thought it best to wait until it had worked out some definite policy on the issue, but this had not been accomplished by the time the Mexico City conference started. Now Rockefeller had to explain to an

21. Draft Resolution on Reciprocal Assistance and American Solidarity, Draft No. 181 CS-PR-5, translaton by State Department, n.d., *SP*.

22. *Diario de la Conferencia Sobre Prolemas de la Guerra y de la Paz*, No. 7, Feb. 28, 1945, p. 94.

angry senator and listen to Austin protest that the treaty would
require Senate approval because it carried over into peacetime,
when Roosevelt's extraordinary wartime powers would have
lapsed.[23]

Even though this discussion embarrassed Rockefeller, it resulted in an idea that solved the entire problem of an inter-
American security treaty. It was suggested by State Department
Legal Adviser Green Hackworth, who recommended that promises
of concrete aid from the body of the treaty be deleted and enforcement measures be affixed to the treaty as possible amendments. In this way, the hemisphere governments could consider
them with the greater care they deserved. It would also lessen
Senate opposition to a treaty which, in its present form, committed
American troops to fight after a simple majority vote of the members of the pact.[24]

By March 1, Hackworth and Senator Austin had forged a new
treaty. Thus the United States, which had originally hoped to postpone decisions on inter-American security until after the United
Nations charter was written, took a major part in working out a
regional security pact. Stettinius informed Grew of these events in
a cable on March 1. He reported that the resolution in the committee had created a dramatic situation and that delegates were talking excitedly about the inter-American security treaty, which the
press called the "Declaration of Chapultepec," after the historic
castle that housed the conference. Stettinius characterized it as "one
of the keystones" of the conference.[25] In a cable to Roosevelt, he
summarized the feeling of the American delegation, "We believe
that the proposal conforms to your objectives as outlined in your
conversations with President Santos and that it is essential to the
success of the Conference."[26]

The document which finally emerged from these maneuvers
was titled The Act of Chapultepec. It declared that, while the war
continued, any act of aggression against the territorial or political
independence of an American state would "constitute an interference with the war effort of the United Nations" and would be met

23. Secretary's Staff Committee, minutes, Feb. 12, 1945; U.S. Delegation,
Committee 3, Inter-American Organization, minutes, Feb. 27, 1945, SP.
24. Ibid.
25. FRUS, 1945, vol. 9, The American Republics, p. 134.
26. Stettinius to Roosevelt, telegram, Mar. 1, 1945, SP.

under the war powers of these countries. There was also a recommendation that the hemisphere nations "consider the conclusion" of a treaty extending these commitments into the postwar era. Finally, the declaration was proclaimed as a "regional arrangement . . . which shall be consistent with the purposes and principles of the general international organization."[27]

The statement relating the inter-American system to the international organization might appear to be a Latin American surrender to the supremacy of the UN as envisioned in the Dumbarton Oaks Proposals. Actually it was not, for at the San Francisco Conference, the Latin American countries made a determined effort to provide broad autonomy for regional arrangements under the UN Charter. A preview of this future struggle occurred at a luncheon that Stettinius hosted on March 2. In their remarks the secretary and Senator Connally emphasized the primacy of the Security Council over regional groupings and stressed that the Act of Chapultepec must be viewed in this light. This brought a quick reaction from Colombian Foreign Minister Alberto Lleras Camargo. If the United States was willing for European states to participate in settling problems of the Western hemisphere, he said, "it would appear that the Monroe Doctrine was being abandoned." Thus, ironically, a Latin American statesman used the Monroe Doctrine as a blackjack over the head of the "colossus of the north." In a quick resurgence of nationalism, Connally proclaimed emphatically that "the United States had no intention of abandoning the Monroe Doctrine."[28] This assurance carried the day, and the luncheon ended in a spirit of goodwill over conference achievements.

The Act of Chapultepec did not end the regional issue at all. The Latin Americans could interpret Connally's remarks as leaning toward regionalism, and certainly since he was chairman of the powerful Senate Foreign Relations Committee, his views carried authority. On the other hand, Stettinius and Pasvolsky could be satisfied that, while things had gone further than they wanted, the United States had avoided definite commitments on a peacetime hemisphere security treaty.

27. Final Act of the Inter-American Conference, Resolution 8, The Act of Chapultepec, *U.S. Delegation Report*, pp. 74–75.
28. Brief Account of the Secretary's Luncheon at the Hotel Reforma Apartment, Mar. 2, 1945, *SP*.

One dangerous aspect of the Act of Chapultepec was that other nations, particularly Russia, might look upon the negotiations leading to the Act of Chapultepec as an American effort to build up a private sphere of imperialism. Even if this traditional Communist suspicion did not win out in Moscow, the Russians at San Francisco could legitimately cite the Act of Chapultepec as a precedent for creating their own security system in Eastern Europe. The Soviet-French treaty of December, 1944, was aimed specifically at preventing a resurgence of German militarism rather than a broad regional system aimed at all potential foes. Nor did it embody the concept of one great power protecting a group of smaller nations. The Act of Chapultepec, unfortunately, carried this connotation, and it gave the impression of the United States setting the Western hemisphere off as its special sphere of influence. Russia might seek its own Monroe Doctrine for Eastern Europe.

At Mexico City, the United States faced another great challenge in the matter of securing endorsement of the Dumbarton Oaks Proposals, for the Latin American governments were very critical about the previous work on the world organization. In his opening address, Stettinius had reassured the delegates that the United States would not compromise the security of the Western hemisphere, but he tried to discourage amendments at Mexico City when he declared: "We have met here in order to carry further our discussions of the world organization before the United Nations Conference in San Francisco. We will not, of course, in the inter-American meeting make decisions on questions of policy that will be explored by all the United Nations together at San Francisco."[29] This desire to avoid making decisions about the structure of the international organization arose from a moral commitment the United States had made to stand with Russia, Britain, and China in supporting the Dumbarton Oaks Proposals.[30]

The Latin American delegates ignored this prescription. They had come to Mexico City determined to push through specific amendments in the Dumbarton Oaks Proposals. While many Latin American nations had already submitted their own amendments to the Big Four Powers, they now rallied behind the 200-page Mexi-

29. Address by Edward R. Stettinius, Jr., U.S. Delegation press release, Feb. 22, 1945, SP.
30. Russell, UN Charter, p. 552.

can document as "the best analysis and expression of the views of Latin America."[31]

The Mexican paper warmly praised the Allies' work at Dumbarton Oaks in drafting an effective system to forestall aggression; and it commended the "happy innovation" of the Economic and Social Council. But Mexico sharply denounced the imbalance between the power of the major states and the small ones in the proposed organization. The Mexicans drew evidence from the other international bodies which had been established during the war and found that "all these international instruments embody the principle that the Supreme Organ is that one on which *all* the member States are represented."[32] It was only logical that the same principle must apply to the UN.

Specifically, the Mexicans objected to establishing a Security Council which would be a closed preserve of the great powers. Mexico saw the advantage in having the major powers act in concert for peace, but argued that there should be no permanent members of the council. Its composition should be flexible to allow for changes in the world balance of power, so that new nations would become "semi-permanent" members when they achieved sufficient stature. No state should have a vote on the council when it stood accused of breaking the peace. Finally, if any nation wished, it should have the right to appeal from the Security Council to the General Assembly. In Mexican thinking, the assembly was really the supreme organ in the organization, and it should have the power to take action on its own initiative or when a member appealed from the Security Council.[33]

It was the difficult task of the United States delegation to prevent the Latin American states from accepting the Mexican ideas and pushing major amendments to the Dumbarton Oaks Proposals through the conference. This problem was complicated because the meetings of the committee on international organization, of which Stettinius was chairman, were open to the public and press. How could delicate points be discussed without risking applause

31. U.S. Delegation, Committee 2 on International Organization, minutes, Feb. 21, 1945, *SP.*

32. Opinion of the Ministry of Foreign Affairs of Mexico on the Dumbarton Oaks Proposals for the Creation of a General International Organization, Oct. 31, 1944, pp. 192–193, *SP.*

33. Ibid.

for Latin American amendments and developing a logrolling atmosphere? Stettinius and his fellow Americans on the committee on international organization hit on a solution: " . . . after a few days of general discussion a drafting committee should be appointed, composed of persons found by then to be the best equipped leaders, the meetings of which should be closed on the ground that they were simply sessions for drafting at a high technical level. Matters not easily discussable in public could be handled in the course of such drafting."[34] By this ruse the Americans hoped to keep a tighter hand on the process of winning Latin American approval of the Dumbarton Oaks Proposals.

There was still the problem of how to handle resolutions amending the Dumbarton Oaks Proposals. The American ambassador to Mexico, George Messersmith, had reported that Venezuela and Ecuador were "spearheading" a movement to include "specific items of dissent" in the conference statement regarding Dumbarton Oaks. As a defense, the American members of the committee on international organization decided not to offer any resolutions, "since our resolutions would be the focus of opposition for all those wishing to express dissent on any point in the Dumbarton Oaks Proposals." The Americans chose to work through another country, and their spokesman was Mexico's Foreign Minister Ezequial Padilla. He was to explain to her other big Allies the commitment of the United States not to negotiate further before the San Francisco conference. Padilla had already worked closely with the Americans in drafting a resolution which called on the conference to endorse the Dumbarton Oaks Proposals, and he would present it as sponsored by Mexico.[35]

The paradox of Mexico offering strong criticisms of the Dumbarton plans and then having her foreign minister assist in behind-the-scenes strategems to win endorsement of those same proposals is explained by the domestic situation that Mexican President Avila Camacho faced. Rising prices of staple foods during the war had created popular dissatisfaction, while in foreign policy many opposition leaders regarded Padilla as too subservient to American interests. Right-wing elements and the Catholic Church were re-

34. U.S. Delegation, Committee 2 on International Organization, minutes, Feb. 21, 1945, *SP.*
35. Ibid.

portedly working hard to undermine Mexican-American interests.[36] Padilla apparently wanted his government to cooperate with the United States, but politically he wanted to avoid the impression that he was a United States puppet—hence Mexico's published criticisms and private collaboration.

The United States could not, of course, block the introduction of opposing resolutions; and some highly critical ones were put before the committee on international organization. By February 28, Cuba's representative, Gutierrez, was leading the attack on the Dumbarton Oaks Proposals. He stressed that President Roosevelt had himself stated in October, 1944, that the proposals were intended only as a basis for discussion, not as a fixed blueprint for the UN. Gutierrez hammered away at the power of the Security Council and called the proposals "more totalitarian than democratic."[37]

At this point the United States plan to have Mexico's endorsement rally support for the proposals fell apart. When the Mexicans put the resolution forward on February 28, they gave away the American strategy by stating that they were acting on behalf of the United States, a blunder which was exceedingly embarrassing to their silent partners. Nelson Rockefeller hurriedly tried to withdraw all copies of the Mexican resolution, for they were marked as being endorsed by the United States, but the harm was done. The situation worsened when the Mexicans suddenly announced a second resolution which was hostile to the purposes of the United States. It proposed that all amendments which the conference accepted should be forwarded to the United Nations conference as representing changes that the Latin American republics wanted in the Dumbarton Oaks Proposals.[38]

Pasvolsky delayed action on this resolution by stating that the United States needed more time to study it. Immediately afterward, when the committee adjourned, Stettinius called his top aides into emergency session. Stettinius angrily told Pasvolsky to see Padilla

36. Austin F. Macdonald, *Latin American Politics and Government*, pp. 248–251; George Messersmith to Stettinius, Jan. 8, 1945, *SP*.

37. Coordinating Committee of Committee 2, minutes, 4:30p.m., Feb. 28, 1945, *SP*.

38. Stettinius, calendar notes, Mar. 1, 1945; notes on United States Delegation, Steering Committee meeting, Mar. 1, 1945; U.S. Delegation, developments from noon, Feb. 28, to noon, Mar. 1, 1945, *SP*.

and discover what was behind this latest development and stress to Padilla "that we must get here a complete endorsement of Dumbarton Oaks." America's ambassador to Mexico, Messersmith, stated he was confident that the Mexican foreign minister had acted in good faith toward the United States and that everything would work out satisfactorily. Padilla revealed that the Mexican delegation had been split about cooperating with the Americans, but Padilla assured Pasvolsky that an acceptable resolution could be developed.[39]

A compromise emerged during the next forty-eight hours whereby the conference would pass a set of "comments and suggestions" which "should be taken into consideration" at San Francisco. The United States escaped from any association with the compromise by insisting that all she would do would be to receive and transmit the proposed amendments to the other Allied nations.[40]

The committee on international organization then concluded its work by approving a resolution which embodied the compromise, and it was accepted by the full conference. It included the desired U.S. endorsement of the Dumbarton Oaks Proposals as "a basis for, and a valuable contribution to the setting up of, a General Organization." The Latin American amendments, which the United States would submit to the other Allies, included seven main points: (1) universal membership; (2) a clearer statement of purposes and principles; (3) a greater role for the General Assembly; (4) broader jurisdiction for the International Court of Justice; (5) creation of an agency to promote "intellectual and moral cooperation" among nations; (6) acceptance of the idea of the Western hemisphere as an integrated region of common security interests with the right to settle disputes by long-established procedures; and (7) representation of Latin America on the Security Council.[41]

By March 5, the United States had thus achieved its primary conference goal of endorsement of the Dumbarton Oaks Proposals.

39. Notes on United States Delegation, Steering Committee meeting, Mar. 1, 1945; Daily Report on Developments Concerning the Work of Commission II, Mar. 1 and 3, 1945, SP.

40. Stettinius to Grew, telegram, Mar. 3, 1945, SP.

41. Stettinius, calendar notes, meeting of Commission 2, Mar. 5, 1945, SP; Russell, UN Charter, p. 558.

Stettinius hailed the success as one that would stand as "a historical contribution to the greatest cause in the world."[42] Additionally, the Americans had coped rather successfully with the Latin American surge for a regional security pact by postponing concrete commitments until a later, indefinite time. Certainly American compromises were partly responsible for these achievements, but other events also contributed to the cooperative atmosphere at Mexico City. One example of this was America's reasonableness in the drafting of an "Economic Charter for the Americas," which described postwar hemisphere goals. The Latin Americans were highly pleased with the promise of the United States to reduce slowly its high levels of wartime purchases of Latin American raw materials. This would help Latin American nations avoid a postwar economic slump.[43]

The most far-reaching event making the delegates cooperative was the reversal of the U.S. policy toward fascist Argentina.[44] Although no Argentine delegates were present in Mexico City, the Argentine case was on everybody's mind. In a cable to Roosevelt, Stettinius vividly described this concern:

On arrival here I found the Argentine situation boiling. The Argentines seemed prepared to desert the Axis and join the good neighbors. They have considerable support in their maneuvering but so far we have been able to hold the line. However, I am convinced that we should take decisive action promptly in order to maintain the initiative. As Argentina meets conditions on which I believe there is consensus of opinion, we can insure the unity of the Americas. Otherwise, while Mexico on the surface might appear to be a success to hemispheric unity, yet basically there would be quicksands that would undoubtedly begin to shift before the Conference is over.

Since our arrival I have reviewed carefully with the FBI our accounts against Argentina, and I am now confident that, while one year ago there was substance relative to Axis

42. Stettinius, calendar notes, meeting of Commission 2, Mar. 5, 1945, SP.

43. Secretary's Staff Committee, minutes, Mar. 9, 1945, SP.

44. This marked the end of Hull's unsuccessful effort to get all members of the United Nations to break ties with Argentina in hopes of forcing out its pro-Nazi government. See Hull, Memoirs, II: 1143–1150 and 1377–1408.

relationships, of recent date it had been more of an emotional feeling on the part of the American people and within our own government, rather than any substantial evidence that there is actual aid to the enemy.[45]

The secretary was convinced that Argentina had demonstrated sufficient contrition to warrant her acceptance back into the ranks of democratic states. Stettinius proposed a formula to Roosevelt which had developed out of private conversations with Pasvolsky and others. It required that Argentina declare war on the Axis; work with the other hemisphere governments to bolster continental defense; remove its troops from the borders of neighboring states; and subscribe to the resolutions passed at Mexico City. Two days after this cable was dispatched, Grew informed Stettinius that Roosevelt had approved this major shift in Argentine policy.[46]

As a basis for this change, Stettinius and Rockefeller had accepted evidence that came from Argentine leaders by way of Colombia. In February, President Lopez of Colombia told American embassy officials that he had conferred with Argentine Vice-President Peron. According to Lopez, Peron had stated that Argentina desperately wanted to be reconciled with the United States and the other American republics and would do "anything" to attain this end. Peron had shown Lopez documents purporting to prove how Argentina had begun to suppress Axis activities, and claiming that much of this action had been kept secret because of the power of fascist elements in Argentina. It had even been necessary to make public gestures of appeasement to the fascists, but this was only a cover for the actual dissolution of Axis ties. Lopez accepted the sincerity of Peron's account, and he urged the United States to reconsider its hostile policy toward Argentina.[47]

This was only one side of the Argentine picture. Intelligence reports, available to Stettinius just five days after he had recommended the reversal of policy, indicated that German influence in Argentina remained at a high level. Extensive German espionage still emanated from Argentina, and German economic warfare against the United Nations in the hemisphere was termed both

45. Stettinius to Roosevelt, telegram, Feb. 23, 1945, SP.
46. Grew to Stettinius, telegram, Feb. 25, 1945, SP.
47. Grew to Stettinius, telegram, Feb. 20, 1945, repeating message from Ambassador Wiley in Bogota, SP.

systematic and highly successful. Intervention in the German firms by the Argentine government, at least up through December, 1944, had been inadequate. In early 1945, moreover, the Farrell-Peron regime promoted the pro-Nazi general Von der Becke to be commander in chief of the armed forces.[48]

Apparently, Stettinius and his advisers were willing to accept the sincerity of Peron's professions that Argentina was really turning the corner toward democracy, and they discounted continued fascist activities. This was a dangerous and expedient gamble and shows the extreme pressure the United States faced at the Mexico City conference. By yielding to the desire of the Latin Americans to renew good relations with Argentina, the secretary of state demonstrated America's willingness to accommodate Latin American interests. This decision paved the way for a successful conclusion of the questions concerning the international organization, which was the cornerstone of American foreign policy in early 1945.

The Mexico City conference registered its decisions on Argentina in Resolution 59. The conference delegates deplored Argentina's failure to purge herself of Axis ties before the conference convened; with inter-American unity "indivisible," Argentina could now take specific steps which would enable her to rejoin the American family. Perhaps the most critical demand was that the Farrell-Peron government adopt the principles agreed upon at Mexico City "identifying itself with the common policy these nations are pursuing, and orienting its own policy so that it may achieve its incorporation into the United Nations as a signatory to the Joint Declaration of 1942 entered into by them."[49] This statement was broad and adjustable and could be interpreted in many ways. As later modified by the United States and its Latin Allies, Resolution 59 became the weapon which the Latin Americans used to force the admission of Argentina as a charter member of the international organization. By its agreement to support Argentina's admission to the UN, the United States took a step that created great embarrassment later and exacerbated Soviet-American relations at a critical moment.

On March 5, Stettinius addressed a crowd jammed in the huge

48. U.S., Department of State, Information for Secretaries Stimson and Forrestal, Feb. 27, 1945, SP.
49. U.S. *Delegation Report*, Resolution 59, pp. 133–134.

salon at Chapultepec Castle for the closing sessions. The secretary made the dramatic announcement of the veto agreement that had been reached at Yalta. Mexico's Foreign Minister Padilla responded on behalf of the Latin nations and stated that Stettinius's words "would warm the hearts of all men of good will." Stettinius left the room feeling that this was "perhaps the most significant occasion of my formal participation in the conference."[50] Yet the achievements of the American diplomacy of postponement at Mexico City were largely illusory. For at the San Francisco Conference six weeks later, the Argentine admission question, the regional issue, and the voting problem created such havoc as to practically destroy the UN policy.

50. Stettinius, calendar notes, meeting of Committee 2, Mar. 5, 1945, SP.

6

The Shift toward Containment

THE ATMOSPHERE IN THE UNITED STATES IN THE SEC-
ond part of February, 1945, was one of excited hope. The administration basked in favorable publicity, the earlier pessimism and
criticism apparently forgotten. Roosevelt arrived home on March 1
after a leisurely ocean voyage aboard the U.S.S. *Quincy*. Although
he appeared worn and thin, his physician, Dr. Ross McIntire, con-
fidently assured reporters that the president's appearance was due
to his diet.[1]

Roosevelt was anxious to move ahead in the atmosphere of
public confidence, and within a day of his return he appeared before a joint session of Congress to report on the Crimean conference. His tone was decidedly optimistic. The significance of the
Big Three meeting was, he claimed, that the bonds of cooperation
among the powers were solid despite the problems of the past two
months. "After a week of frank discussion on every point, unanimous agreement was reached. . . . We achieved a unity of thought.
. . . Never before have the major Allies been more closely united

1. *New York Times*, Feb. 26 and Mar. 1, 1945; Henry E. Bateman, "Observations on President Roosevelt's Health during World War II," *Mississippi
Valley Historical Review*, 46 (June, 1956): 82–102.

not only in their war aims but also in their peace aims." Calling the Crimea conference a "turning point" in history, Roosevelt said that the American people and the Senate would soon have to decide about joining a new international organization. This decision, he said, "will determine the fate of the United States—and of the world—for generations to come. There can be no middle ground here. We shall have to take the responsibility for world collaboration or we shall have to bear the responsibility for another world conflict." Calling up the soldiers' sacrifices of two world wars and the broken dream of Woodrow Wilson, the president continued:

Twenty-five years ago, American fighting men looked to the statesmen of the world to finish the work of peace for which they fought and suffered. We failed them then. We cannot fail them again, and expect the world again to survive.

The Crimean Conference was a successful effort by the three leading nations to find a common ground for peace. It ought to spell the end of the system of unilateral action, the exclusive alliances, the spheres of influence, the balances of power, and all the other expedients that have been tried for centuries—and have always failed.

We propose to substitute for all these, a universal organization in which all peace-loving nations will finally have a chance to join.[2]

This was what Americans wanted to believe, and these bright prospects reinforced the hopes of many people.[3] Allied forces were overrunning Germany, the First Army reaching the Rhine on March 8. Berlin reported that Russian tanks were within twenty-five miles of the Nazi capital. In the Pacific, Americans were dying on Iwo Jima, and soon Okinawa would imprint a bloody memory in his-

2. Rosenman, ed., *Public Papers of Roosevelt*, 13: 573, 585–586.
3. Statistics compiled by the Department of State showed a marked increase in the percentage of people satisfied with Allied relations as a result of the Crimea Conference:

Allied cooperation	Jan., 1945	Feb. 1945
satisfied	46%	64%
dissatisfied	43	25

Among those dissatisfied, twice as many people picked Britain as picked Russia as the nation most responsible for unsatisfactory relations. See U.S., Department of State, Division of Public Liaison, Latest Public Opinion Trends, Feb. 23, 1945, SP.

tory. As women counted their never adequate supply of ration
stamps, as old men and boys hoed little "victory gardens," as wives
and mothers read the terse messages of death from the War Department, there developed an insistent mood across the nation
that American foreign policy must create an enduring peace.

The new popularity of the State Department was reflected by
opinion polls that showed an upswing of public confidence in
Allied relations and approval of the manner in which the department was publicizing foreign policy. This reflected, in part, the
more effective organization that Stettinius had developed in the
department. He had learned a great deal from the mistakes he had
made in his reorganization a year earlier, and his second organization plan made many improvements. Top officials met daily in the
staff committee to discuss current problems. Bohlen's liaison in the
White House provided a window for the department, and Stettinius saw to it that the president had a daily report on major actions of the department. Cooperation between the department and
the White House was at an all-time high. Even though Stettinius
was away from Washington much of the time, he kept in close
touch with the department. When he was in Washington, his white
phone to the White House was seldom idle, and he used spare moments in his car to dictate urgent notes and personal thoughts to his
secretary. Even when Stettinius took a few days' rest at Horseshoe,
he often called aides down to his farm; and the "rest" turned into
country working sessions.[4]

On March 10 Stettinius flew into Washington's National Airport. His mood was buoyant, and his airport statement reinforced
Roosevelt's speech of the preceding week. He stressed the vital
importance of unity among the Allies, which events at Yalta had
shown in action. The UN Conference in San Francisco, he predicted, would be "a turning point in the history of the world and of
America," and he compared it to the Constitutional Convention of
1787. There would be difficulties, and the American people must
take a long realistic look at them: "Like a great many Americans, I
have been brought up in business and I have been trained to look

4. U.S., Department of State, Division of Public Liaison, Latest Public
Opinion Trends, Mar. 10 and May 3, 1945, SP; for an interesting sketch of
Stettinius's habits see Bob Considine, "Stettinius—Dynamo in the State Depart-
ment," Readers Digest, 46 (Mar., 1945): 11–14.

reality squarely in the face. But I share also with most Americans an abiding faith in the power for good of our people and in the aspirations for which America stands."[5]

Underlying the statements of both the president and secretary of state was their faith in the UN policy. Their expression of this commitment was being repeated by dozens of government agencies in the weeks just prior to the UN conference. The UN was the topic of countless speeches, forums, programs, and articles. Their common denominator was idealism, creating a national mood of expectant optimism.

The public rhetoric bore little resemblance to the realities of Allied politics. By early March it was becoming clear to American leaders that Russia was acting in eastern Europe with scant regard to the Yalta pledges of democratic procedures. The Russians tried to hide their pattern of operation. Rumania is an example. The ground for Russian intervention was subtly laid by the Rumanian Communist party. It launched a campaign against the government of Prime Minister Nicolai Radescu, charging neglect of land reform, incompetency, and favoritism to Nazi sympathizers.

By early March the Radescu government teetered on the brink of collapse. Just at this moment Russian Deputy Foreign Minister Vyshinsky fortuitously arrived in Bucharest. He demanded that King Michael replace the Radescu ministry with one "based on the truly democratic forces of the country." The ideal candidate was Peter Groza, who was closely associated with the Rumanian Communist party. Powerless against Russian warnings that a refusal would result in the Red army being unable to control its soldiers, the King appointed Groza prime minister on March 6. His appointment marked Rumania's entry into the Soviet orbit.[6]

The White House was fully aware of these developments. The president received daily situation reports prepared from State Department cables, which plainly showed that the Kremlin had forced Radescu out. A personal appeal had reached the Office of Strategic Services from King Michael. Directed to the president, it somehow did not reach the White House until April. Too late to change the *fait accompli*, the King's letter, nonetheless, added interesting details on the tactics which the Russians had employed to place the

5. *New York Times*, Mar. 10, 1945.
6. Feis, *Churchill, Roosevelt, and Stalin*, pp. 564–566.

Radescu government in an untenable position. In reality there was little new in the pattern of Russia's pursuit of power in the reports of February and March. The Roosevelt administration had been receiving similar information prior to Yalta which, in part, was what lay behind the president's willingness to write off Eastern Europe.[7]

Still the American government had not expected Russia to move in so blatant a fashion, and it decided that the moment had come to invoke the Declaration on Liberated Europe.[8] Accordingly, Harriman called on Molotov and asked for a special Allied investigation of the Rumanian situation. He was rebuffed, and other United States protests brought no better response. The Russians simply delayed until Groza had been firmly seated in power, then told Harriman that there was no need for Allied inquiry in Rumania because "the Soviet Government considers that the formation of a national democratic government makes unnecessary any special consideration of the Rumanian situation at this time."[9] Clearly the Soviet government had its own ideas regarding the use of the Declaration on Liberated Europe. Groza remained in power, and the only action the British and Americans took was to withhold recognition of his government.[10]

Having gone through the motions, the American government rested its efforts. Far to the north of Bucharest, Molotov was meeting in Moscow with ambassadors Clark Kerr of Britain and Harriman of the United States as the special commission created at the Crimea conference to reorganize the Polish provisional government. This regime had been established by Russia but recognized by neither the British nor Americans. From the outset of their deliberations on February 22, it was apparent that serious difficulties existed over interpreting the Crimea agreement on Poland. By March 10, the Russians were demanding that Polish participants in the reorganization talks must be acceptable to the Polish provi-

7. *FRUS, 1945*, vol. 5, *Europe*, pp. 465–466. The memorandum detailing Soviet harassment is not published in *FRUS*, but a copy of it is in the Stettinius Papers. For Russian activities in Rumania, see *FRUS, 1944*, vol. 4, *Europe*, pp. 253–254, 257–260.

8. U.S., Department of State, Information for Secretaries Stimson and Forrestal, Mar. 13, 1945, *SP*.

9. U.S., Department of State, Special Information for the President, Mar. 19, 1945, *SP*.

10. Feis, *Churchill, Roosevelt, and Stalin*, p. 567.

sional government in Warsaw. The Western Allies objected that this amounted to allowing the Warsaw government a veto and violated the Yalta agreements.[11]

The delay this deadlock caused was politically embarrassing to the West, especially America. It had been expected that some face-saving compromise could be achieved that would still the criticisms of Americans of East European descent. There was also pressure from the Catholic Church, whose American prelates had already publicly warned against Russian expansion.

The American government's problem was that it had succeeded too well at Yalta. By binding Russia to democratic procedures in eastern Europe, the United States had subscribed the Russians to a goal they could not honor. It contradicted Russian security needs, particularly in Poland, which had been Germany's invasion corridor into Russia. Given the historic enmity between Russians and Poles, there was little chance that a politically free choice would yield a pro-Russian government. Doubtless at Yalta, Stalin had gone along with Western demands in deference to American sensitivity on domestic politics, and certainly out of a desire for postwar Western economic help.

While the fact of Soviet power was clearly recognized by the American government, and its use expected, the unwillingness of Russia to adhere at least to democratic form upset the Roosevelt administration's timetable. Russia's disdain for the politics of appearances created serious difficulties for the American government because it threatened to disrupt the UN policy that the Americans counted on to afford time and means for working out postwar cooperation. The Russians were being obstinate.

Even though the deterioration of the Yalta agreements seriously disturbed Roosevelt, he maintained a surface optimism. This facade was also apparent in the State Department and was presented both to the public and Congress.[12]

11. *FRUS, 1945, 5, Europe*, pp. 123–167; Llewellyn Woodward, *British Foreign Policy*, pp. 500–505; Rozek, *Allied Wartime Diplomacy*, pp. 363–364.

12. *FRUS, 1945, 5, Europe*, p. 209; Polish leaders and Congressmen from regions with a heavy Polish concentration were vociferous in expressing doubts about Roosevelt's policy on Poland. See, Rozek, *Allied Wartime Diplomacy*, pp. 298–302; prominent Catholic leaders expressed their fears to Secretary Stettinius in a private meeting in March. See Stettinius to Lynch, n.d., about 1948, SP; Werth, *Russia At War*, pp. 943–948, 1016–1020. Werth shows

Privately, a deepening gloom gripped American leaders, as if Churchill's grim forebodings at Malta had taken hold of their minds. Relations among the Allies grew more acrimonious with each passing day as the April 25 opening of the UN conference approached. On March 29 word came that Molotov would not attend the conference and that Russia would be represented by Ambassador Gromyko. The UN policy appeared to be on the brink of disaster, for its strength depended on the continued collaboration of America, Britain, and Russia.

Out of this mood of despair developed a reappraisal of American policy toward Russia. Several important characteristics of this development are clear. It was not ordered by Roosevelt, nor did it have any channel of operation. Second, it was the maturation of fears about Russia's intentions that had been suppressed while the UN policy dominated official thinking. Third, the review process, which lasted from late March to May 10, was not anticommunist at the outset, but after Truman became president the hand of the anticommunist hardliners was measurably strengthened. Finally, this reappraisal was the germinating ground from which much of Truman's containment policy evolved.

Revisionist historians have seen a sharp break in policy from Roosevelt to Truman, with the latter abandoning the wartime policy of collaboration. The most detailed explanation has been offered by Gar Alperovitz in his *Atomic Diplomacy: Hiroshima and Potsdam.* His analysis of Truman's reliance on the atomic bomb as a diplomatic weapon is quite significant, but he failed to see the disintegration of the UN policy as a closely linked factor. He puts forward an awkward thesis of an immediate and delayed showdown strategy to explain Truman's actions in the spring of 1945. Actually, the president's policy developed slowly in the months after he became president. The review of Russian policy casts

---

the strong rivalry between the Communist party and the Red Army, with party leaders striving to assure ideological correctness as the war drew toward a close. Stalin was entering a period of increased suspiciousness in 1945, and the situation in Poland fed the party's worst fears. Stalin told Hopkins on June 1, 1945, that he believed the British government was conspiring with the London Poles against Russian interests. Earlier he had warned against returning to the prewar concept of a *cordon sanitaire* using eastern Europe as a hostile buffer against Russia. *FRUS, Conference at Potsdam, 1945* I: 39, 59 [Hereinafter: *FRUS, Potsdam*].

doubts on the validity of Roosevelt's UN policy. Truman gradually abandoned that policy in favor of the atomic diplomacy dominant in the summer and fall.

A major source of the American reappraisal is to be found in military discontent with the Roosevelt administration's provisions for safeguarding the nation after the war. Both Secretaries Stimson and Forrestal had serious misgivings about the wisdom of providing for national safety through the collective security apparatus of the UN. Forrestal feared that overemphasis on the UN would sap public support for a powerful postwar navy, and he lamented the influence of "all of the pacifists and do-gooders." His fear was that America would demobilize its two-ocean navy in a wave of false hope in the UN.[13] Stimson approached the UN policy gingerly. He regarded Stettinius, who had so much responsibility for guiding execution of the policy, as "thoroughly ignorant" of past events regarding the League of Nations, and he never fully trusted Stettinius as a policymaker.[14] Stimson regarded the administration's diplomacy at Dumbarton Oaks as premature, and he took every opportunity to forward this view. He argued that public excitement engendered by the UN policy might hinder achieving goals vital to America's postwar military security.[15]

The military leaders typically wanted the U.S. to rely on its own forces for postwar security and to acquire a network of overseas bases in the Pacific and Atlantic to guard against any potential aggressor. Stimson and Forrestal reluctantly went along with the State Department at Dumbarton Oaks out of necessity, not choice. At the insistence of the Joint Chiefs the American negotiators dropped the trusteeship question from the conference agenda. The JCS wanted no agreements limiting acquisition of overseas bases for airfields and naval facilities.[16]

Paradoxically, it was Stettinius's coming into the secretaryship that facilitated presentation of the military viewpoint. Through his

13. Forrestal to Harriman, Oct. 3, 1944, Forrestal Papers; Forrestal to Robert Matter, Nov. 29, 1944 and Forrestal to Baruch, Dec. 31, 1944, Forrestal Papers; Vincent Davis, *Postwar Defense Policy and the U.S. Navy, 1943–1946,* pp. 106, 158; Forrestal to James B. Carey, Jan. 12, 1945, Forrestal Papers.

14. Stimson, Diary, July 31, 1945, Stimson Papers.

15. Stimson, Diary, Jan. 21, 1945, Stimson Papers.

16. *FRUS, 1944,* 1, *General,* pp. 699–703, 705.

creation of the State-War-Navy Committee, machinery came to exist that was a powerful medium for military thinking. By January, 1945, this new vehicle was being utilized to persuade the new secretary along lines amenable to the military position.

On January 21 there was a top-level meeting of Stimson, Forrestal, and the JCS at the Pentagon. Here it was decided to discuss future Pacific security with Stettinius, pointing out the need for bases and raising the issue of how the atomic bomb might be a factor in the forthcoming Yalta conference.[17]

The following morning Stimson and Forrestal met with Stettinius. Vannevar Bush, chairman of the National Defense Research Committee, the man most responsible for coordinating the development of the atomic bomb, was also present. The discussion centered on America's postwar military needs and the timing of a conference to establish the United Nations. Stettinius, who had known of the bomb project since late December, was given an *aide-memoire* by Bush to use in case the Russians inquired about the atomic bomb at Yalta. There was also discussion of the American need for bases in the Pacific. Stimson stressed that all matters pertaining to the UN should be postponed "until certain underlying problems had been ironed out and solved among the four major powers." Stimson claimed that had Woodrow Wilson cemented an alliance among Britain, France, and America before plunging ahead with the Covenant of the League of Nations, the first world organization "would have been far easier and more successful." Forrestal gave "vigorous" support to Stimson's arguments.[18]

It should not be inferred from this meeting that the secretaries of War and Navy wanted to delay any UN conference until the end of the war when America possessed an atomic capability. If this had been the case, America could have negotiated from a position of even greater strength on the matter of Pacific bases and other political issues in the Far East. Stimson's emphasis on "underlying problems" implies his concern that premature discussion of Far Eastern problems with Russia might encourage her to demand a more extensive role in postwar Japan than the United States desired. Stimson left the meeting pleased with Stettinius's grasp of

17. Stimson, Diary, Jan. 21, 1945, Stimson Papers.
18. Stettinius, *Roosevelt and the Russians,* pp. 33–34.

these problems.[19] But is is misleading to argue that Stimson, Forrestal, and Stettinius were concocting any brand of "atomic diplomacy" at this early date. This seems to have been the only time prior to Roosevelt's death that the atomic potentiality was raised in regard to diplomacy. Had the atomic bomb been seen as a diplomatic weapon this early, it would have cropped up in the policy review carried out in early 1945, but this did not occur until after Roosevelt's death.

After the Yalta conference, where it had been agreed to hold later joint talks on trusteeships, the review of America's postwar security continued in meetings of the State-War-Navy Committee. Much attention centered around postwar bases and their control. The State Department wanted to create a UN Trusteeship Council to exercise broad powers over all dependent territories placed under the international organization's jurisdiction. The council would establish multinational commissions to administer trust territories, require regular reports, conduct site investigations, and dismiss insubordinate trust officials.[20]

Such ideas frightened American military leaders who feared that other nations might use the Trusteeship Council to pry into security arrangements that the United States established on islands that it had captured from Japan and that the military was determined to retain after the war. Stimson warned, on February 20, that any consideration of trusteeships at the forthcoming United Nations Conference would provide a forum for "discussion before a large number of nations of matters relating to the Pacific over which many of the nations would have no legitimate interest, as well as no appreciation of the security interests of the United States."[21] The Joint Chiefs deemed control over the Japanese mandated islands "essential to our security." The islands should come "under the sole sovereignty of the United States." Since they were being captured by United States forces, "there appears to be no valid reason why their future status should be the subject of discussion with any other nation."[22]

Stettinius appreciated the need to provide for American secur-

19. Stimson, Diary, Jan. 22, 1945, Stimson Papers.
20. Russell, UN Charter, pp. 573, 606–607.
21. Committee of Three, minutes, Feb. 20, 1945, SP.
22. Leahy to Hull, Mar. 11, 1944, SP.

ity and to time negotiations on international organization so that
the Russians could not use the trusteeship question to undermine
American national security in the Pacific. Yet he knew that the
United States could not hold off vital negotiations for establishing
the United Nations until every element of timing (such as the successful conclusion of the atomic project) gave the United States
the ideal bargaining position that the military desired. In its search
for a solution, the State Department in mid-March hit upon the
idea of specifying strategic areas in trust regions which would not
be altered unless all of the permanent powers on the Security Council concurred. It was hoped this would be acceptable to the JCS,
but departmental experts "agreed that it [trusteeships and Pacific
islands] was an important but probably insoluble problem." Outright annexation was recognized as the best answer, but this would
create the impression that the United States was violating the
promises of the Atlantic Charter and of the Cairo Declaration,
which rejected territorial aggrandizement. Also such action might
be used by other nations as an excuse to develop control over areas
that they captured.[23]

By late March the discussions over America's postwar security
in the Pacific broadened into the larger issue of reassessing all
Soviet-American relations. Stettinius and Hopkins recommended
that Roosevelt send an old friend of Churchill's, Bernard Baruch,
to London to confer with the prime minister on relations with Russia. Baruch went, but his report was shunted aside after Truman
came into office.[24]

The problem of Russia was raised by Stettinius in the State-
War-Navy Committee meeting on April 2. The secretary reviewed
the elements of what he called "a serious deterioration in our relations with Russia,"[25] and expressed concern that a rupture with
Russia might occur. That evening Stimson called Stettinius to report that he and General Marshall had discussed the secretary's as-

    23. Secretary's Staff Committee, Document No. 79, Mar. 17, 1945; Co-
ordinating Committee, minutes, Mar. 29, 30, 1945, and Secretary's Staff Committee, Document No. 102, Apr. 17, 1945, SP.
    24. Bernard Baruch to Byrnes, memorandum, Dec. 24, 1945, Baruch
Papers. In this paper Baruch adds that he had offered to aid the new President by providing the wisdom of his experience in two wars, but "no interest
was shown in these suggestions."
    25. Millis, ed., Forrestal Diaries, pp. 38–39.

sessment. They had expected this turn and thought the United States would have to put up with it for the present.[26]

There was much talk during this first week of April about canceling the UN Conference, a prospect that was regarded only as a last resort. The State Department was most reluctant, the military less so. All along, the secretary of War had advocated securing a harmony of interests among the great powers first, and afterward creating the UN organization. Had his been the decision, the United States would openly have acknowledged the realities of power, that Russia would dominate in postwar eastern Europe, and that the United States would grow in power in the Far East. This was the point he tried to impress on Stettinius the night of April 2: "I told Stettinius that in retrospect Russia had been very good to us in the large issues. She had kept her word and carried out her engagements. We must remember that she has not learned the amenities of diplomatic intercourse and we must expect bad language from her."[27] He expressed the belief that Russia wanted to get along with the United States.

It was not that the Roosevelt administration did not recognize Russia's intentions. Military and diplomatic sources had constructed a picture of calculated Russian attempts to build up a security buffer zone. Rather the men in Washington feared adverse public reaction if the United States openly acknowledged the legitimacy of Russian ambitions in eastern Europe. American officials were therefore engaged in an intensive search for ways to break the deadlock with Russia over Poland and to work toward more cordial relations. The answer that American leaders gradually developed was the strategy of economic coercion as an alternative to calling off the UN conference and the rupture such action might cause. Its chief proponent was Ambassador Harriman, who was summoned home for the policy review.

Harriman saw Russia as having "three lines of foreign policy." One, overall collaboration in a world organization; two, creation of a "unilateral security ring" on its western border; three, exploitation of democratic processes to penetrate other nations and create an atmosphere favorable to Soviet policies. The United States had

26. Stimson, Diary, Apr. 2, 1945, Stimson Papers.
27. Ibid.

"been hopeful that the Soviets would, as we have, place number one (international organization) as their primary policy and would modify their plans for two (the security ring) if they were satisfied with the efficacy of plan one." Recent events showed that Russia had reversed its approach and was moving to assure its security in Europe regardless of what this did to the UN. Harriman speculated that Stalin may have believed that by accepting generalized language for the agreement over Poland and the Declaration on Liberated Europe, the United States was tacitly accepting the Soviet policies regarding eastern Europe.[28]

Harriman had several explanations for the difficulty the United States now encountered. One was the well-known Russian suspiciousness toward foreigners. Another was that the Americans had tried to counter this by showing "goodwill by generosity and consideration." This approach had failed, and now friendship could be achieved only by a new tactic, which was to deal firmly and frankly with the Russians. "As you know, I am a most earnest advocate of the closest possible understanding with the Soviet Union so that what I am saying only relates to how such understanding may best be attained."

Harriman then outlined the policy of economic coercion. It involved the building of closer relations with Britain and other friendly nations. They should be assisted economically and made to feel independent of the Soviet Union. This would affect the Russians, "as I believe they fear more than anything else a close understanding among the western nations and I believe they will be more ready to deviate from their unilateral policies if they find that they cannot play one against the other and that they are not indispensable to us."[29] Congress should empower the administration to use American economic and financial power to achieve this goal.

28. Harriman was typical of the best type of American capitalist in overseas activity. From a wealthy, prominent family, he was well educated, intelligent, and had dealt closely with the Russians in a private business capacity for many years. He was keenly aware of American international economic interests and alive to the need of discovering ways in which capitalism and communism could coexist in peaceful economic competition. Stettinius, though less experienced than Harriman in overseas trade, appreciated the same problems and possibilities: Stettinius, *Roosevelt and the Russians*, p. 286; *FRUS, 1945*, 5: 821–824. Harriman found Stettinius under no illusions about the difficulties Russian relations posted, Harriman interview, Dulles Oral History Collection.

29. Ibid.

At the time there was consideration being given to Soviet requests for long-term, low-rate loans for recovery. Harriman incorporated this into his program, saying that he fully agreed with the idea of postwar loans; but he wanted Congress to give the administration blanket authority to lend money to nations, not to authorize a specific loan for aid to Russia. The president should have the control over credits to "restrict or reduce them as we may see fit." We should then make clear to Russia that our aid depended entirely on the extent to which we could achieve understanding in other areas of mutual interest.[30]

Harriman still believed that Russia wanted to cooperate with the West in establishing an international organization. Russia desired the world's respect and feared an outright showdown with Britain and the United States. The Russian people were friendly toward the Western democracies, and Soviet leaders were "sensitive to public demands," but Harriman told the State Department staff committee that "the time had come to eliminate fear in our dealings with the Soviet Union and to show we are determined to maintain our position." One way to be firm was in handling all the little areas of Allied relations, particularly in day-to-day military relations in Europe. Returning to his advocacy of economic pressure, Harriman said the ultimate weapon to force Russia to live up to her Yalta commitments was the economic cudgel. Russia depended on American Lend-Lease. Without it the Soviet Red army was " . . . a disorganized mass of human beings. . . . The country Russia is still fantastically backward. There is no road system, railroad mileage is very inadequate, and ninety percent of the people of Moscow live in a condition comparable with our worst slum areas." Mr. Harriman said he was therefore not much worried about the Soviet Union's taking the offensive in the near future. But they will take control of everything they can by bluffing. Harriman suggested that the United States curtail Lend-Lease aid and hold Russia strictly accountable for explaining how this aid was utilized.[31]

Before any decision could be made on using economic coercion

30. Harriman to Stettinius, telegram, Apr. 11, 1945, *SP*; Thomas G. Patterson, "The Abortive American Loan to Russia and the Origins of the Cold War, 1943–1946," *Journal of American History*, 56 (June, 1969): 70–81.

31. Harriman's views are covered in Special Information for the President, Apr. 5, 1945; Stettinius, Record, sec. 8, pp. 38–39; Secretary's Staff Committee, minutes, Apr. 20 and 21, 1945, *SP*.

on Russia, the shocking news of Roosevelt's death came. The unbelievable events of that April 12 stamped themselves indelibly on the memories of all Americans. Roosevelt had raised the power and scope of the presidency to unsurpassed heights during his twelve years in the White House. The nation had come to rely on his firm direction; he seemed the very heartbeat of national affairs.[32] The white phone on Stettinius's desk rang at 5:10 p.m., bringing an urgent request for the secretary to come immediately to the White House. Stettinius received the word of the president's passing from Mrs. Roosevelt, who, he noted, seemed more calm and composed than anyone else: "Everything was completely disorganized and nobody knew exactly where to turn. I spoke up and said a Cabinet meeting should be held immediately, and Anna Boettiger asked where. I said it should be in the Cabinet room at 6 p.m. Truman then asked me if I would make the arrangements."[33]

The meeting was held, but many extra officials were now crowding into the White House and the meeting accomplished little. As he waited with Truman for the chief justice to arrive for the swearing-in ceremony, Truman and Stettinius talked. Truman stated that the death had come as a surprise and he was "shocked and startled." Stettinius said he felt certain that inner strength would come: "I had full confidence that the American people would rally around and see us through. I said we are well on the road to defeat of the enemy and we must win on the world organization. Truman said 'I understand thoroughly, and you will have my fullest support in everything.' "[34]

The following day, as arrangements were being completed for Roosevelt's funeral on the 14th, Stettinius gave Truman a more candid report that stressed the crisis in Soviet relations: "I then told the president that our relations with the Soviet Union since Yalta had deteriorated. He said he understood this, but asked why. I said

32. William E. Leuchtenburg, *Franklin D. Roosevelt and the New Deal, 1932–1940,* chap. 14; Bernard Asbell, *When F.D.R. Died,* chaps. 9–13.
33. Stettinius, calendar notes, Apr. 12, 1945, *SP.*
34. Stettinius also talked with Roosevelt's personal physician, Dr. McIntire, who had not gone to Warm Springs. McIntire said the President's death "was a complete shock to him—it was something absolutely new and came as a complete surprise. The President's blood pressure was all right and had been for some time, and there was absolutely no apparent cause for the stroke," Stettinius, calendar notes, Apr. 12, 1945, *SP.*

that there was no explanation other than the fact that Stalin had his own political problems within the Soviet Union and perhaps certain influences were being brought to bear on him from within his own country. The president emphasized, as he had the day before, that we must stand up to the Russians at this point and that we must not be too easy with them. He gave me the impression that he thought we had been too easy with them."[35]

Stettinius recommended a twofold approach. The Americans should bend all efforts to hold the UN conference and simultaneously dispatch a special envoy to talk over problems with Stalin. Stettinius recommended Hopkins as he knew Stalin and had been close to Roosevelt. Truman concurred, and on the way back from Hyde Park after Roosevelt's funeral, Truman asked Hopkins if he would undertake a special mission. Stettinius did not elaborate on specific measures of economic coercion as these were still being explored.[36]

The paramount significance for U.S. policy of Truman's accession to the presidency was his decision to continue implementation of the UN policy. His first act was to announce that the San Francisco conference would meet on schedule. Through the next two months Truman constantly stressed avoiding any showdown with the Soviets until the Americans knew the outcome of the UN conference.[37] The American aim was still to develop the UN policy to a successful conclusion, a subject Alperovitz largely ignores. In the framework of this goal, American leaders, in reassessing the UN policy, paid primary attention to postwar American security

35. Stettinius, Record, sec. 9, pp. 36–39, SP.
36. Stettinius, calendar notes, Apr. 13, 1945, SP; Truman, Memoirs, I: 221, 234–235.
37. This does not mean that Truman was averse to taking a firmer stand in dealing with Russia. He soon adopted a tougher position on Poland and accepted the advice of the State Department to use economic leverage as a means of attaining U.S. goals on Poland. But Truman was not, contrary to Alperovitz's contention, applying any "immediate showdown" strategy when he met with Molotov on April 22 and 23, when the foreign minister stopped in Washington on his way to San Francisco. Alperovitz misreads the evidence in developing his hypothesis. Truman approved the cut in lend-lease after the point at which Alperovitz claims Truman had decided to adopt the delayed showdown; and the Hopkins mission to Russia was in Truman's mind from the very day he took office. Alperovitz, Atomic Diplomacy, chaps. 1 and 2; Stettinius-Truman, transcript of phone conversation, May 11, 1945; Stettinius, calendar notes, April 12, 1945, SP.

in the Pacific and Far East. They did not want the Russians to have any voice in determining the future of Japan, and there was growing doubt about the need to have Russia join the Pacific war. The high point of this reassessment came in a meeting of the State-War-Navy Committee on May 11, during which it was decided by Acting Secretary of State Grew and Secretaries Stimson and Forrestal to determine if there was any way the United States might abrogate the Far Eastern provisions of the Yalta agreement.[38]

Alperovitz further dismisses Western fear of Communist subversion in western Europe too lightly. This was the chief political fear among all Western statesmen throughout the spring of 1945. Communist parties were potent in France, Italy and Greece, as well as the Low Countries. The specter of the Russian army controlling eastern Europe, plus political subversion in the West, raised prospects of Soviet domination of the European continent and the Mediterranean. This was unacceptable to any Western government.[39]

The American government, then, was focusing on its UN policy and seeking ways to confine Russian power to eastern Europe. The new U.S. administration was not trying to drive Russia out of eastern Europe. Truman was concerned first with postwar Pacific security, second with preserving democracy in western Europe and the Mediterranean, and only lastly with eastern Europe. It was natural for Truman to talk of Poland as the "symbol" of East-West cooperation, but the use of Poland was to keep Russia off balance, to protect western Europe, while the Americans waited to see what emerged at the UN conference and sought to secure their interests in the Pacific. This was the strategic picture at the time Truman became president.

This leads finally to the question of Truman's consideration of the atomic bomb as a diplomatic weapon. Alperovitz at this point makes a major contribution to understanding American diplomacy in the spring of 1945. He has demonstrated, even though he cannot cite much direct evidence, that Stimson did connect possession of

38. State-War-Navy Committee, memorandum by Joseph Grew, May 11, 1945, SP.

39. Alperovitz, *Atomic Diplomacy*, pp. 25, 131–132; *FRUS, 1945*, vol. 4, *Europe*, p. 686; *FRUS, Potsdam* 1: 67–81; 256–262, 269–280; *FRUS, 1945*, vol. 5, *Europe*, pp. 866–867.

the bomb with American goals. He viewed the bomb as of possible benefit in helping America obtain better relations with Russia throughout the world. With Russia's awareness that America had the bomb it would be easier to persuade Russia to stay within bounds in eastern Europe while America held sway in the Pacific.[40]

It was not necessary to have any significant change in policy to pursue the advantages afforded by the atomic bomb because Truman had already decided to postpone any rupture with Russia until after the UN conference ended. Since this would coincide closely with the anticipated testing of the first bomb and the Potsdam conference, Truman had no need to adopt any immediate showdown. He followed, instead, a program of careful policy review, accepted the recommendations to pressure Russia by the use of economic means, and waited until the atomic bomb was ready. It was then—the summer of 1945, as Alperovitz shows—that Truman went on the offensive. By this time, Truman had largely abandoned the UN policy of his predecessor. He began to move rapidly, from July, 1945, through the spring of 1946, to substitute an Anglo-American bloc for the internationalist approach of the UN.

There is little question that Truman's accession speeded the process of eroding the UN policy because Truman was inherently more suspicious of communism than was Roosevelt, but in the spring of 1945 he was not ready for a precipitous break. He had much to learn, and when he became president the UN policy still dominated the American foreign policy intentions. But increasingly the UN policy was to become a facade behind which the American government searched for alternative means of security.

These policy reviews were unknown to the American public. In fact, the reappraisal of Soviet relations, which ultimately led into the postwar containment policy, coincided with the high-water mark of official support for the UN policy. The building of the masquerade peace that had begun in December, 1944, now reached its strongest point in the spring of 1945. The efforts of the U.S. government to reassure the people about the correctness of the UN policy attest to the primacy of this goal among official plans.

Preparations for the UN conference proceeded on two levels after Yalta. One was the announcement of the American delegation. Roosevelt and Stettinius carefully selected delegates to pre-

40. Alperovitz, *Atomic Diplomacy*, chap. 3, Appendix 1.

serve the bipartisan spirit that Hull had inaugurated a year earlier. Two senators stood out as easy choices for the American delegation. Vandenberg was selected for his role as Republican spokesman on foreign policy in the Senate and because of his active interest in the international organization. The choice was popular among Republicans. The GOP Senate steering committee unanimously endorsed his attending the United Nations Conference, and party floor leader Senator Wallace H. White wrote to him, "Your views respond more completely to the composite judgment and conscience of Republicans in this international field than do those of any other Senators."[41] Connally, representing Senate Democrats, would be a real asset because of his position as chairman of the Senate Foreign Relations Committee. From the House came Sol Bloom, Democratic chairman of the Foreign Affairs Committee, and Clement Eaton, the ranking Republican on the same committee.

Two delegates were selected from the ranks of American private citizens. One was Harold E. Stassen, whom Stettinius recommended to the president as appropriate because of his stature as a liberal Republican political leader from the Midwest. A break with tradition was made by the appointment of Virginia Gildersleeve, the first woman to represent the United States at a conference. Miss Gildersleeve, dean of Barnard College, was a widely respected educator. Hull was named senior delegate, a post which proved to be largely honorary, as the former secretary was too ill to make the trip to San Francisco.[42]

Out of eight briefing sessions before the conference, the State Department accepted two changes suggested by the delegation. First, its congressional members wanted to strip the Security Council of the right to impose terms in peaceful settlement cases. This power allowed the great powers to force unfavorable decisions on smaller powers in territorial disputes, as Germany had forced a de-

41. Senator Robert A. Taft was quoted as saying, "I believe all the Republican Senators are agreeable to his selection as a delegate whether they agree with the Dumbarton Oaks Proposals or not," *Washington Times-Herald*, Feb. 18, 1945; Wallace H. White to Vandenberg, Apr. 12, 1945, Vandenberg Papers.

42. (Stettinius), Discussion of the Composition of the United States Delegation, ca. Feb. 8, 1945; Stettinius, calendar notes, Feb. 8, 1945, and Roosevelt to Hull, Feb. 10, 1945, SP; Stettinius, *Roosevelt and the Russians*, pp. 186–187; Virginia Gildersleeve, *Many A Good Crusade*, p. 321.

cision on Czechoslovakia in 1938. The delegation decided to work for a change in the Dumbarton Oaks Proposals in Section VIII-B, which would make it clear that the council had no right to impose terms in peaceful settlement disputes.

Congressional pressure also secured the second change. The four U.S. senators and representatives spoke out vigorously when they learned that the Department of State favored the World Court determining whether a dispute was domestic. Since domestic matters normally were preserved for the individual nation's sovereignty, this would be a major break with precedent. In supporting this change, the State Department was combating years of congressional opposition to any international agreement limiting America's right to decide what constituted a domestic matter. Faced with a storm of protest by the congressional delegates, the State Department accepted a revision whereby each nation would determine whether it or the world court would rule on its domestic matters. This protected the sovereignty of the United States, for the Senate would resist all attempts to put very much power into the hands of the court in handling cases involving America.[43]

Of concern to Stettinius was the American promise to support Russia's bid for extra seats. Roosevelt had not revealed this commitment to the people in his report to Congress. He apparently hoped to find some way to escape the pledge made at Yalta. Certainly both Roosevelt and Stettinius had second thoughts about the wisdom of the extra-seats decision, and no sooner had Stettinius returned from Mexico City than he warned the President that the United States ought to get out of this bad situation: "I . . . told the President that I was extremely apprehensive and had not discussed the matter in the Department, but I had come back from this trip with an intuitive feeling that it would be much better not to let the X matter come up in San Francisco if we could possibly avoid it. He said he had come to the same conclusion."[44]

The two men decided that they would extricate the United States from its promise if possible. Then Stettinius learned that some foreign newspaper correspondents knew about the agreement and that rumors were circulating around Washington. This convinced Stettinius that positive action must be taken. Stettinius

43. Russell, *UN Charter*, pp. 599–607.
44. Stettinius, calendar notes, Visit to the President, Mar. 12, 1945, *SP*.

asked Ambassador Gromyko to call on him to discuss reports that the Soviet government was preparing to send three delegations to San Francisco and Stettinius wanted some explanation. Gromyko, immediately on guard, nonetheless opened the way for the secretary by stating that at Yalta it had been "completely agreed to" that Belorussia and the Ukraine would be invited to the conference to become members of the United Nations alongside of Russia. Stettinius disagreed. The Soviet interpretation was erroneous. The president and secretary of state had reviewed the notes on the conference " . . . and he must believe me that neither the President nor I nor any of our advisers ever had any idea that the conversations in the Crimea would result in the Soviet Union having more than one Delegation in San Francisco." Gromyko protested that the United States had agreed to having the two Soviet republics as initial members of the United Nations. But, Stettinius replied, the ambassador must remember that it had been understood that the meeting in San Francisco "was a universal meeting of the United Nations who will sign the United Nations Declaration." Once the organization is functioning "that these *extras* would take their place at the table at the first meetings of the Assembly."[45]

There can be little doubt that Gromyko left this interview enraged. He had curtly told the secretary, "Well, there is something totally wrong because this is not at all our understanding." Russia would "proceed as planned." The exchanges which ensued over this problem showed the Soviet irritation over a matter in which they certainly thought they were correct.[46] If the United States was practicing dubious diplomacy in regard to the admission of the two Soviet republics to the United Nations, understanding, if not justification, could be found in the administration's fear that the American public would turn against the international organization if the republics were seated in San Francisco. Stettinius then ordered his executive aide, Bob Lynch, to discuss the problem with other Stettinius advisers: " 'My feeling,' Stettinius said, 'is that you should very seriously consider . . . whether the President shouldn't send for the members of the San Francisco delegation who are in Washington in the next few days and tell them the whole truth about

45. Stettinius-Gromyko, memorandum of conversation, Mar. 20, 1945, *SP.*
46. *FRUS, 1945,* 1, *General: The United Nations,* pp. 113–114; 124–125; 147–148; 327–328; 379–384.

this "X" matter, about the whole business . . . and then put it up to them for their guidance and advice as to how we ought to handle [the Soviets]. It takes them into the camp, it makes them feel a sense of responsibility. . . .' "[47]

The president accepted Stettinius's advice, and he met with the American delegation in the White House on March 23. He did not mention the history of the "X matter" prior to Yalta, merely describing how it had arisen at Yalta and emphasizing the Russian argument that the suffering which the two republics had endured warranted separate membership in the organization. As to the American support of this procedure, Bohlen reported to Stettinius that Roosevelt "rather slithered over the fact that there was a commitment on the part of this Government to support" the admission of Ukraine and White Russia. The president, instead, left the impression "that if he were a delegate at San Francisco that he would personally favor the Soviet proposal," and he ended the meeting by saying that this was "all there was to the subject." Roosevelt had ignored Stettinius's suggestion that the delegation be asked about the handling of the crisis. Bohlen noted in his report of the meeting, "the delegates in general received this announcement in silence and it was not evident that they fully appreciated immediately the degree to which the United States Government was committed to support the Soviet proposal."[48] Indeed, Roosevelt complicated the situation by misleading the delegates, for they were given the impression that each one could vote individually and according to his own conscience at San Francisco on this issue. Thus the administration was playing a game of double deception trying to extricate itself from a commitment made to the Russians at Yalta and seeking at the same time to make it appear to the delegates that no commitment existed.

The storm broke on March 29, when the *New York Herald Tribune* published a report that the United States had agreed at Yalta to give Russia three votes in the organization instead of the expected one. Immediately the dam of secrecy broke unleashing a

47. Stettinius-Lynch, transcript of phone conversation, Mar. 21, 1945, *SP*.

48. Report of the Meeting of the U.S. Delegation to UNCIO with the President, Mar. 23, 1945, Stettinius-Grew, memorandum of phone conversation, Mar. 23, 1945, Grew Papers.

flood of indignation and confusion. Papers across America treated the story as a "secret deal." Editors protested that the American people had been duped since Roosevelt's report to Congress had given the impression of revealing all the agreements made at Yalta. The *Washington Post* expressed a widespread feeling, "We can think of nothing more calculated to sow seeds of suspicion throughout the Allied world than delay in, and the way of making announcement" of the extra-votes agreement. Columnist Arthur Krock charged that Roosevelt had lost the Senate's confidence by his secrecy, and some observers publicly wondered whether the San Francisco conference should be held at all. Under a barrage of hostile questioning, the White House admitted that Roosevelt had definitely committed the United States to support a Soviet request for the admission of two republics as charter members of the organization.

In the initial flurry of excitement, confusion reigned in the government. Vandenberg publicly protested that Roosevelt had promised the delegates that they were free to "do as they please" about the issue at San Francisco, warning: "I would deeply disagree with any proposal which . . . would destroy the promised 'sovereign equality' of the nations in the peace league's assembly. . . . This applies to extra votes for us as well as to extra votes for anyone else."[49]

The secretary's staff committee searched for an answer to calm the public storm, and it initially decided to release a statement promising that the United States would not go along with Russia's request at the UN conference. On learning of the frank White House admission that the nation was committed, the State Department had no alternative except to reiterate what had already been stated from the executive mansion. Stettinius bore the brunt of the reaction for the government when he met the press in a news conference the day after the story was made public. The newsmen handed him a list of thirty-three questions which ranged over the

49. *New York Herald-Tribune,* Mar. 29, 1945; *New York Post,* Mar. 30, 1945; *Philadelphia Inquirer,* Mar. 31, 1945. Radio commentators were quite critical, among them Martin Agronsky, Raymond Swing, and Richard C. Harkness. U.S., Department of State, Division of Public Liaison, Summary of Press and Radio Comment on Announcement of Voting in United Nations Assembly, n.d., SP; *Washington Post,* Mar. 30, 1945; *New York Times,* Mar. 31, 1945; *New York Herald-Tribune,* Mar. 30, 1945.

entire scope of the Yalta conference and posed many blunt questions. It was a ticklish assignment, but Grew told the staff committee the next day that, although he had never seen a secretary put so much "on the spot," Stettinius "had handled the situation beautifully."[50]

The secretary moved quickly to convince the American delegates that the administration had not intended to make them party to some dark conspiracy that had occurred at Yalta. On March 30, the day he faced the reporters, Stettinius explained that Roosevelt had kept the agreement quiet because he did not think that it had been a wise one and it "was his desire, if possible, to have further discussions with the Soviets that might possibly lead to a modification of their position." The secretary assured them there were no other secret agreements except for certain military matters which he could not disclose. Vandenberg and Connally criticized the administration's handling of this affair, but the delegation voted to support Roosevelt's actions.[51]

Aside from quieting the delegates, Stettinius was engaging in a frantic effort to find some way in which the government could recoup its prestige. After numerous conversations between the Department of State and White House officials, it was decided that the best hope was to have the president announce that the United States had decided not to ask for extra representation. Roosevelt concurred,[52] and on April 3, Stettinius announced this decision to reporters. He carefully pointed out that while the United States was obligated to support Russia's bid for extra seats, the decision to accept the idea rested with the entire San Francisco conference. He stressed that Roosevelt had acted out of the "utmost respect" for the suffering which the peoples of the Ukraine and White Russia had endured. The American people must look at this issue in perspective, Stettinius warned, for it was but one of many prob-

50. Secretary's Staff Committee, minutes, Mar. 30 and Mar. 31, 1945, *SP*; *New York Post*, Mar. 30, 1945. That Stettinius took his vacation trip indicates he hoped the whole matter would be kept out of public view.

51. U.S. Delegation to UNCIO, minutes, Mar. 30, 1945, *SP*. In stating that there were no other secret agreements, Stettinius misled the delegation unintentionally since he did not know about the secret Yalta agreements regarding the Far East.

52. Stettinius, summaries of phone conversations with William D. Hassett, Vandenberg, and Connally, Apr. 2, 1945, *SP*.

lems that the United Nations conference would explore. America must keep its eyes on the greater goal, "the effort to eliminate future wars."[53]

This attempt to set the facts straight quieted the furor of the previous week. Some newspapers remained critical for awhile longer,[54] but the major big-city papers welcomed Stettinius's statement as clarifying matters. The *New York Times* noted that he had indicated that there were no other secret agreements, and it welcomed the news that the United States would not seek extra votes for itself.[55]

Undoubtedly the suspicions unloosed by revelation of the extra-seats promise would have been more damaging were it not for the extensive groundwork the State Department had done to publicize the Dumbarton Oaks Proposals. Every possible means was employed to enlist the support of private organizations. Large amounts of literature were made available, speakers provided, and organizational advice given to enable private groups to rally public support. The grass roots impact was reflected in a strong public outpouring of mail to Congress backing American participation in the UN, causing Senator Robert Taft (R-Ohio) to complain that the Congress was being flooded by a government campaign of "super propaganda."[56]

The government consciously suppressed its rising doubts about future relations with Russia, choosing instead to focus on the prospects of great power cooperation represented by the coming UN conference. Stettinius was the highest government official to take a leading role in this campaign. He took out time from the policy review to deliver two major addresses, one in Chicago on April 4, the second in New York two days later. In his first speech, broadcast nationwide on the Mutual Broadcasting System, the secretary struck at isolationism. Two wars and a major depression had taught the people that "political isolationism and economic nationalism are utterly unrealistic and can only lead to complete disaster for our

53. U.S., Department of State, Press Release No. 285, Apr. 3, 1945, *SP*.
54. Mobile (Ala.) *Press*, Apr. 4, 1945; Providence (R.I.) *Bulletin*, Apr. 4, 1945.
55. *New York Times*, Apr. 4, 1945; the *Baltimore Sun*, and the *New York Herald-Tribune* also joined in cautious approval.
56. Divine, *Second Chance*, p. 283.

country and for the world." He referred to Allied tensions as "temporary difficulties," and called on the people to remember that the Allies had repeatedly overcome "far more serious" problems, that the area of agreement was much wider than the peripheral differences, and their common interests required them to cement their wartime alliance in the UN.[57] In his New York address, Stettinius warned against perfectionism and impatience. "All too many" Americans are easily upset at any sign of trouble. "They show a lack of stability, a susceptibility to fear and despair which is disturbing."[58]

The State Department climaxed its drive with Dumbarton Oaks Week, April 16–22. This was sponsored by leading private internationalist groups and sixteen governors proclaiming the observance in their states. The response was measured by the jump in State Department mail from 400 letters per day in early April to more than 5,000 per day by the end of the special Dumbarton Oaks Week.[59]

Even President Roosevelt's death worked to further the UN cause, as it moved many Americans to look on a successful UN conference as a holy task, a memorial to the fallen president's dreams. Yet analysis of the public outpouring raises serious questions about the "triumph of internationalism" in America. This is shown in the continuing lack of public knowledge about the Dumbarton Oaks Proposals right up to the opening of the UN conference. In early January, Assistant Secretary Archibald MacLeish reported widespread confusion in the country as to exactly what the proposals said and meant. The displeasure over British and Russian actions in Europe had caused a turn toward isolationism which was partly explainable because only 43 percent of the public had heard of the proposals even after three months of publicizing them, and only 50 percent of this group had any idea if the proposals provided a practical basis for establishing an international organization to maintain world peace.

A month later, despite intensive educational efforts by the State Department, the Office of War Information, and private

57. U.S. Department of State, Press Release No. 290, Apr. 3, 1945, SP.

58. Remarks of the Secretary of State before the Americans United, New York City, Apr. 6, 1945, SP.

59. Divine, Second Chance, pp. 283–284.

groups, it was found by the State Department that " . . . it is evident not only from opinion polls but from comments of individuals from all professions and all walks of life, that the essential character of the Proposals is not yet understood. The country, in other words, does not have before it the information to make the most important decision in its recent history."[60]

State Department officials felt that the people placed too much emphasis on the UN's ability to keep peace. Top officials agreed that the UN was only a start, "the embryo of order in the world," as Acheson put it. The UN could not stop big wars, and its ultimate success rested on the ability of the great powers to arrive at a political accommodation outside the UN framework. Rockefeller advocated honesty in putting this to the people. "If we should follow this policy of candor, the American people would probably feel at first a sense of shock, but this would be followed by a feeling of much greater realism."[61] In fact, just the opposite was taking place. A department study in early February concluded that the UN was being oversold "by the highest officials of the American government" as the means of ending all wars when an end to war could not be guaranteed unilaterally by the UN. State Department officials worried about this lack of candor, but they never found a way to meet it, fearing the public would not understand a UN of limited powers.[62]

U.S. public opinion continued to support the UN policy, bolstered by the official optimism in reporting success at the Yalta and Mexico City conferences. From late February through the opening of the UN conference polls showed constant and greater public support than had existed prior to Yalta. Generally the public remained hopeful about long-run cooperation among the powers, even through the disquieting post-Yalta developments. Americans also continued to support membership in the UN by percentages in favor of membership running from 64 to 80 percent. Two-thirds of the backers wanted UN participation even if the peace treaties fell short of American expectations. This grew out of a flexible public view of the Yalta agreements. On the controversial Polish government reorganization, surveys in the two weeks after Yalta showed about 56

60. Secretary's Staff Committee, Document No. 48, Feb. 6, 1945, *SP*.
61. Secretary's Staff Committee, minutes, Feb. 9, 1945, *SP*.
62. Secretary's Staff Committee, Document No. 48, Feb. 6, 1945, *SP*.

percent thought it "about the best possible under the circumstances." Apathy characterized public opinion on Poland. Sixty-three percent of the people had no knowledge of what had been decided, and only 17 percent had a clear understanding of the Yalta communique on Poland. There was widespread acceptance of the voting compromise. The State Department found that thirty-seven major papers supported it as "practical rather than perfect," while only four expressed open disapproval.[63]

Underlying this acceptance was a continuing lack of comprehension about the actual working of the UN. The Division of Public Liaison of the State Department concluded on the eve of the San Francisco Conference that "The significant increase in popular support for American participation in an international peace organization has not been accompanied by widespread familiarity with the facts about America's record of international cooperation. Despite public discussion of the League of Nations and other international organizations, the general public remains largely uninformed as to whether the United States has participated in the most outstanding international organizations."[64]

This lack of public comprehension raised questions in the State Department about the stability of American commitment to the UN policy. In fact, events showed that public commitment was shallow. The war conditioned Americans to think in black and white terms. In the shock of the early cold war the public easily transferred its antipathy from fascism to communism, thereby missing almost completely the noncommunist force of revolutionary nationalism that was at work.

In the spring of 1945, the UN policy was becoming increasingly illusory. To most people it offered an easy means of avoiding hard thinking about foreign problems. It was easy to support the general idea without knowing what responsibilities membership would entail. The UN promised a maximum of security for a minimum American military investment. And in its idealistic cloak, it appealed to the utopian streak in Americans.

The American government continued to rely on the UN pol-

63. U.S., Department of State, Division of Public Liaison, Latest Opinion Trends, Feb. 23, 1945 and Mar. 10, 1945; Public Reaction to the Voting Formula for the Proposed Security Council, Mar. 27, 1945, SP.
64. Ibid.

icy, but was now using it to cover its secret review of Soviet relations. This review was undermining the UN policy, but the government simultaneously assured the public that all was well. Thus in the spring of 1945 the gap between public rhetoric and private fears grew ever wider.

7

The Emergence of Regional Blocs
at San Francisco

RELATIONS AMONG THE GREAT POWERS HAD NEVER been more strained than they were as delegates from the fifty Allied nations arrived in San Francisco for the April 25 conference. While the UN policy was the official guideline of American action, Truman had already indicated that he would not sacrifice American interests to Russia just to achieve success of the UN. Truman was much less interested in internationalizing American political processes than either Hull or Roosevelt. He gave his blessing to the UN partly out of a feeling of obligation to the fallen Roosevelt but largely because he could not fly in the face of public faith in its success, particularly before he had worked out an alternate policy.

Truman believed that the language of power was the most effective way to deal with Russia, and he adopted a belligerent tone toward Russian leaders from the outset of his administration. When Molotov stopped in Washington en route to San Francisco, Truman chastised him over the Polish deadlock, stating the Yalta agreement was clear and that the Russians, not the Americans, had broken their promises. The American government was not willing to have cooperation, he angrily told Molotov, on the basis of unilateral concessions. When Molotov protested, "I have never been talked to like that in my life," the president retorted, "Carry out your agreements and you won't get talked to like that."[1]

Truman adopted this tough line even though he knew the Polish agreement at Yalta was so ambiguous that different interpretations were quite possible.[2] Truman was even willing to risk a breakup of the UN conference before it began. He told Harriman that America would not adhere to the UN unless Russia acknowledged the American view on Poland, and at a top-level policy review on April 23, just before his confrontation with Molotov, Truman said that America would proceed with the UN conference and that if his statements on Poland upset the Russians, they "could go to hell."[3]

This expression was more one of momentary exasperation than of reckless willingness to precipitate a rupture with Russia. Truman accepted his advisors' view that the time had come for standing up to Russia to counter the assumption of Stalin that Russia could "do as it pleased" in eastern Europe while America meekly acquiesced.[4] He also believed that Russia's dependency on American economic aid for postwar recovery made any Soviet retaliation unlikely. Truman's confrontation over Poland was a symbol of his attitude. He pursued a dual approach toward Russia during May. On the one hand he gave the green light to proceed with cutting back Lend-Lease aid to Russia, bringing to bear the economic sanctions that had been recommended by his top officials.[5] Simultaneously, he prepared to dispatch Hopkins to Moscow in the hope that Hopkins would be the emissary of a firm yet acceptable American policy.

These developments coincided with Germany's surrender plus the growing belief by the Joint Chiefs of Staff that Russia's military role in the Pacific was no longer essential. Thus the bonds that had held the Allied coalition together were loosening in early May during the first stages of the UN conference.[6] It is an important testimony to their desire for postwar cooperation that after Germany's

1. Truman, *Year of Decisions*, p. 80–82.
2. Stettinius, *Roosevelt and the Russians,* p. 302.
3. *FRUS, 1945,* 5: 253.
4. Truman, *Year of Decisions,* p. 70; Leahy, *I Was There,* p. 351.
5. George C. Herring, Jr., "Lend-Lease to Russia and the Origins of the Cold War, 1944–1945," *Journal of American History,* 56 (June, 1969): 106–107.
6. McNeill, *America, Britain, and Russia,* pp. 577–579.

defeat the Allies still made major concessions to bring the UN into existence. Many historians have missed this significant fact.

Watching the acrimonious exchanges that marked the organizational sessions of the San Francisco conference, one could justifiably wonder if the UN Charter would ever see the light of day. The Russians began by insisting that there be four presidents of the conference to indicate equality among the four sponsoring nations. Molotov ominously threatened to go home unless his view prevailed. The Americans steadfastly refused. Stettinius told Truman that he feared the Russians were trying to set a precedent for the permanent organization of the executive machinery of the United Nations. He warned Truman that it might prove impossible to have one executive officer for the United Nations if Molotov won his point. Fortunately, Eden proposed a compromise acceptable to both sides. By it there were four presidents of the conference, but Stettinius would double as the chairman of the presidents. This artificial device kept the responsibility for running the conference securely in Stettinius's hands, and it apparently satisfied a point of pride with Molotov.[7]

Immediately under the presidents was the steering committee, composed of the chairman of each delegation. Much of the actual work was done by an executive committee composed of the five permanent nations plus the chairmen of other delegations. There were four main commissions charged with drafting UN Charter provisions: general provisions, General Assembly, Security Council, and judicial. Controversial issues were worked out by the executive committee, and the full plenary sessions received commission reports and acted on UN Charter provisions.

In practice most of the crucial decisions of the conference occurred in Secretary of State Stettinius's penthouse atop the Fairmont Hotel. Here Stettinius met with other members of the Big Four (soon the Big Five, when France, as a permanent member of the Security Council, was asked to participate, even though she was not a sponsor of the conference). These meetings were the heartbeat of the conference, where the divisions among the great powers

7. Stettinius, San Francisco Conference Diary, Steering Committee Meeting, Apr. 26, 1945; Truman-Stettinius, transcript of phone conversation, Apr. 26, 1945; Stettinius-Hull, transcript of phone conversation, Apr. 26, 1945, SP; Russell, UN Charter, pp. 634–635.

were hammered out. The penthouse was also the site of numerous private conferences between Stettinius and other delegation chairmen. This concentration of power caused wide discontent during the conference, but Stettinius never hesitated to employ whatever pressure was necessary to hold the smaller delegations in line, in the case of his chief critic, Foreign Minister of Australia Herbert Evatt, even appealing to the Australian prime minister to order Evatt to ease up his opposition.

After the flare-up over the presidency of the conference, a second crisis arose that engendered deep suspicion and bitterness between the Americans and Russians and between the Latin American bloc and Russia. This concerned the seating of Poland, the two Soviet republics, and Argentina. It had been assumed that as soon as a new Polish government was constituted it would be recognized and invited to the San Francisco conference. The deadlock in Moscow on this matter scuttled this hope, but Molotov tried to force the seating of the Warsaw government. He held several private talks with Stettinius before the steering committee considered the question, only to hear Stettinius insist that the Yalta agreement must be met. Molotov appealed to Stettinius on the ground that it was vital to Russia to have a Polish regime "friendly to the Soviet Union." In an unusually frank revelation of Soviet interests, Molotov "concluded by saying that if the Soviet Union was forced to accept anything but a friendly government in Poland after all the Russian blood that had been shed for Polish liberation, any other solution would mean for them that this blood had been shed in vain and they had lost the war. He said that aggression had come to Russia through Poland twice in a generation and that they could not abandon the interest of their state."[8] Molotov failed to move Stettinius. The United States delegation refused to support seating of the Warsaw government, and Molotov's bid was soundly defeated in the steering committee.

Furthermore, Russia almost lost its effort to seat the two Soviet republics, owing to its stand against the admission of Argentina. The Latin American delegates threatened to block the seating of Belorussia and the Ukraine unless Argentina was admitted. Molotov and Mexico's Foreign Minister Padilla exchanged bitter charges,

8. FRUS, 1945, 1, General: The United Nations, p. 384.

while Stettinius worked feverishly behind the scene to persuade the Latin Americans to vote for seating the Soviet republics. In return, he promised that the United States would publicly back Argentina's admission. The secretary's efforts resulted in a unanimous vote to accept the two republics, while United States support for Argentina secured its seating despite Molotov's strong objections.[9]

The refusal to seat Poland, so closely coupled with Argentina's admission to the conference, created much unfavorable publicity for the American delegation. Poland was the nation over which the European war had started, while Argentina was regarded as a bastion of fascism and Nazi influence. The American public was incredulous, and two of the Senate's strongest UN supporters, Carl Hatch and Joseph Ball, termed the United States action on Argentina "a cynical repudiation" of the cause for which the Allies were fighting."[10] Hull bitterly denounced the decision and concluded privately that Stettinius was not especially capable in his post.[11] The available evidence indicates that the Argentine episode created genuine misgivings in Moscow about American intentions in the UN. Later in May, when Hopkins discussed tensions in Allied relations, Stalin went on at great length about how the Argentine case justified Russian suspicion of Western motives.[12]

These early crises delayed the work of the conference by a full week, for Russia refused to agree on organizing the commissions until these matters were settled. Even after solutions were arrived at, fear of a major new disruption hung oppressively over the delegates. Molotov, who soon returned to Moscow, leaving Ambassador Gromyko in charge of the Russian delegation, had made many enemies. His repeated rudeness to a number of Latin American representatives spurred them into open expression of their dislike and fear of Russia. Finally, the inability of the sponsoring powers to

9. *Ibid.*, p. 444; Stettinius, San Francisco Diary, Second Steering Committee meeting, Apr. 27, 1945, *SP*; Stettinius-Hull, transcript of phone conversation, Apr. 27, 1945, *SP*; Stettinius, San Francisco Diary, Apr. 28, 1945, *SP*; U.N. Information Organizations and Library of Congress, *United Nations Conference on International Organization* (16 vols.), 5: 80 and 1: 345, 357–358. [Hereinafter cited as *UNCIO Documents.*]

10. Senators Hatch and Ball to Stettinius, May 1, 1945, *SP.*

11. Grew-Hull, memorandum of phone conversation, May 3, 1945, Grew Papers; Arthur Krock, *Memoirs, Sixty Years on the Firing Line,* p. 210.

12. *FRUS, Potsdam,* 1: 32, 36–37, 72.

unite over Argentina and Poland boded ill in view of the many other complex subjects which awaited the diplomats' consideration.

Secretary Stettinius sought to conciliate. On May 5 he addressed a meeting of American consultants, who represented the views of broad sections of national opinion. Speaking of the Polish impasse, Stettinius urged calm. "Regardless of any situation we must succeed in San Francisco in agreeing on the foundation and framework and building on that. Let us get over this hurdle and get unanimity on the basic thinking of a world organization and then let's take up these world political problems one by one as we come to them."[13] The secretary's faith was increased by the successful agreement among the great powers on amendments they would present to the conference on the Dumbarton Oaks Proposals. He reported to Acting Secretary Grew that all was now "speeding along" toward success on the Charter.[14]

His optimism turned into frustration almost immediately with the eruption of a bitter quarrel over regional security blocs within the UN structure. Before the issue was settled, two weeks had passed and the critics of the UN policy—the Latin American nations, working with United States regionalists, chiefly the military and congressional elements of the American delegation—had devised a formula which went far to thwart the universalist nature of the original UN policy.

The regionalists' opportunity came in an amendment agreed to by the sponsoring powers, which exempted Russia's bilateral European security treaties from Security Council control. Molotov had argued that, until the UN demonstrated its capability of preventing a German resurgence, Russia needed these treaties.[15] The request had caused a brief debate among the American delegates which Stettinius squelched in the interest of speedy action. He had promised Truman to move the conference along rapidly, and this matter erupted on May 4, the day the sponsoring powers were scheduled to announce their amendments.

When the Latin American leaders learned that the exception would be allowed for Russia's security treaties while no recognition

13. Consultants to U.S. Delegation, transcript of meeting, May 5, 1945, SP.

14. Stettinius-Grew, summary of phone conversation, May 4, 1945, SP.

15. FRUS, 1945, 1: 605.

was granted for the inter-American system, they reacted furiously. Stettinius sent Pasvolsky and State Department Latin American expert Avra Warren to talk with the Latin American delegation chairmen in a futile effort to placate them. Speaking for his colleagues, Colombian Foreign Minister Alberto Lleras Camargo complained that the United States was trying to scuttle the Act of Chapultepec. As it now stood, he charged, regional arrangements were at the mercy of the permanent members of the Security Council. Any disputes in South or Central America would find each opponent seeking the support of a permanent Council member. Such a Pandora's box would constitute an open invitation for nations " . . . to become mixed up in the affairs of this hemisphere to an extent which had never happened before." He concluded that South America might easily become the seedbed of World War III.[16]

The meeting ended on this discouraging note. Pasvolsky phoned Stettinius that his pleas had gone unheeded. The situation was explosive, with the Latin Americans wanting a regional bloc "completely free of world arrangements."[17] Stettinius told Pasvolsky to hold fast and count on the unanimity of the great powers to force it through. His timetable was soon disrupted by Senator Vandenberg. Vandenberg was as concerned as Stettinius and Pasvolsky, but, unlike them, he wanted to find new ways to safeguard the inter-American system, fearing that otherwise the Monroe Doctrine would soon be a dead issue. The same day that Pasvolsky was meeting Latin American representatives, Rockefeller, a strong backer of the inter-American system, arranged to have dinner with Vandenberg. During their meal, Rockefeller stressed that the Latin American delegates were "up in arms."[18] This information led the Michigan senator to write a letter to Secretary Stettinius outlining the dilemma and demanding action "before it is too late." He warned that if the Monroe Doctrine were undermined it would pose " . . . a threat to the confirmation of the entire San Francisco Charter by the Senate of the United States."

16. Pasvolsky, Warren, et al., memorandum of conversation, May 5, 1945, Pasvolsky Papers.
17. Stettinius-Pasvolsky, memorandum of phone conversation, May 5, 1945, SP.
18. Vandenberg, *Private Papers,* p. 189.

He went on to compare the inter-American system to the European pacts Russia had set up against Germany. He had no objection to Russia's desire for security through bilateral treaties. "But what can we say in defense of our action in requiring at the same time that Pan-America must depend upon this new Peace League . . .?" Was the United States abandoning the inter-American system which it had just "vigorously reasserted" at Chapultepec? Vandenberg rejected the notion that recognition of the inter-American system undermined the UN. If America acceded to Russia's desire for an independent security system against Germany, it should demand a similar exception for the Western hemisphere "until such time as the [United Nations] Organization may, by consent of the Governing Board of the Pan-American Union, be charged with this function."[19]

Vandenberg's letter angered Stettinius. He fully appreciated the necessity of Vandenberg's support in obtaining Republican votes in the Senate, and he was cognizant of the uproar caused in 1919 by those who believed that the Covenant of the League of Nations inadequately safeguarded the Monroe Doctrine. Already irritated over Rockefeller's support of regionalism, Stettinius called him and demanded to know if he had drafted the Vandenberg letter. Rockefeller assured the secretary that he had not, but neglected to say that it had been his initiative that had spurred the senator's action.[20] Stettinius had to act, for Vanderberg's political power was too potent to be ignored, and on May 7 the secretary brought the question before the full delegation.[21]

The delegates' discussions between the regionalists and universalists were edged in sharp tones and placed great weight on national power, specifically Russia's role in Europe and that of the United States in the Western hemisphere. Vandenberg's special adviser, John Foster Dulles, took issue with the senator's emphasis on the inter-American system. He said that Russia wanted a free hand throughout Europe. He predicted that the Russians would acquiesce to a United States demand for exempting the inter-American system and use this to justify excluding the Americans

19. Vandenberg to Stettinius, May 5, 1945, SP.
20. Stettinius-Rockefeller, summary of phone conversation, May 6, 1945, SP.
21. FRUS, 1945, 1: 625–628.

from a voice in European matters. Pasvolsky and Harriman agreed with Dulles that the United Nations provided the soundest basis for dealing with Russia and restricting communism within acceptable limits.[22] Pasvolsky warned that any further provision for excluding regional pacts from United Nations jurisdiction would loose an avalanche of regional exceptions, in turn wrecking the organization. In defending this view, Leo Pasvolsky claimed that the Western hemisphere would be protected because if a veto prevented the Security Council from handling a crisis, the United States had the inherent right to act in self-defense.

This alternative had first been suggested in the May 4 delegation meeting when Stassen indicated that any nation possessed the inherent right of self-defense. At that time Senator Vandenberg expressed worry about an adverse impact should such a right be explicitly recognized in the United Nations Charter. He thought it would encourage nations to ignore the international organization and rely on their own power. At the same time Vandenberg realized that the United States Senate might demand that this right be written into the Charter. He recalled for his delegation colleagues the intense Senate debate on this very point when the Kellogg-Briand Treaty had been considered in 1927. Dulles reassured Vandenberg by pointing out that under the Kellogg-Briand Treaty the right of self-defense had been very narrowly construed. On the other hand nothing in the proposed United Nations Charter limited the right of self-defense, and Vandenberg could point this out in the Senate.[23]

For the moment the congressional and military proponents of the inter-American system were forced to admit the logic of not doing anything that might lead to the expansion of Russian influence into western Europe, and an ad hoc committee was appointed to study the dilemma.[24] Their deliberations stressed self-defense as the answer to the problem. State Department experts frequently referred to a member's right to resort to self-defense and unilateral military force if the United Nations failed to handle a world crisis. This prompted Representative Bloom to ask if this could be inter-

22. Ibid., pp. 619–640.
23. Ibid.
24. The committee members were Dunn, Rockefeller, McCloy, Pasvolsky, and Dulles; ibid., p. 626.

preted as indicating that the Monroe Doctrine "still remained un-
touched." Pasvolsky answered affirmatively, but Senator Connally
broke in to demand how that could work. Pasvolsky replied " . . .
that the Monroe Doctrine is protected by our right of veto and by
the obligation assumed by all the states, including the big powers,
not to intervene. The old [whole?] system, he said, rests upon the
good faith of the big powers and their willingness to behave. If
they fall out there is no opportunity to keep the peace."[25]

Dulles and Stassen endorsed this interpretation, but Senator
Vandenberg dissented. He thought there was a general renuncia-
tion of the right to use force; and "he was now convinced that the
people would be disillusioned beyond words when they realized the
plan." Vandenberg here revealed a fundamental misconception of
how the UN was supposed to work. He was confusing the enforcement power of the UN with its role as an agency to promote international law. He was unable to reconcile his desire to protect the
sanctity of the Monroe Doctrine with his vision of a legally comprehensive UN.

If the United States delegation seemed unable to resolve its
decision about how best to safeguard the Monroe Doctrine, its
Latin American colleagues had no such doubts. On the morning of
May 8 Stettinius met with a number of Latin American delegation
chairmen. The day was damp and dark, the swirling fog around the
penthouse atop the Fairmont seemed to match the despair in the
hearts of the assembled group. Victor Andrade, Bolivian ambassador to the United States, presented a statement which, he said, the
Latin American delegates had all agreed upon: "If the Security
Council is permitted to manage American affairs it would mean
the end of the Monroe Doctrine. The Act of Chapultepec meant
the perfection of the American system without interference from
outside powers. The inter-American system disappears if the Security Council rules."[26] He said that the Latin American nations were
unwilling to trust their security to an "untried" United Nations and
were "resolute that they must not sacrifice the American system."
There were further similar warnings, with the common theme
stressed that by shackling the inter-American system to the veto,

25. Ibid., p. 637.
26. Stettinius and advisers and Latin American Foreign Ministers, minutes
of meeting, May 8, 1945, SP.

the United States was inviting hemisphere nations to "seek the favor" of the great powers.

At the heart of this situation, in which the United States stood accused of abandoning the Monroe Doctrine that Latin Americans had so long viewed as a cloak for oppression, was the Latin American governments' fear that communism would gain a foothold in their countries if the United States became preoccupied with the United Nations. Lleras Camargo minced no words in stating this clearly and prophetically:

> Any country seeking to attack the United States in the future would attack through the weakest point which is in South America. The next war will be between Russia and the United States, not between any two countries in Europe. [An] attempt will be made to flank the United States through South America. Penetrations would be made in South America, similar to the ones made by Germany in this war, when she planted the seeds of fascism in surrounding countries by utilizing small minorities. We must retain the independence of action of the inter-American system, particularly with reference to the veto in the Security Council which will [preserve] this freedom of action.[27]

Stettinius protested emphatically that the United States had no intentions of weakening the inter-American system. His assurances elicited little confidence and the meeting ended on a note of stalemate. In a mood of depression afterwards, Stettinius asked Rockefeller why the Latin Americans had lost confidence in the United Nations organization. Rockefeller replied that it was essentially fear of the Russians and communism reinforced by the shock of Roosevelt's death.[28]

The secretary now decided the time had come to turn to Washington for assistance. He asked Dulles to prepare a memorandum that he could submit to the president. Dulles hit the issue

27. Ibid.; Lleras Camargo attempted to leave a different impression when, in his first report as Secretary General of the Organization of American States in November, 1949, he claimed that stories charging that the Latin Americans at San Francisco were anticommunist were "basically erroneous and dangerous": "Annual Report of the Secretary General," *Annals of the Organization of American States*, 2 (1950): 6.

28. Stettinius, San Francisco Conference Diary, May 8, 1945, *SP*.

squarely. The cold fact was, he wrote, that to reject the Latin American contentions "would seriously impair our good Latin American relations," but the alternative was even more dangerous for it invited Russian domination of all Europe: " . . . from the standpoint of world peace [a regional exception for the inter-American system would] greatly weaken the position of the Security Council, and from the standpoint of practical politics will invite a European regional arrangement which will include Western Europe as well as Eastern Europe and which the Soviet Union will dominate and where we will through the Security Council have no voice."[29]

The timing of Stettinius's call to Washington for help on the regional issue is significant, for it coincided with the climax of the government's review of relations toward Russia. May 8 was the same day that the secretary and Harriman were agreeing to recommend that Truman cut back Lend-Lease aid; Harriman then flew to Washington to take part in the final crucial decisions. Agreement came, on May 10 and 11, during top-level meetings of civilian and military officials. Also on May 11 American officials decided to see if there were any means to undo the American commitments on the Far East made at Yalta. The minutes on this last subject were considered so sensitive that Grew personally burned them, jotting down only a brief summary for his files.[30]

It was in this setting of a new and greater urgency to protect American interests through means other than the UN, that the regional controversy was considered. Although no formula was suggested, the Washington policymakers gave strong backing to protecting the inter-American system from Security Council interference.[31] Stimson, Forrestal, and the Joint Chiefs pushed this view very strongly all during the regional review. Stimson had long believed that Hull's UN policy was dooming the Monroe Doctrine. Now that he had gotten State Department acquiescence to a trusteeship policy that gave America control over Pacific bases, Stimson and his colleagues sought to push their regionalist sentiments to the

29. John Foster Dulles to Stettinius, with memorandum for the President, May 8, 1945, SP.
30. "Entry of the Soviet Union into the Far Eastern War . . . ," 68–71; Stettinius, summaries of phone conversations, May 10, 1945, SP; Grew-McCloy-Harriman-Stettinius, memorandum of phone conversation, May 12, 1945, Grew Papers.
31. Stimson Diary, May 10, 1945, Stimson Papers.

forefront. In the deliberations of the American delegation in San Francisco, John J. McCloy, speaking for the JCS, had said that American military security was in jeopardy because of the veto and the subjugation of regional arrangements to the Security Council. The JCS wanted "a wider rather than narrower latitude to the regional organization in enforcement action." Stimson urged McCloy to stand firm "because of national security reasons" to empower America "to move in the first instance in the hemisphere free of any veto of the Security Council."[32]

No solution developed in Washington because American leaders realized that to demand special exemption for a Western hemispheric bloc from the Security Council would make it easier for Russia to claim similar rights in Europe. And Harriman had already warned that Russia intended "to try to ride roughshod over her neighbors in Europe."[33] Thus the same dilemma was realized by American policymakers both in San Francisco and Washington.

With every door apparently shut, American leaders became increasingly resentful of Latin American intransigence. Cordell Hull voiced the opinion that the Latin Americans were seizing leadership that should rightfully belong to the United States. Stettinius underscored this view when he told the United States delegation that "the time has arrived when we must not be pushed around by a lot of small American republics who are dependent on us in many ways —economically, politically, militarily; . . . we must provide leadership."[34]

Then, at this low point, a possible solution appeared. A new formula had been drafted by Dulles, Pasvolsky, Dunn, and Bowman which utilized the concept of self-defense: "In the event of an attack by any state against any member state, such member state shall possess the right to take measures of self-defense. The right to take measures of self-defense against armed attack shall apply to arrangements, like those embodied in the Act of Chapultepec,

32. Stimson Diary, May 2, 1945, Stimson Papers; Instructions for the Guidance of the United States Military Advisers at the San Francisco Conference, memorandum, n.d.; McCloy to Stettinius, May 3, 1945, SP; FRUS, 1945, 1: 547; Stimson-McCloy, memorandum of phone conversation, May 8, 1945, SP.

33. Stimson Diary, May 10, 1945, Stimson Papers.

34. Hull-Pasvolsky, transcript of phone conversation, May 10, 1945, Pasvolsky Papers; Stettinius, San Francisco Diary, May 11, 1945, SP.

under which all members of a group of states agree to consider an attack against any one of them as an attack against all of them. The taking of such measures shall not affect the authority and the responsibility of the Security Council under this charter to take at any time such action as it may deem necessary in order to maintain or restore international peace and security."[35]

The American delegation considered this formula during two long meetings on May 11 and 12, and it was sent to Washington for comment by the Joint Chiefs. Forrestal and Stimson objected that it opened the door too far to regional blocs. In San Francisco, Assistant Secretary of the Navy Artemus Gates reported that there was fear "that it will throw the door open to arrangements elsewhere which might weaken the international organization." Even so, the military was willing to take the risk.[36]

The only strong opposition came from Hull. In a call to Stettinius he expressed his conviction that the new proposal would impair the international organization, " . . . that we are being led away from our own national interests and intent on the Dumbarton Oaks Proposals."[37] His objection was insufficient to prevent the weary delegation from accepting the advisers' memorandum as the basis for formal discussion with the other sponsoring nations.

In his haste to get the formula before the sponsoring powers, Stettinius neglected to provide them with advance copies. This was particularly a risk in the case of Eden who earlier had brusquely turned aside Stettinius's request for British aid in finding a loophole to protect the Monroe Doctrine. When the Americans read their proposal on the afternoon of May 12, Eden angrily attacked it as a paper "clearly of Latin American origin. It would result in regionalism of the worst kind." He predicted it would wreck the conference: "I am frank to say I dislike it intensely. . . . It makes me extremely unhappy. Either we have a world organization or we don't. There would be regional movements all over the world. How do you define aggression? . . . I would rather not sign the Charter. . . . That this should come so late in the day."[38]

35. *FRUS, 1945,* 1: 674.
36. Ibid., pp. 672, 675; Stettinius-Grew, memorandum of phone conversation, May 12, 1945, Grew Papers.
37. *FRUS, 1945,* 1: 678; Hull-Pasvolsky, transcript of phone conversation, May 10, 1945, Pasvolsky Papers.
38. *FRUS, 1945,* 1: 692.

Vandenberg, always ready for a good fight, flashed back that the British were hardly new at seeking special consideration where their interests were concerned. Connally tried to restore some equilibrium by launching into a long account of the history of the Monroe Doctrine, but an impasse clearly threatened. During the indecisive conversation Eden slipped a note to Stettinius asking to talk privately, and the secretary declared a short recess.[39]

With the Russians out of earshot, Eden came straight to the real point for his outburst. He agreed that a way must be found to safeguard the inter-American system, but he wanted the British to have the same right for western Europe and the Mediterranean. The United States formula, he thought, was wrong in specifying the Act of Chapultepec because this limited British action in a situation such as an attack by Russia on Turkey or Bulgaria. Eden had naturally not revealed this idea in front of Gromyko, but if any regional exception were to be made now, it must be strong enough to allow Britain "to act at once" as "a matter of self-defense of the Empire." Both Dulles and Stassen quickly caught the regionalist approach in Eden's remarks. Dulles pointed out that "Mr. Eden wanted to go further in his proposal than the United States did and that if he understood correctly, Mr. Eden disliked the United States proposal because of its limitations on the right of self-defense." Stassen added that "with a proviso such as suggested by the British draft, the international organization would fall before it started."[40]

Since the forces of regional autonomy were growing stronger with each passing day this prospect seemed less important than protecting prospective regions from Russia. So experts from the British and U.S. delegations worked to modify the American draft. It omitted all reference to the Act of Chapultepec. This upset Stettinius, who bluntly repeated his earlier statement that unless the Monroe Doctrine were integrated into the United Nations without impairing it "there was a good possibility that the treaty could not be approved by the Senate."[41] After it appeared that the United States could not insist successfully on a specific reference to the Act of Chapultepec, Vandenberg spoke out: "I warned Eden

39. Stettinius, San Francisco Diary, May 12, 1945, SP.
40. FRUS, 1945, 1: 700, 703.
41. Ibid., 698.

that if any such language is adopted, the Senate (with my approval) will attach an interpretive reservation saying we construe the language to specifically include Chapultepec." The senator gained Eden's consent to this and was satisfied that the Americans had obtained a working compromise. He confided to his diary that although it was the best they could hope for, "it is *no good* unless it is acceptable to the Pan-Americans."[42]

Since the new formula interfered in no way with their bilateral security treaties, Russia and France accepted the proposal. China concurred and Stettinius quickly tried to bring the regional matter to an end. The United States delegation approved the Anglo-American formula on "collective self-defense," but when Stettinius summoned the Latin American foreign ministers to secure their approval, he ran into trouble. An atmosphere of suspense prevailed as he sought to impress on the ministers the loyalty of the United States to the inter-American system. They must remember that the rest of the world should not get the idea that by protecting the hemisphere system the United States was moving toward isolationism. Unfortunately, he said, this charge was heard with increasing frequency. The secretary then read the formula which the British and Americans had worked out. Vandenberg spoke out and promised that the Senate Foreign Relations Committee would attach a reservation making it clear that the reference to collective self-defense meant the Act of Chapultepec. His voice rose to an emotional shout as he concluded, "The Senate of the United States will nail this down so nobody on earth can misunderstand it."

Then Colombia's Lleras Camargo spoke "very quietly and coolly" but in unmistakable terms. He insisted that specific mention be made of the Act of Chapultepec. The statement of the Senate might satisfy nations in the Western hemisphere, but it did not insure that the rest of the world would take the same view. Stettinius stuck to his point, and called for Lleras Camargo to assume a position of "world leadership," not a "small hemispheric view."[43] Although Stettinius's determination and Vandenberg's assurances seemed to mollify the Latin Americans to some extent, the meeting adjourned without agreement.

With Latin American fears about to nullify the progress that

42. Vandenberg Diary, May 13, 1945, Vandenberg Papers.
43. Stettinius, San Francisco Diary, May 14, 1945, SP.

the Americans and British had made, Stettinius decided to consult with the president. Earlier Truman had approved the compromise formula. He now agreed that in order to secure Latin American backing, Stettinius should privately tell the chairmen of the Latin American delegations that the United States would call a hemispheric conference in the near future to implement the promise made in the Act of Chapultepec. Stettinius conveyed this message to the Latin American leaders on May 15. This proved to be the step which broke the logjam. For the first time since the regional question had arisen, there was now full harmony between the United States and its southern neighbors.

Although some days passed before final agreement on wording was worked out on a basis acceptable to Russia, the end result was Article 51 of the UN Charter, which provided the legal basis of the postwar blocs that marked the Cold War: "Nothing in the present Charter shall impair the inherent right of individual or collective self-defense if an armed attack occurs against a Member of the United Nations, until the Security Council has taken the measures necessary to maintain international peace and security."[44]

Thus was the universalist orientation of America's UN policy fundamentally altered during the San Francisco conference, largely as a result of the tensions associated with the crumbling of the grand alliance in the early cold war days as each nation sought new avenues to security.

44. U.S., Department of State, *Charter of the United Nations and Statute of the International Court of Justice,* Publication 2368 (Washington, D.C., 1945).

8

The Great Veto Crisis

THE REGIONAL COMPROMISE WAS SENT TO THE TECH-
nical committee, where it was approved after several weeks of discussion and minor attempts to revise it.[1] Although a major crisis
had existed during the first two weeks of May over this question, the outcome demonstrated the ability of the conference to
devise flexible principles accommodating diverse security needs.
That a solution was found relatively quickly was a tribute to Secretary Stettinius's persistence and his willingness to forget ordinary
working limitations for the sake of securing agreement. He had, on
occasion, bemoaned the difficulties that the Latin American nations
were causing, but throughout the negotiating he kept his eyes fixed
on the broader goal of moving ahead to finish the Charter of the
United Nations. Senator Vandenberg, who initially thought that
Stettinius was letting American interests be pushed around, gradually changed his view and became an admirer of the secretary's dy-
namic drive. *Time* magazine, which had often criticized Stettinius,
noted in its May 14 edition that his actions at San Francisco had
won respect of many seasoned diplomats.[2]

1. Russell, *UN Charter*, pp. 703–712.
2. Stettinius, San Francisco Diary, U.S. Delegation Meeting, May 11 and
14, 1945, SP; U.S. Delegation Meeting, May 11 and 14, 1945 *FRUS, 1945,*

No sooner had the regional problem been settled than the second great crisis of the conference developed over interpreting the exact use of the veto in the Security Council. The sponsor nations had achieved agreement on the role of the veto at Yalta, but the small nations, angered over not being consulted about these substantive decisions, now launched a determined campaign to liberalize the voting provisions of the Security Council. The New Zealand delegation raised the question in technical committee on May 17 and asked for an interpretation: " . . . how far . . . can a matter in which a permanent power is involved be taken before that Power can exercise its right to vote and veto any important matter? . . . How far can the Security Council go? Can it discuss matters freely and without limitation? Can it suggest proposals for settlement of a dispute? Can it inferentially throw upon the Power concerned the responsibility of refusing to accept and [of] nullifying that decision of the Council? Can the Security Council designate one of its five permanent members as an aggressor or can it simply point in that direction without such designation?"[3]

Small-power representatives listened approvingly and voted to submit a list of twenty-three questions to the Big Five, asking that the veto power be precisely defined. They admitted the necessity of allowing a veto right for enforcement decisions, but they wanted no veto on any decision which dealt with peaceful settlement procedures.[4]

When Stettinius learned of this development, he insisted in the meeting of the U.S. delegation on May 17 that the Big Five discuss the matter immediately in order "to nip this thing in the bud."[5] He found the U.S. delegation divided as to the proper course of action. The point was raised that if the issue had to be reviewed minutely, Russia might find some new argument for a total veto, which could disrupt the conference. It was soon apparent that the permanent powers must confer to prepare answers to the small nations' questions, for without satisfying the forty-five other nations there

1, *General: United Nations,* pp. 663–674, 707–712; Vandenberg, *Private Papers,* pp. 191–193; *Time,* 45 (May 14, 1945): 38.

3. UNCIO Documents, 11: 318.

4. Ibid., 316, 699–709; Charles W. Yost to Stettinius, memorandum, May 17, 1945, *SP.*

5. Stettinius, San Francisco Diary, U.S. Delegation Meeting, May 17, 1945, *SP.*

was no hope the conference would approve the voting formula. Further discussion among the U.S. delegates showed that they favored abolishing the veto on all peaceful settlement decisions. This position was adopted by the delegation, putting the United States in line with the forty-five small nations on this major revision of the veto.[6]

Secretary Stettinius, more aware than the other delegation members of how much difficult negotiation had preceded the Yalta agreement, was reluctant to press the Russians on a change in the hard-won voting formula. He also feared that any difference among the sponsoring nations would cause a delay in completing the Charter. Already his original estimate for the president, that the work of the conference might be concluded in a month, seemed beyond realization. Timing was significant because Truman did not want to force any showdown with the Russians before the UN Charter was completed, and he was watching developments at San Francisco closely as a bellwether of Soviet-American relations.[7]

Before he could pursue the veto matter further, Stettinius learned, on May 21, that Hopkins would shortly depart on a mission to Moscow. Stettinius was perturbed that Truman had not kept him informed about plans for the mission he had suggested.[8] He decided that the time had come for him to return to Washington for a talk with the president to clarify his relationship with the White House. For some time he had been disturbed about widespread speculation in the press and radio that Truman was ready to replace him with James F. Byrnes after the San Francisco conference ended.

Stettinius saw the president in Washington for nearly an hour on May 23. Their talk dealt primarily with the unresolved questions of the conference. Stettinius reported that the American delegates favored altering the voting procedure to prohibit vetos in peaceful settlement of disputes. Truman favored this change, but he thought it would be difficult for the United States to depart from

6. Stettinius to Grew, cable, May 17, 1945, *SP.*
7. Truman-Grew, memorandum of conversation, June 4, 1945, Grew Papers.
8. Truman, *Memoirs,* I: 258; Alperovitz, *Atomic Diplomacy,* Appendix 2, offers an elaborate but unfortunately erroneous explanation of the origins of the Hopkins mission; Stettinius-Grew, summary of phone conversation, May 23, 1945, *SP.*

the position which had been agreed upon at Yalta. This question occupied much of their time; and, although Stettinius had been prepared to discuss a number of questions related to Europe and Soviet-American relations, the president ended the meeting without having brought these up. Truman's only remark on overall policy was that he had "great confidence" that Hopkins would clarify relations with Stalin. "He said he was not worried about things in Europe."[9]

Truman's failure to review all aspects of foreign policy with Stettinius is a strong indication that the president, who had already decided on Byrnes as his new secretary of state, was not taking Stettinius into his full confidence. It is also possible that Truman was satisfied that Stettinius was occupied with the many problems in San Francisco and had adequate access to policy decisions in Washington through Acting Secretary Grew and the voluminous reports passing from Washington to Stettinius in San Francisco. The main influence that Stettinius exerted upon the president during this period was his support of the United Nations as a cornerstone of United States policy; he symbolized the internationalist aspect of the foreign policy of the late FDR and Cordell Hull. Truman, however, did not treat Stettinius as a trusted adviser, nor did he ask Stettinius to offer his views on overall Soviet-American relations. Throughout Stettinius's tenure as secretary of state, Truman was searching for ways other than the UN policy to model postwar American foreign policy. His treatment of Stettinius clearly indicates this.

The secretary had told Truman that he believed the demands of the smaller nations for altering the veto could be kept from disrupting the conference, and on returning to San Francisco Stettinius held several conversations with Ambassador Gromyko to this end. It was apparent from these talks that Russia would not shift her position on the veto formula as agreed upon at Yalta. The secretary was not especially perturbed, since he did not want any basic change.[10]

Meanwhile, experts of the sponsoring powers had completed a reply to the small powers' questions. It explained in minute detail how the veto would work and cited examples to illustrate each

9. Truman-Stettinius, summary of conversation, May 23, 1945, *SP.*
10. Stettinius, San Francisco Diary, May 26, 1945, *SP.*

question. The day before, Gromyko had given his tentative approval, and Stettinius told the Big Five meeting that they could "just sail right through with this." Closer discussion revealed serious disagreement among the Big Five. The problem lay in paragraph 3 of the interpretive statement: "Since the Council has the right by a procedural vote to decide its own rules of procedure, it follows that no individual member of the Council can alone prevent a consideration and discussion by the Council of a dispute or situation brought to its attention. Nor can parties to such dispute be prevented by these means from being heard by the Council."[11] Gromyko objected that discussion of a dispute almost certainly would lead to decisions being demanded by an aggrieved party and that it was absolutely essential for the permanent members of the Security Council to retain their veto in deciding whether to discuss a dispute.[12]

Stettinius denied that Gromyko's interpretation was correct, and Gromyko cabled Moscow for new instructions. On June 1, Gromyko told the Big Five that he was prepared to present Russia's "final position" on the matter: Russia would stick by the Crimea agreement and insist that the veto apply to discussion as well as decisions.[13]

On June 2, Stettinius set forth the position of the United States, Britain, and China. He referred to an interpretive statement that the State Department had issued on March 24, which held that, under the Yalta agreement, a permanent power could not employ its veto to prevent discussion of an issue but only in deciding what action should be taken.[14] Stettinius noted that Russia had not taken exception to this view; but Gromyko, irritated, interrupted that this was a "retreat from Yalta." He claimed that the decision for discussion must be covered by the veto, for it launched "a chain of responsibilities." He then started to read from the Dumbarton Oaks Proposals to illustrate his point. Stettinius heatedly broke in " . . . to say that we had stated our position and our efforts would result

11. Ibid.; *FRUS, 1945*, 1: 889–892; Statement by the Delegations of the Four Sponsoring Governments on Voting Procedure in the Security Council, draft, May 26, 1945, *SP.*

12. *FRUS, 1945*, 1, 889–892.

13. Ibid., pp. 1071–1094.

14. Ibid., pp. 1094–1117.

in no Charter at all if the Soviet view should prevail. I did not mince matters at all at this point but talked to the Soviet representative in as firm, emphatic, and unmistakable terms as possible so that the importance of our stand could not be misunderstood."[15]

Although the secretary's strong language made the American position clear, it brought the impasse no nearer solution. Stettinius decided to move swiftly and boldly. Several days earlier, Lord Halifax, the British ambassador, had suggested that Stettinius could request Truman to direct Hopkins to appeal to Stalin. Stettinius had rejected the idea,[16] but after the bitter exchange in the Big Five meeting on June 2, he decided to try it. He cabled Ambassador Harriman a directive to hand to Hopkins, explaining the deadlock, and stating that he had conferred with the president:

> . . . and he confirms my own feeling . . . that the United States could not possibly accept an organization subject to such a restrictive procedure. . . . With the president's approval I am bringing this matter to your attention urgently. I know that in the past Marshal Stalin did not know himself of some of the decisions that were being taken and communicated to us. I feel therefore that it would be most helpful if you and Harry could meet with Marshal Stalin as soon as possible and ask him whether he fully realizes what the instructions sent to Gromyko mean and what effect the Soviet proposal would have upon the character of the world organization we are all trying to work out. Please tell him in no uncertain words that this country could not possibly join an organization based on so unreasonable an interpretation of the provision of the great powers' veto in the Security Council.[17]

Stettinius asked that Hopkins reply quickly "since we will have to

15. Stettinius, San Francisco Diary, Big Five Ministers' Meeting, June 2, 1945, *SP.*

16. Dulles to Hayden Raynor, memorandum, May 29, 1945, with attached memorandum on American reaction, *SP.*

17. Grew to Harriman, telegram, June 2, 1945, *FRUS, 1945,* 1: 1117–1119, relays message from Stettinius for Hopkins's use in conversation with Stalin; Byrnes, *Speaking Frankly,* p. 64, erroneously claims credit for the idea of asking Hopkins to approach Stalin on the veto. Herbert Feis, who constantly underrated Stettinius in his writings, entirely omits Stettinius from this episode. See Herbert Feis, *Between War and Peace, the Potsdam Conference,* p. 177.

take the necessary steps to wind up the Conference here if we have nothing favorable from you in this regard."[18]

Stettinius had determined to avoid leaks on his message to Hopkins, and had told only a few State Department officials about it. Consequently, the other American delegates were ignorant of this maneuver and soon began grumbling over Stettinius's apparent inaction. Then on June 3, an article by Reston on the front page of the *New York Times* minutely described the blowup within the Big Five meeting; and rumors spread throughout the conference that a breakdown was imminent. In the American delegation there was talk of completing agreement on other aspects of the Charter and leaving the veto open for later adjustment "because the prestige of the United States is diminishing daily under the present circumstances."[19]

Across the country the mood was one of disillusionment. In the wake of Allied tension and conference crises, a late May survey showed that 40 percent of the American people doubted the conference would succeed. Within a month of the start of the conference, the percentage of Americans who believed the UN could prevent war for fifty years had slipped from 49 to 32 percent. Still, having no acceptable alternative, 85 percent of the people surveyed believed that the United States should join the UN.[20] State Department officials attributed the pessimism to a decline in public trust of Russia. Only 45 percent of the people believed Russia "can be trusted to cooperate" after the war, a slippage of 10 percent since late February. American officials also noted an increasing public desire to gain overseas bases and to keep America's military "stronger than any others."[21]

Americans also feared division among the Western Allies. This

18. Stettinius to Harriman, cable, June 2, 1945, *SP*.
19. *New York Times*, June 3, 1945; the leak apparently came from John Foster Dulles: Stettinius-Pasvolsky, transcript of phone conversation, June 3, 1945; Notes on Meeting in Dining Room of Penthouse Following Big Five Meeting, June 3, 1945, *SP*.
20. U.S. Delegation, Daily Summary of Opinion Developments, June 4 and 7, 1945, *SP*. Data was prepared by the Princeton University Office of Public Opinion Research.
21. U.S., Department of State, Division of Public Liaison, Latest Opinion Trends in the U.S.A., May 31, 1945; U.S. Delegation, Special Memorandum, Recent American Opinion on U.S.-Soviet Relations, May 30, 1945, *SP*.

involved France's intrigues in Syria and Lebanon aimed at restoring French influence in the postwar years. The French exerted diplomatic pressure in the spring of 1945 and in May dispatched more troops to Lebanon, moves that greatly upset the Arab nations. This embarrassed Britain and the United States, who were bent on keeping the region stable and were already facing a dangerous situation regarding Zionist efforts to secure a postwar Jewish state in the face of Arab determination to keep Jews out of Palestine.

For a permanent Security Council member to act as France was doing portended badly for the role of the UN as an agent of peace, a dilemma that Loy Henderson, director of Near Eastern Affairs in the State Department, cogently summed up: "While we in San Francisco are talking about world security and are devising methods for combating aggression, France is openly pursuing tactics which are similar to those used by the Japanese in Manchukuo and by the Italians in Ethiopia. It will be difficult for any small nation or any great power to have any confidence in the effectiveness of the International Security Organization if, at the very time that it is being built, we close our eyes to what is taking place in Syria and Lebanon. . . ."[22] France was the only Western power since the war had begun to "deliberately set out by force and threats of force to work its will upon smaller powers. . . ."[23] This was a particularly black mark because the aggressor was a democratic nation, and it damaged the democratic West in world eyes. This came at a bad time because it diverted the attention of world opinion from Soviet actions in Eastern Europe.

The Levant crisis finally burst into open warfare between French forces and the Syrian populace on May 29 and 30, with French artillery and bombs killing hundreds of people. The President of Syria, joined by the heads of other Arab nations, charged France with violating the 1942 UN Declaration; they bitterly asked Secretary Stettinius, "Where now are the Atlantic Charter and the Four Freedoms? What can we think of San Francisco?"[24] While the Truman administration hesitated, Churchill seized the lead and sent a curt ultimatum to De Gaulle on May 31. Churchill warned that British military forces would act to restore peace and urged

22. *FRUS, 1945,* vol. 8, *The Near East and Africa,* pp. 1093–1094.
23. Ibid.
24. Ibid., 1118.

that French troops cease fire "in order to avoid collision between British and French forces."[25]

The swift action by Churchill restored peace and ended a serious threat to the proceedings at San Francisco. The legacy of French actions was momentous. Not only were Franco-British relations seriously impaired, but the division among the Western powers provided Russia further opportunity to enter into Middle Eastern affairs. It was no accident that just at this time Russia initiated demands on Turkey to revise the Montreux Convention controlling the use of the Dardanelles Straits and asked for bases to assure Soviet access from the Black Sea to the Mediterranean.[26]

These ominous events coincided with the despair at San Francisco over the veto deadlock. The delegates were supposed to be building a United Nations on the theory of close cooperation between the major powers when it was obvious that no real identity of interests existed.[27] Yet like so many other leaders of the day, Vandenberg was trapped by the knowledge that there was little alternative to persisting to the end in the hope of some success. "I feel that even 'wishful thinking' is preferable to the devastating shock the country and the world would get if Frisco were to produce nothing at all."[28]

Neither Truman nor Stettinius yielded to the rising pressures and criticisms. In a conversation with Acting Secretary Grew on June 4, the president said that while Hopkins was negotiating in Moscow and so long as the conference was in session in San Francisco, "it would be desirable not to exert too much pressure" in Soviet-American relations. A few days earlier, Stettinius had delivered a worldwide radio address, billed as a major pronouncement on U.S. policy. In it Stettinius reiterated the tenets of international cooperation that Roosevelt had set forth and called on the American people to realize that their interests extended to the entire world. The United States would have to "maintain those interests in our relations with other great powers" and mediate between them when their interests conflict among themselves: "We in America can never again turn our backs upon the world. For we are not

25. Ibid., 1124.
26. *FRUS, Potsdam,* 1: 1020.
27. Vandenberg, Diary, May 31, 1945, Vandenberg Papers.
28. Ibid., June 7, 1945.

only a part of it—we are one of the most important parts. If we do not assume our new responsibilities willingly, then we shall be compelled to assume them by the brutal necessities of self-preservation. There is no possibility of retreat."[29]

Rhetoric did not replace deeds, and the secretary had difficulty in restraining the panic within the delegation. Vandenberg thought everything was collapsing. He complained to Stettinius that the world's nations were choosing sides between Russia and America, and that increasingly they believed they could not rely on the United States. He warned Stettinius that, if action were not taken soon to restore confidence, the Republicans might have to end their bipartisan cooperation and publicly condemn the course of events. This persuaded the secretary to reveal his secret appeal to Stalin in order to keep the volatile senator from acting rashly.[30]

After four days of nerve-racking waiting, a dramatic break occurred. On June 6 Hopkins wired that he had concluded a cordial series of talks with Stalin and had won the premier's acceptance of the American position on the veto. According to Hopkins, Molotov had kept rigidly to the position argued by Gromyko, but when Stalin quizzed his foreign minister about the matter, Molotov was overruled. Stalin "remarked that he thought it was an insignificant matter and that they should accept the American position."[31]

Word had reached Stettinius before Gromyko learned of the changed Soviet position, and the secretary had the unique duty of explaining to Gromyko a major action of his own government. Stettinius said he took this step "because of our friendship and I feel I owe it to you in all friendliness to tell you immediately of this word I had received." Gromyko appreciated the gesture and seemed more cordial than at any previous time during the conference. After the Soviet ambassador received his instructions on the 7th, he met with Stettinius, and they worked out the details for a joint press release announcing the end of the veto crisis.[32]

The news was met with wild enthusiasm in San Francisco. The American delegates devoted their next meeting to mutual con-

29. *Vital Speeches of the Day,* 61 (June 15, 1945): 524–528.
30. Stettinius, San Francisco Diary, June 4, 1945; Stettinius-Charles Ross, transcript of phone conversation, June 4, 1945, *SP.*
31. Sherwood, *Roosevelt and Hopkins,* p. 910.
32. Stettinius, calendar notes, conversation with Gromyko, June 6 and 7, 1945, *SP.*

gratulations, and messages of satisfaction passed between Stettinius, Truman, Grew, and Hull. On the evening of June 7, Stettinius joined close friends for a dinner in celebration of the veto break-through.[33]

A major result of the veto dispute among the Big Five was to end any chance that the forty-five smaller nations could win curtailment of the veto on peaceful settlement decisions. In this matter the forty-five smaller countries were responsible, for it was their probing questionnaire that had first revealed the unsuspected cleavage in the thinking of the permanent powers. In the ensuing crisis, the Americans had dropped all notions of modifying the veto and thereafter would not consider any attempt along this line.[34]

The American actions after June 7 clearly demonstrated the determination of the Big Five to defeat all efforts to alter the voting procedure. In the technical committee, Australia, Belgium, the Netherlands, and the Latin American nations still fought to end the veto on pacific settlement. At one tense point, Senator Connally told the committee that the Big Five would not change: "You may go home from San Francisco . . . and report that you have defeated the veto. . . . But you can also say, 'We *tore up the Charter.*' At that point I sweepingly ripped the Charter draft in my hands to shreds and flung the scraps upon the table."[35] Stettinius, applying his own pressure, called several chairmen of small-power delegations to his penthouse and told them privately that unless they accepted the voting formula as presented by the sponsors there would be no United Nations. He also ordered Rockefeller to warn the Latin American leaders to vote with the United States or face an uncooperative attitude by the United States in the future.[36]

This stiff line succeeded, and the conference accepted the Yalta veto formula without change. The spectacular failure of the

33. Stettinius-Truman, transcript of phone conversation, June 7, 1945; Stettinius, San Francisco Diary, June 7, 1945, SP.

34. Sir Charles K. Webster, "The Making of the Charter of the United Nations," *History*, 32 (Mar., 1947): 342–345.

35. Connally, *My Name is Tom Connally*, pp. 282–283; *UNCIO Documents*, 11: 493.

36. Stettinius-Auguste de Schryver (Belgium), memorandum of conversation, June 12, 1945; Stettinius-Alexander Loudon (Netherlands), memorandum of conversation, June 12, 1945; Stettinius-Rockefeller, memorandum of conversation, June 12, 1945, SP.

forty-five smaller nations to win modification of this cardinal principle tended to obscure their solid success in helping to mold a charter more liberal than the Dumbarton Oaks Proposals. These successes were the product of quiet committee work, and the gains were often overlooked by the public which generally read stories only about the great controversies of the conference.

Stettinius had emphasized the cooperative aspect of planning for the organization on May 5 when he informed reporters about the amendments to the Dumbarton Oaks Proposals which the conference would consider. He noted the worldwide discussion which had taken place during the interval since October: "Seldom has there been a greater demonstration of respect for democratic rights or a fuller proof of the value of democratic procedures."[37]

The secretary hoped that the permanent powers and the forty-five other nations would reach easy harmony, but these hopes were rudely jolted. Australia, Canada, and New Zealand frequently embarrassed Britain by leading small-power drives to liberalize the provisions being written into the Charter; and the United States found a similar embarrassment when the Latin American countries joined this effort. Both Britain and the United States had thought that their friends and allies could be more easily controlled.

The loggerheads between the sponsoring nations and the other delegations annoyed Stettinius. When he had referred to democratic consultation among the Allies since October, he meant discussions where the smaller nations took a back seat. Now that the moment had arrived for concrete agreements, Stettinius found that he had little patience with the small powers' efforts to broaden the framework of the organization which had been drafted at Dumbarton Oaks. He was largely interested in expediting the conference and securing approval of a charter basically like the Dumbarton Oaks plan. He used his authority and prestige to speed up meetings and decision making. While he wanted topics fully discussed, he quickly grew tired of the seemingly endless debate, which he often regarded as repetitious quibbling.

In large part this drive for rapid accomplishment stemmed from the American desire to create the UN so that it could tackle the problems that were straining the Allied coalition. Truman put constant pressure on Stettinius to fix a definite date for the termi-

37. U.S. Delegation, Press Release, No. 10, May 5, 1945, SP.

nation of the conference.[38] This made the secretary particularly sensitive to delaying tactics, and he believed that the leaders of the small-power delegations were obstructing this goal. Several times he moved quickly to smash opposition to the Big Five. At one point toward the end, when Australia's Herbert Evatt was driving hard to win approval of a veto-free amendment process for the Charter, Stettinius successfully asked President Truman to pressure Australian Prime Minister Forde to instruct Evatt to cooperate.[39]

Stettinius's pressure kept the American delegation united most of the time, and under his guidance the Big Five resisted any major change in the power structure of the organization as it had been planned at Dumbarton Oaks. That significant change in the Dumbarton Oaks Proposals was avoided is well illustrated by examining the modifications made in the operation of the Security Council. The small nations won assurance that in selecting the six nonpermanent rotating members of the council, "due regard" would be given to those countries that had effectively contributed to keeping the peace by making forces and bases available to the organization. The powers of the council were broadened so that it could recommend terms of settlement as well as methods in cases of peaceful disputes. But since this latter amendment had been proposed by the Big Five, it could hardly be credited to the forty-five small nations.[40] Finally they failed entirely in their drive to eliminate the veto in cases of peaceful settlement.

An indirect assault on the supremacy of the Big Five in the Security Council was made when the small nations pressed to increase the authority of the General Assembly. They championed the assembly as their chief protection against the misuse of power by the Big Five in the Security Council. To assure this protection, the small powers sought to limit the power of the council by making it more responsible to the General Assembly. This was a natural

38. Stettinius, calendar notes, Meeting with President Truman, May 23, 1945, *SP*.

39. Stettinius-Grew, transcript of phone conversation, June 13, 1945; Big Five Ministers' Meeting, minutes, June 11, 1945; Stettinius-Department of State Advisers, meeting in penthouse, June 11, 1945, *SP*.

40. Johnson, "Stettinius," in Graebner (ed.), *Uncertain Tradition*, 222; *UNCIO Documents*, 3: 624; Summary Analysis of the Charter for an International Organization, 10, June 22, 1945, *SP*.

desire, since in the assembly each state had only one vote regardless of its size or power. New Zealand introduced a resolution requiring assembly concurrence before the Security Council could take enforcement action except in instances of "extreme urgency." Even then, the council would have to report immediately to the assembly and secure its approval.[41] Such a radical invasion of the province of Big Five power had no chance of acceptance, however, and even a number of smaller powers realized that the council must have freedom to act swiftly in time of crisis.

Thus, the small powers failed to increase the assembly's sphere of influence regarding security; but they did win adoption of stronger texts on the ability of assembly members to speak out on matters of peace and security. The assembly was granted the power to make recommendations "on any questions pertaining to the maintenance of international peace and security" so long as the same issue was not being considered by the Security Council at the same moment.[42] The small powers, joined by the United States, also preserved the right of the assembly to "discuss *any* questions or matters within the scope of the Charter," resisting a Soviet move to have the assembly limited to considering only matters affecting peace and security.[43]

This last point assured member nations that the new organization could seek ways to promote the positive aspects of peace, such as fostering international economic, social, and educational advancement. With the exception of the Russians, who argued that the organization must focus only on threats to the peace in order to be effective, the preponderant opinion at San Francisco held that the United Nations would be most concerned in its first decade in preparing the economic and social foundations of lasting peace. The smaller powers also succeeded in securing a broader statement of principles to govern the operation of the Economic and Social Council, enabling it to promote higher standards of living, improved

41. *UNCIO Documents*, 3: 488.

42. Ibid., pp. 4–5; Russell, *UN Charter*, pp. 752–764.

43. The American Position on the Right of the General Assembly to Discuss Any Matter Within the Sphere of International Relations, memorandum, June 15, 1945; Big Five Foreign Ministers Meeting, minutes, June 13, 1945; Stettinius-Gromyko, memorandum of conversation, June 16, 1945; Notes on a Meeting in the Penthouse, Stettinius, Halifax, and Evatt, June 17, 1945, *SP; UNCIO Documents*, 9: 234–235.

health, and full world employment.[44] The big powers accepted these areas as being important to the promotion of world stability, and Russia acquiesced to the wishes of its cosponsors.

The controlling interests of the great powers, particularly of the United States, were fully demonstrated with the establishment of the Trusteeship Council. Russia, which had no overseas colonies or military bases, joined the small nations in seeking to have specific dependent areas placed under the trusteeship of the organization.

Owing to the able representation of Harold Stassen on the technical committee and the unity of the United States delegation, the powers of the Trusteeship Council were narrowly limited. It could operate only in areas formerly under a League of Nations mandate, lands detached from the Axis, or in territory voluntarily placed under its jurisdiction by a colonial power. In keeping with the interests of the American military leaders, the whole stand of the United States was to limit the actual control exercised by the council as much as possible. Thus the council could receive reports "of a technical nature relating to economic, social, and educational conditions," but it could not infringe on the security interests of the country which controlled the territory. The United Nations could make inspection visits to trust territories only when the trustee nation approved. The restricted power of the council was covered by promises of the member nations to work for the "well-being" of dependent peoples and pledges to guard against abusing them and to act according to standards of "good-neighborliness."[45]

Indeed, the entire charter abounded with appeals to justice and promises to uplift man's life in a dozen ways. These trimmings had great appeal to the American delegates and advisers, whether they were Department of State officials such as Stettinius or veteran congressmen such as Vandenberg. For American foreign policy was deeply engaged in fulfilling the Wilson-Hull brand of "missionary diplomacy." Axiomatic to this concept was the belief that by setting the example of faithfully adhering to democratic principles the United States could convert the world to peace by example.

44. Russell, *UN Charter*, pp. 778–788; Gildersleeve, *Many A Good Crusade*, pp. 340–345.
45. Russell, *UN Charter*, chap. 31; Gromyko to Stettinius, June 20, 1945; Stettinius to Gromyko, June 23, 1945; *SP*; Charter of the United Nations, as reproduced in Russell, *UN Charter*, pp. 1047–1050, chaps. 11 and 12.

Stettinius outlined this policy on May 28, when he reported to the American people on the first month of the conference. He alluded to the regional and veto crises as transitory and stressed that the sponsor nations had met at San Francisco: "to form an organization for peace . . . not to conspire for war. . . . Their intentions are honorable and their necessities for peace are fully as urgent as those of any other nation, large or small. To assume that they seek to violate pledges rather than to enforce them is to oppose the existence of any organization for peace and to resign the world to an endless succession of wars."[46] Stettinius emphasized there was no choice but for the United States to assume the responsibilities commensurate with its power.[47]

The secretary's address was almost a creed that the United States must rely on the United Nations as its chief instrument for preserving national security and the peace of the world. But it was highly misleading because Stettinius presented an overconfident picture of great-power cooperation at the conference table and glossed over Allied rifts about the course of events in Europe.

Stettinius and his State Department colleagues had found it difficult to uphold principle at San Francisco for Allied discord over Europe menaced the embryonic plans for a new peace organization. During the entire course of the conference, information poured into the State Department showing unmistakably that Russia was acting in Europe as if prior Allied agreements on cooperation had never existed. The Western Allies had continued a stream of protests to Moscow, and Stettinius and Eden had several discussions with Molotov about Allied relations; but nothing indicated any early change in Russia's attitude.[48]

Churchill was not content to wait to see if the creation of the United Nations could rescue the deteriorating Big Three coalition. Instead, he suggested that British and American armies maintain their advanced lines in central Europe, which at that moment (May 3) extended far east into the agreed areas that Russia was scheduled to administer in eastern Germany, Czechoslovakia, Aus-

46. *Vital Speeches of the Day*, 61 (June 15, 1945): 524–528.
47. Ibid.
48. Summary of Current Foreign Developments, May 23, 1945, SP; Feis, *Between War and Peace*, p. 36; Stettinius-Molotov-Eden, memorandum of conversations, May 3 and 4, 1945, SP.

tria, and the Baltic region. The Western Allies now had a strategic advantage in Europe, Churchill argued; and they must use this to force Russia to live up to its political commitments at Yalta concerning Allied cooperation in eastern Europe. He prophesied that unless they extracted strong agreements, "there are no prospects of a satisfactory solution and a very little hope of preventing a third world war."[49]

The Truman administration refused to use the power of Western armies to bring Russia to heel. Instead it had decided upon subtle economic pressure, to use Lend-Lease curtailments as a threat to let Russia know what might occur if she failed to mend her ways. Meanwhile Truman would stick to diplomatic contacts, such as sending Hopkins to Stalin to revive the earlier atmosphere of cooperation. But ineptly, all Lend-Lease aid was suddenly halted on May 12, and the Russians quickly saw the move as a public effort to humiliate them.[50]

Stettinius had supported Churchill's idea of keeping British and American forces at their forward positions in Europe, but Truman had overruled this notion. The secretary had also favored pressuring Russia by using Lend-Lease as a weapon, but he thought it should be employed as a threat to Russia; and he disapproved of the sudden stopping of Lend-Lease shipments as doing more harm than good.[51]

Two important considerations dictated a moderate policy toward Russia. The first was military. American military leaders still counted on Russia's support against Japan, even though Russian aid seemed less urgent than it had in late 1944. The atomic bomb project was still an unknown factor; the bomb had not been tested, and estimates varied widely about its value in defeating Japan.[52] A second essential reason for moderation was the ardent American desire to maintain an atmosphere conducive to success at the San Francisco conference.[53]

49. Stettinius to Truman, cable, May 11, 1945, SP.
50. Stettinius-Harriman, memorandum of conversation, May 9, 1945; Stettinius-Truman, transcript of phone conversation, May 10, 1945, SP; Herring, "Lend-Lease to Russia and the Origins of the Cold War," pp. 100–101.
51. Stettinius, Roosevelt and the Russians, pp. 318–319.
52. Feis, Churchill, Roosevelt and Stalin, pp. 638–639; Herbert Feis, Japan Subdued, pp. 3–14.
53. Secretary's Staff Committee, minutes, May 9, 1945, SP.

It is unmistakably clear that American foreign policy relied heavily on the successful creation of the United Nations as the principal means of solving its conflicts with the Soviet Union. This accounts for the steady pressure that Stettinius exerted on the delegation leaders to move speedily in completing the Charter.

On June 25 the Charter was completed after last minute delays over translations and phrasing. When the plenary session adopted the Charter, the delegates and audience rose to their feet and cheered. Halifax, who was presiding, expressed the common emotion when he fervently spoke, "I think, Ladies and Gentlemen, we may all feel that we have taken part in, as we may hope, one of the great moments of history."[54]

Much of the credit for that moment must go to Secretary Stettinius, who had brought to the conference a driving will that the work would succeed. He had used his authority with great force to break deadlocks at crucial moments. He balanced the employment of sheer power with a talent for instilling faith in those around him as to the ultimate success and worth of the international organization. His abilities had helped shape many of the decisions that were indispensable to the creation of the Charter. America's long-sought goal now seemed assured. Out of the chaos of war would come an organization capable of ensuring world political stability. On Stettinius's last night in San Francisco he watched the flickering lights as a line of ships moved under the Golden Gate toward the far distant Pacific war. In his mind he went over the many days so full of worries and trials as well as great hope and success. He could well think of Halifax's closing words to the plenary session, " . . . one of the great moments of history."

54. *UNCIO Documents*, 1: 631.

9

America's UN Policy
and the
Onset of the Cold War

EUPHORIA PREVAILED AS PRESIDENT TRUMAN ARRIVED to take part in the Charter-signing ceremonies on June 26. Amid a great fanfare of publicity and celebration, Truman optimistically reaffirmed America's UN policy. In his address before a packed San Francisco's Opera House, Truman proclaimed that he would utilize the United Nations as a central instrument in America's foreign policy. Renouncing the path of great power domination, he declared, "By their own example the strong nations of the world should lead the way to international justice. . . . Let us not fail to grasp this supreme chance to establish a worldwide rule of reason. . . ."[1]

Truman's subsequent actions during 1945 raise doubts about his convictions that the UN would really operate effectively. His reorientation away from Roosevelt's UN policy was underscored by bringing Byrnes in as secretary of state and moving Stettinius to the new post of American representative to the United Nations. Truman assured Stettinius that his new job " . . . is the biggest job in the world today for an American outside the United States. . . ."

1. Truman, *Memoirs*, 1: 291–293.

and pledged full cooperation from himself and Byrnes; but in the year Stettinius served in the UN the president never gave substance to his promise. Stettinius found himself uncomfortably on the outer rim of decisionmaking.

In part this development can be explained by the difficulties inherent in establishing administrative procedures of a major new post. It was December before Congress passed legislation regulating America's legal relationship to the United Nations. Truman seemed in no hurry to decide on the precise structure of the American delegation to the UN. When he did act in the spring of 1946, neither he nor Byrnes brought Stettinius into the process during the crucial decision-making stages. Stettinius's rising frustration also partly reflected Secretary Byrnes's determination to maintain State Department control over foreign policy formulation, as opposed to Stettinius's view that the American UN representative should have a role almost coequal to that of the secretary of state. Finally in June of 1946 Stettinius resigned, charging that Truman had not given him the wide powers that were originally promised.[2]

These personal considerations were secondary to the disillusionment Stettinius felt as he watched Truman shunt the United Nations aside. Stettinius repeatedly urged the importance of getting the UN into operation quickly, but in his work on the UN Preparatory Commission in London in the late summer and fall of the year, Stettinius found that the UN was already becoming a battleground between East and West. The British seemed even less interested in the UN than earlier although they insisted now that UN headquarters be located in Europe. The British spokesman, Philip Noel-Baker, privately told Stettinius that if the UN settled in America, pressure would arise to develop a strong regional organization in Europe. Russia would almost certainly dominate it, and "The British might have difficulty pulling their weight against the Russians."[3] Stettinius found himself working in isolation for, even though the first foreign ministers' meeting was in session in London, Byrnes

2. Stettinius, calendar notes, July 19, Sept. 2, 7, 1945, Mar. 20, May 15, and June 4, 1946; Stettinius-Easton Rothwell, memorandum of phone conversation, May 21, 1946; Stettinius to Byrnes, May 18, 1946, SP.
3. Staff Meeting of U.S. Delegation to Preparatory Commission, memorandum, Sept. 4, 1945; Stettinius, calendar notes, Sept. 12, 1945; Easton-Rothwell-Martin Hill, memorandum of conversation, Sept. 26 and 27, 1945, SP.

made almost no effort to coordinate his efforts with those of Stettinius.[4]

When illness necessitated Stettinius's return to America in late October, he went to the White House before entering the hospital in an effort to impress his concern on Truman. He told the president he had found the British Labour government indifferent to the United Nations. The atmosphere was "completely different" from that of the San Francisco conference. The British and French wanted to postpone further action on the UN until their problems with Russia were resolved. Stettinius attributed the change in atmosphere to the acrimonious disputes at the foreign ministers' meeting and to uncertainities about controlling the atomic bomb. To counter this trend he said it was "absolutely vital" for America to stand firm on the UN, and he urged the president to take a strong lead in obtaining an early convening of the General Assembly and Security Council. He warned that Truman must provide leadership and vigor or watch the UN fail. "The President replied very earnestly, 'I am with you a hundred percent. You say the word—I'll give you anything you ask for. I'm with you all the way.'" Truman was emphatic that the United Nations would be made to work. The failure of the foreign ministers, he went on, was no great surprise to him; he had expected a letdown in relations after the war ended. Many of the really difficult problems had been postponed during the war. He did not think current difficulties should be too greatly emphasized, but that it was preferable to settle these differences publicly now. "He said that we did have some real problems with the Russians but we had every hope that we could work them out amicably if we gave ourselves time." He envisioned the UN playing a major role as a forum in which to achieve compromise. The only alternative, the president feared, "was a bitter armament race with the Russians."[5]

This led Stettinius to raise the problem of controlling atomic weapons. He had long since regarded this as the overriding question, and he had found almost all British leaders pessimistic about how to handle it. Stettinius made it clear that he believed that the proper place to raise atomic energy questions was in the UN. He

4. Stettinius, calendar notes, Sept. 25, 1945, SP.
5. Notes on conversations between the President and Mr. Stettinius, by Charles P. Noyes, Oct. 22, 1945, SP.

expressed hope that the United States would sufficiently decide its policy by the time the first General Assembly met so that it could exert real leadership on this vital matter. The president concurred and said that he would soon meet with Canadian Prime Minister King and Britain's Attlee to discuss controlling the atomic bomb. Truman added that he disagreed with the popular view in the United States that the bomb was a "precious secret" which the nation must hoard. The scientific knowledge was easily available; the United States possessed only an industrial and technological advantage, which he saw lasting no more than "perhaps four to ten years." Truman said "that his present thinking was that we ought to be able to outlaw the use of atomic bombs in the same way we outlawed the use of gas. He said that any bombs we had would be placed at the disposal of the United Nations Security Council."[6]

This discussion between Truman and Stettinius offers interesting insight into the president's thinking at an important point in the nascent Cold War days. Truman placed great emphasis on the UN. He had become president on the threshold of the San Francisco conference, "The event," Feis has written, "that was in the center of American thought at the time. . . . Most American officials were at one with the American people in believing this more meaningful than the troubles over European frontiers or the alignment of the smaller European states."[7]

Planning for the UN had influenced all of America's diplomatic decisions since 1944. It was because Russian cooperation along the lines envisioned by the Dumbarton Oaks Proposals was so important that any deviation by Moscow was seen as an ominous threat. Measured by the democratic yardstick of the Dumbarton Oaks Proposals, Russia's moves from the summer of 1944 on seemed to belie her professions of support for the UN. As they watched the political patterns emerging in Poland, Rumania, and Hungary, many American officials began to doubt whether the UN policy would work. This haunting fear had produced the revolt in the State, War, and Navy Departments against Roosevelt's acceptance of the Morgenthau plan to dismember Germany. Despite the temporary hope created by the Yalta accords, American officials found themselves

6. Ibid.
7. Feis, *Between War and Peace,* p. 85.

increasingly sympathetic to British efforts to develop a Western bloc.

By the opening of the San Francisco conference the American shift away from the UN policy was already well-advanced. Whether justified or not, American leaders had convinced themselves that they faced a dramatic communist expansionism that would threaten American interests on a global scale in the postwar years.[8]

Faith in the UN as a keystone in America's postwar security had never been very strong at any time. Those who shared Hull's strong hope in the international organization's ability to keep the peace were limited largely to a few devoted individuals in the State Department, most notably Leo Pasvolsky. Even Secretary Stettinius, who shared Hull's broad philosophical commitment to the UN policy was, in Harriman's words, "under no illusions" about the difficulties in dealing with Russia on an amicable basis.[9] Undersecretary Joseph Grew, who took part in nearly all of the policy review meetings in the spring of 1945, summed up the mood of disillusionment:

> The world organization for peace and security now being built at San Francisco will be incapable of preserving peace and security because, through the agreement at Yalta to give the right of veto to the great powers against the use of force in disputes to which one of them is a party, the organization will be rendered powerless to act against the one certain future enemy, Soviet Russia. In practice the main purpose of the organization will be annulled. We shall have no confidence in it whatsoever. Its power to prevent a future world war will be but a pipe dream. . . . A future war with Soviet Russia is as certain as anything in the world can be. It may come within a very few years.[10]

When Truman suddenly became president the missing factor in the anticommunist equation was dramatically added. Because Roosevelt did not keep Truman fully apprised of developments,

8. Millis, *Forrestal Diaries*, pp. 37–59; Grew, *Turbulent Era*, 2: 1444–1447; Averell Harriman, *America and Russia in A Changing World, A Half Century of Personal Observation*, pp. 40–44; *FRUS, 1945*, vol. 7, *China*, pp. 342–344, 347–348.

9. Harriman interview, Dulles Oral History Project.

10. Grew, *Turbulent Era*, 2: 1446.

many authors have pictured Truman as groping uncertainly during the spring of 1945.[11] Several writers suggest that because of his inexperience Truman was reluctant to tamper with Roosevelt's policies, and some see a basic continuity in policy from Roosevelt to Truman.[12] This view places more emphasis on Truman's inexperience than is warranted and overlooks Truman's decisiveness and quick action. The significant fact about Truman's early days in the White House is the extent to which he shared the fear of communism that pervaded the thinking of his top advisers.

Out of this mutual perspective on the Russian problem evolved five major actions that fundamentally altered America's UN policy:

One: The decision to proceed with economic pressure against Russia which resulted in ending Lend-Lease aid to Russia on May 12. More significant was the continued hedging on extending postwar credits to Russia. "The American use of the loan as a diplomatic weapon, at the same time that Great Britain was granted a handsome loan at below two percent interest, fed exaggerated Soviet fears, but fears nevertheless, that the United States was creating an international bloc. . . ."[13]

Two: American support for allowing regional blocs the right to initiate measures of collective self-defense. This was a complete turnabout in American thinking since the Dumbarton Oaks Conference and represented the start of the American pilgrimage toward building the postwar Anglo-Saxon alliance system first publicly called for by Churchill less than a year later in his iron-curtain address at Fulton, Missouri.

Three: The delay of any full confrontation with Russia during the proceedings at San Francisco.

Four: Truman's acceptance of Stimson's view that the atomic bomb should be considered as a bargaining factor in dealing with Russia.

Five: Truman's effort to reverse Roosevelt's abandonment of Eastern Europe. This decision was implemented only in the months

11. Gaddis Smith, *American Diplomacy During the Second World War,* p. 154; Ulam, *Expansion and Co-existence,* p. 384; Kolko, *Politics of War,* p. 381; Paterson, "The Abortive American Loan to Russia," p. 80.

12. Feis, *Churchill, Roosevelt and Stalin,* pp. 599–600; Williams, *Tragedy of American Diplomacy,* pp. 238–239.

13. Paterson, "The Abortive American Loan to Russia," p. 91.

after the Postdam Conference when the UN Charter was completed
and the atomic bomb was a known quantity.

These decisions by Truman marked a shift away from Roosevelt's efforts to secure Russian cooperation through America's UN
policy, and they contributed significantly to the onset of the Cold
War.

Truman fully intended to use unparalleled military power to
achieve a long-lasting strategic advantage for America. There were
to be no challengers to America's domination of the Pacific; Britain
and western Europe must be made secure against Russia's increased
power; and America would resist all Russion efforts to increase its
influence in countries bordering the Mediterranean. American diplomacy continually hardened during the last six months of 1945 to
achieve this last goal. Once he possessed the atomic bomb, Truman
launched a vigorous program to reduce Russia's influence in eastern
Europe, but there is little real evidence to show that this was Truman's major objective.[14] If atomic diplomacy existed, it was used not
primarily to undercut Russia's role in eastern Europe although the
American government did oppose Russian efforts to cut the West
out of all access to eastern Europe. American criticisms of Soviet
actions in eastern Europe were largely a means of keeping Russia
on the defensive and to discourage communist subversion in western Europe. The chief diplomatic significance of the atomic bomb
was as an agent that would make Russia halt short of trying to ex-
tend itself into western Europe and the Mediterranean. During de
Gaulle's visit to Washington shortly after Japan surrendered, both
Truman and Byrnes specifically spoke of this concept of the bomb's
utility. More importantly they stressed that de Gaulle should look
to the United Nations as the primary means of attaining lasting
security.[15]

The hard line in dealing with Russia was abundantly clear at
the fall London Foreign Ministers' Conference. Secretary Byrnes
turned aside all Russian efforts to obtain a voice in occupying Japan
and went back on an earlier American promise to support Russia's
request to have a trusteeship role. In the latter instance, the Ameri-

14. Adam Ulam, "On Modern History: Re-reading the Cold War," *Interplay Magazine*, 2 (March, 1968): 51–53.
15. Memorandum of conversation between Mr. Georges Bidault and Mr.
James F. Byrnes, Aug. 23, 1945, Byrnes Papers.

can duplicity was almost forced when Russia talked about administering former Italian colonies in North Africa.[16] The London Conference ended in abysmal failure and heightened tension was the chief result. The American government was convinced that it was facing a new Russia—one that was bent on establishing suzerainty in eastern Europe and the Balkans and expanding elsewhere as far as it could.

Despite his assurances to Stettinius of support for the UN policy, Truman turned to employing the UN as an instrument in America's emerging power contest with Russia. This development is clearly seen in the Iran crisis which dominated the first meetings of the UN Security Council in the winter of 1946. The issue arose out of a 1942 treaty between Iran and the Big Three powers, providing for the stationing of troops in Iran to protect that nation's oil resources and its function as a vital supply route for Lend-Lease goods into Russia. After hostilities ended, Russian troops did not evacuate the northern part of Iran as provided by the treaty. Instead Russia encouraged a separatist movement in the province of Azerbaijan. It was feared in Washington and London that the Russians were fomenting this movement in hope of gaining oil concessions from Iran. The matter remained deadlocked throughout the two sessions of the foreign ministers' conference in London and Moscow, with Russia refusing to allow Iranian troops into the rebellious region.[17]

The Iranian delegation filed a complaint with the secretary general on January 19, 1946, and the United Nations had its first showdown between East and West.[18] The Russians quickly tried to

16. Herbert Feis, *Contest Over Japan*, pp. 33–50; The original American support had been in response to Russia's request for support of Russia's having a role as a trust nation. Although the Russians mentioned no specific territory, Gromyko's request pointed toward a definite area of interest. Stettinius replied that " . . . your point of view was eminently reasonable and that we would be happy to support in principle the Soviet proposal as to the eligibility of your Government as a potential administering authority." Stettinius went on to note that Gromyko's letter of June 20 implied specific territories and that this matter would have to be discussed after the San Francisco Conference ended; *FRUS, 1945*, vol. 1, *General: The United Nations*, pp. 1235–1236, 1398–1399, 1428–1429; *FRUS, 1945*, vol. 2, *Political and Economic Matters*, pp. 163–166, 191, 200–201, 297.

17. Richard W. Van Wagenen, *The Iranian Case, 1946*, pp. 17–18, 23–28.

18. Ibid.; Byrnes, *Speaking Frankly*, p. 123; United Nations Security Council, Official Records, First Year, First Series, Supplement No. 1, pp. 16–17.

shift attention from their presence in Iran by asking the Security
Council to investigate the presence of British forces in Greece.[19]
These developments led to bitter clashes between Vyshinsky and
Bevin, in which the honor and prestige of the two great powers
quickly overshadowed the issues at stake. At a secret meeting of
the Security Council on February 5, Bevin exchanged heated words
with the Soviet deputy foreign minister; and it appeared that the
Security Council might end in disaster before it accomplished anything. After listening to two hours of bitter tirades, Stettinius criticized both sides for losing their sense of compromise. Stettinius then
suggested that the assertions of both sides regarding British troops
in Greece be officially published and that the matter be regarded
as closed. Since the British had already promised to withdraw their
troops after elections were held, this should suffice as a commitment
to return Greece to its own ways.[20]

The mediating attempt was followed later that day and the
next morning by private conversations, which resulted in Stettinius's
recommendations being accepted. The way for compromise had
been forged when the Security Council agreed that bilateral negotiations between Russia and Iran looking forward to withdrawal of
Russian troops from that country should take place.[21]

Truman did not trust the United Nations' formula to achieve a
solution satisfactory to America. He saw Russia's moves in Iran as
part of an aggressive policy to outflank the West in the Mediterranean. Earlier he had told Byrnes: "There isn't a doubt in my
mind that Russia intends an invasion of Turkey and the seizure of
the Black Sea straits to the Mediterranean. Unless Russia is faced
with an iron fist and strong language another war is in the making.
Only one language do they understand—'how many divisions have
you?'"[22] In his *Memoirs* Truman commented on Russian activities
in Iran: "It all seemed to add up to a planned move on the part of
the Russians to get at least northern Iran under their control. To-

19. George Curry, *James F. Byrnes*, (vol. 14 in Robert H. Ferrell, ed.,
The American Secretaries of State and Their Diplomacy), p. 194.
20. Record of the Secret Session of the Security Council, Feb. 5, 1945,
SP.
21. Security Council Records, First Year, First Series, Fifth Meeting, pp.
49–70; Tenth Meeting, p. 173.
22. Truman to Byrnes, memorandum, Jan. 6, 1946, photocopy in Truman,
Memoirs, 1: 551–552.

gether with the threat of a communist coup in Greece, this began to look like a giant pincers movement against the oil-rich areas of the Near East and the warm-water ports of the Mediterranean."[23]

Throughout February evidence mounted in Washington indicating a rapid buildup of Russian troops in northern Iran. At a March 7 meeting of high State Department officials, Byrnes was shown a map that showed Russian armies deployed in positions aimed at the borders of Turkey, Iraq, and toward Tehran and the oil fields beyond. Byrnes remarked that "it now seemed clear that the U.S.S.R. was adding military invasion to political subversion in Iran. . . . Now we'll give it to them with both barrels."[24]

The American government moved on two planes. It pressed the Iranian government to bring the situation back to the Security Council, and it directly queried the Soviet government, as Undersecretary Dean Acheson put it, "to let the U.S.S.R. know that we were aware of its moves, but leave a graceful way out if desired to avoid a showdown."[25] But while the public efforts went ahead at the UN, Truman wrote Stalin on March 21 and threatened American military action if Russian troops were not out of Iran within six weeks.[26] Four days later, March 25, the Russian government announced that it had reached an agreement with Iran to withdraw all Russian forces within five to six weeks.

The American government and press interpreted Russia's pullout from Iran as a major victory for the United Nations.[27] If indeed there was a victory involved it was not a UN victory but one for the United States. The Iranian crisis showed that both America and Russia were employing the United Nations for their own narrow ends. The Cold War had experienced its first direct clash between the two former allies.

The pinnacle of hope for achieving world peace through the United Nations had come in the Charter-signing ceremonies that

23. Ibid., p. 523.
24. *FRUS, 1946*, vol. 7, *The Near East and Africa*, p. 346.
25. Ibid., p. 347.
26. Herbert Druks, *Harry S. Truman and the Russians*, p. 125. Truman later cited this crisis as an example of how the Russians "backed down" when faced with a tough American stand. Harry Truman, *Truman Speaks*, p. 132.
27. *FRUS, 1946*, vol. 7, *The Near East and Africa*, pp. 563–567; *Newsweek*, 27 (Apr. 15, 1946): 40–41; ibid., (Apr. 22, 1946): 16; *Time*, 47 (Apr. 1, 1946): 26–27; ibid., (Apr. 15, 1946): 27.

closed the San Francisco conference. Gabriel Kolko has written in *The Politics of War* that American war aims "postulated an ideal world order that would emerge from the chaos of the war, one not wracked by social and economic disorder, hunger, and radical changes in the conditions that had defined the prewar world." American leaders, Kolko claims, "did not anticipate radical frustrations in the immediate postwar realities."[28] That statement seems to overlook the important shift in view from Roosevelt to Truman.

Roosevelt, Hull, and Stettinius all believed that the UN policy offered the best way to control the forces of radical change they saw emerging after the war. The State Department, and Stettinius in particular, ardently pushed plans to get the UN in operation as quickly as possible because they viewed the UN as the only instrument sufficiently comprehensive and flexible to offer any real hope of dealing with the revolutionary condition of the postwar world. This is a primary reason why the Americans placed such great emphasis on the Economic and Social Council which they envisioned as bringing international resources to bear on rooting out the causes of war.

Under Roosevelt this sophisticated UN policy had a chance of success. For all his shortcomings, Roosevelt possessed important assets. Foremost was his sense of political timing and his skill in congressional tactics. He also had immense prestige at home and abroad. Roosevelt, although more cautious and less visionary than Wilson, enjoyed the same charismatic appeal, which would have been of great value in gaining continuing support for the UN. Even Roosevelt's caution and political dissembling would have aided in the difficult leadership required to hold America patiently to the wheel of cooperation until the UN grew strong enough to command support on its own.

As it became apparent that the American government could not count on Russia to cooperate with the UN policy, Truman felt compelled to emphasize a more nationalistic approach of its own. America's worldwide economic interests demanded a vigorous diplomatic posture. Truman could not afford to wait on the infant United Nations. His instincts were narrower than those of Roosevelt. He was willing to seize on the atomic bomb as a diplomatic agent

28. Kolko, *The Politics of War*, p. 347.

because, as he later wrote, "Dropping the bomb ended the war, saved lives, and gave the free nations a chance to face the facts."[29]

Some writers emphasize the Cold War's inevitability, arguing that it was an impersonal clash of competing systems. The quest for power, and the chaos created by the hot war just ending led naturally to the Cold War.[30] Granting that there were great forces in conflict, Truman preferred to employ economic coercion. And he utilized the atomic bomb indirectly in diplomacy because it offered a promise of dramatic gains. As president, he had the choice to support the UN strongly and grant some concessions to Russia. By choosing a belligerent approach he alienated the Russian government at a time when it was militarily weak. Fear and isolationism governed much of Stalin's action in 1945–1946.[31] Internal needs prevailed. It is one of the tragic ironies of the 20th century that Russia and America were rapidly demobilizing their armies at the same time each country's leaders feared the other nation might unleash war.

Thus the UN was born as a child of the masquerade peace that marked the early atomic age. Despite its crippled birth the UN has been of real significance in assisting many of the limited steps toward world peace that have occurred since 1945. If the past has some value in futhering man's understanding of himself, this story indicates that the UN should now, in the twilight of the Cold War, be given the serious support by East and West that was envisioned at the time of its conception.

29. Truman to James L. Cate, Jan. 12, 1953, photocopy in W. L. Craven and James L. Cate, eds., *The Army Air Forces in World War II*, vol. 5, *The Pacific: Matterhorn to Nagasaki, June 1944 to August, 1945*, pp. 712–714.

30. William L. Neumann, *After Victory—Churchill, Roosevelt, Stalin and the Marking of the Peace*, pp. 182–189.

31. Ulam, *Expansion and Co-existence*, pp. 397–405, 414–415.

Bibliography

Manuscripts

The Papers of Bernard Baruch, Princeton University Library.
The Carnegie Endowment Archives, Columbia University Library.
The Papers of the Department of State, National Archives.
The Papers of John Foster Dulles, Princeton University Library.
The Papers of James Forrestal, Princeton University Library.
The Papers of Joseph C. Grew, Houghton Library, Harvard University.
The Papers of Cordell Hull, Library of Congress.
The Papers of Breckinridge Long, Library of Congress.
The Papers of Leo Pasvolsky, Library of Congress.
The Papers of Robert P. Patterson, Library of Congress.
Records of the Committee on Foreign Relations, National Archives.
The Papers of Franklin D. Roosevelt, Hyde Park.
The Papers of Edward R. Stettinius, Jr., University of Virginia Library.
The Papers of Henry L. Stimson, Yale University.
The Papers of Arthur H. Vandenberg, Clements Library, University of Michigan.

Public Documents

Publications of the United States Government

Congressional Record, 78th Cong., 1st sess. through 79th Cong., 1st sess. Washington, 1944–1945.
Department of State. *Bulletin,* vol. 10 (June 3, 1944) through vol. 12 (Mar. 11, 1945). Washington, D.C., 1944–1945.

———. *Foreign Relations of the United States, 1943, Conferences at Cairo and Teheran,* Washington, D.C., 1963.

———. *Foreign Relations of the United States, 1943,* Vol. 1, *General,* Washington, D.C., 1963.

———. *Foreign Relations of the United States, 1944,* Vol. 1, *General,* Washington, D.C., 1967.

———. *Foreign Relations of the United States, 1944,* Vol. 5, *The Near East, South Asia, Africa, the Far East,* Washington, D.C., 1965.

———. *Foreign Relations of the United States, 1945, Conferences at Malta and Yalta,* Washington, D.C., 1955.

———. *Foreign Relations of the United States, 1945, Conference of Berlin* (Potsdam), 2 vols., Washington, D.C., 1960.

———. *Foreign Relations of the United States, 1945,* Vol. 1, *General: The United Nations,* Washington, D.C., 1967.

———. *Foreign Relations of the United States, 1945,* Vol. 2, *General: Political and Economic Matters,* Washington, D.C., 1967.

———. *Foreign Relations of the United States, 1945,* Vol. 3, *European Advisory Commission,* Washington, D.C., 1968.

———. *Foreign Relations of the United States, 1945,* Vol. 5, *Europe,* Washington, D.C., 1967.

———. *Foreign Relations of the United States, 1945,* Vol. 7, *China,* Washington, D.C., 1969.

——. *Foreign Relations of the United States, 1945,* Vol. 8, *The Near East and Africa,* Washington, D.C., 1969.

———. *Foreign Relations of the United States, 1946,* Vol. 7, *The Near East and Africa,* Washington, D.C., 1969.

———. *Report of the Delegation of the United States of America to the Inter-American Conference on Problems of War and Peace,* Washington, D.C., 1946.

Congress. Senate. *Hearings before the Committee on Foreign Relations the United States Senate, 78th Cong. on the Nominations of Joseph C. Grew et al.,* Washington, D.C., 1944.

Publications of Foreign Governments

Correspondence between the Chairman of the Council of Ministers of the U.S.S.R. and the Presidents of the U.S.A. and the Prime Ministers of Great Britain. 2 vols. Moscow: Foreign Languages Publishing House, 1957.

Publications of the United Nations

U.N. Information Organizations and U.S. Library of Congress. *Documents of the United Nations Conference on International Organization,* New York, 1945.

United Nations. *Security Council, Official Records, First Year, First Series, Supplement, No. 1,* London, 1946.

Newspapers

Albany (N.Y.) *Knickerbocker News,* 1944.
Atlanta *Constitution,* 1944.

Baltimore *Sun*, 1944–1945.
Barron's Weekly, 1941.
Brooklyn *Eagle*, 1944.
Brooklyn *Citizen*, 1944.
Boston *Herald*, 1944.
Bristol (Conn.) *Press*, 1941.
Chicago *Sun*, 1943.
Chicago *Daily Tribune*, 1944.
Cleveland *Plain Dealer*, 1937.
Christian Science Monitor, 1944.
Chicago *Polish Daily News*, 1944.
Danville (Va.) *Register*, 1941.
Daily Worker, 1940.
Detroit, *Free Press*, 1944
El Universal (Mexico City), 1945.
Fort Wayne (Ind.) *Journal Gazette*, 1944.
Knoxville *Journal*, 1944.
Lewiston (Me.) *Journal*, 1941.
Little Rock (Ark.) *Democrat*, 1944.
Mobile *Press*, 1945.
Memphis *Commercial Appeal*, 1943.
Minneapolis *Star Journal*, 1944.
New York *Herald Tribune*, 1937, 1940, 1944–1945.
New York *Journal American*, 1939.
New York *Mirror*, 1944
New York *Post*, 1944–45
New York Times, 1937–1945.
New York *World*, 1944–45
New York *World Telegram*, 1944.
Newport News *Times Herald*, 1944.
Norfolk *Pilot*, 1944.
Philadelphia *Inquirer*, 1944–1945.
Philadelphia *Record*, 1941.
Pittsburgh *Post Gazette*, 1944.
Pittsburgh *Press*, 1937.
Providence (R.I.) *Bulletin*, 1945.
Richmond *News Leader*, 1941, 1945.
Richmond *Times Despatch*, 1943.
Rochester *Times Union*, 1944.
St. Louis *Post-Dispatch*, 1944–45
San Antonio *Express*, 1944.
Savannah *Press*, 1944.
Seattle *Press*, 1944.
Seattle *Times*, 1944–45
Sioux City *Journal*, 1943.
Springfield (Mass.) *News*, 1944.
Tampa *Tribune*, 1944.
Topeka *Capital*, 1943.
Wall Street Journal, 1939.
Washington *Daily News*, 1943.
Washington *Post*, 1943–1946.
Washington *Star*, 1944–45

Washington *Times Herald,* 1944–1945.
Zanesville (Ohio) *Times Recorder,* 1944.

Periodicals

American Peace Society *Bulletin,* 1944.
Colliers, 1944.
Journal of Commerce, 1926.
Nation, 1944.
Newsweek, 1944.
New York Times Magazine, 1932, 1944.
Public Opinion Quarterly, 1945.
Reader's Digest, 1945.
Time, 1944–1945.
Vital Speeches of the Day, 1945.

Secondary Works

Asbell, Bernard. *When F.D.R. Died.* New York: Holt, Rinehart and Winston, Co., 1961.

Alperowitz, Gar. *Atomic Diplomacy, Hiroshima and Potsdam.* New York: Simon and Schuster, 1965.

Adler, Selig. *The Isolationist Tradition, Its Twentieth Century Reaction.* London: Abelard Schuman, 1957.

Bateman, Henry E. "Observations on President Roosevelt's Health during World War II," *Mississippi Valley Historical Review,* 46 (June, 1956): 82–102.

Biddle, Francis B. *In Brief Authority.* New York: Doubleday and Co., 1962.

Bor-Komarowski, Gen. O. T. *The Secret Army.* London: Victor Gollancz, 1950.

Burns, James MacGregor. *Roosevelt: The Soldier of Freedom, 1940–1945.* New York: Harcourt Brace Jovanovich, 1970.

Byrnes, James F. *Speaking Frankly.* New York: Harper & Row Publishers, 1947.

Churchill, Winston. *The Second World War,* Vol. VI: *Triumph and Tragedy.* Boston: Houghton Mifflin Co., 1953.

Coffin, Tristram. *Missouri Compromise.* Boston: Little Brown and Co., 1947.

Connally, Thomas T., and Alfred Steinberg. *My Name Is Tom Connally.* New York: T. Y. Crowell, 1954.

Considine, Bob. "Stettinius—Dynamo in the State Department," *Readers Digest,* 46 (Mar., 1945): 11–14.

Craven, W. L., and James L. Cate, eds., *The Army Air Forces in World War II,* vol. 5, *The Pacific: Matterhorn to Nagasaki, June 1944 to August 1944.* Chicago: University of Chicago Press, 1953.

Curry, George. *James F. Byrnes,* vol. 14 of *The American Secretaries of State and Their Diplomacy,* ed. Robert H. Ferrell. New York: Cooper Square Press, 1965.

Divine, Robert A. *Second Chance, The Triumph of Internationalism in America during World War II.* New York: Atheneum, 1967.

Druks, Herbert. *Harry S. Truman and the Russians.* New York: Speller and Sons, 1966.

Drury, Allen. *A Senate Journal, 1943–1945.* New York: McGraw-Hill Book Company, 1963.

Dulles, John F. *War or Peace?* New York: Crowell-Collier-Macmillan Co., 1950.

Eagleton, Clyde. "The Charter Adopted at San Francisco," *American Political Science Review,* 39 (Oct., 1945): 934–942.

Eden, Anthony, Earl of Avon. *The Memoirs of Anthony Eden* (3 vols.), vol. 3: *The Reckoning.* Boston: Houghton Mifflin Co., 1965.

Feis, Herbert. *Between War and Peace, the Potsdam Conference.* Princeton: Princeton University Press, 1960.

————. *Churchill, Roosevelt, and Stalin: The War They Waged and the Peace They Sought.* Princeton: Princeton University Press, 1957.

————. *Contest Over Japan.* New York: W. W. Norton Co., 1967.

————. *Japan Subdued, The Atomic Bomb and the End of the War in the Pacific.* Princeton: Princeton University Press, 1961.

Gervasi, Frank. "Greece, Proving Grounds for Peace," *Colliers,* 114 (Dec. 9, 1944): 20–21.

Gildersleeve, Virginia C. *Many a Good Crusade.* New York: Crowell-Collier-Macmillan Co., 1954.

Graebner, Norman A., ed. *Uncertain Tradition, American Secretaries of State in the Twentieth Century.* New York: McGraw-Hill Book Company, 1961.

Grew, Joseph C. *Turbulent Era, A Diplomatic Record of Forty Years* (2 vols.), Walter Johnson, ed. Cambridge: Harvard University Press, 1952.

Groves, Leslie R. *Now It Can Be Told, the Story of the Manhattan Project.* New York: Harper and Row, Publishers, 1962.

Harriman, W. Averell. *America and Russia in A Changing World, A Half Century of Personal Observation.* New York: Doubleday & Co., 1971.

Herring, George. "Lend-Lease to Russia and the Origins of the Cold War, 1944–45," *Journal of American History,* 56 (June, 1969): 93–114.

Hewlett, Richard G., and Oscar E. Anderson, Jr. *A History of the United States Atomic Energy Commission,* Vol. I: *The New World, 1939–1946.* University Park, Pa.: The Pennsylvania State University Press, 1962.

Houston, John A. *Latin America in the United Nations.* New York: Carnegie Endowment for International Peace, 1956.

Hull, Cordell. *The Memoirs of Cordell Hull* (2 vols.). New York: Crowell-Collier-Macmillan, 1948.

Israel, Fred L. (ed.) *The War Diaries of Breckinridge Long, Selections from the War Years, 1939–1944.* Lincoln: University of Nebraska Press, 1966.

Johnson, Walter. "Edward R. Stettinius, Jr." in *Uncertain Tradition, American Secretaries of State in the Twentieth Century,* ed. Norman Graebner. New York: McGraw-Hill Book Company, 1961.

Kennan, George F. *Russia and the West Under Lenin and Stalin.* Boston: Little, Brown and Co., 1961.

Kolko, Gabriel. *The Politics of War, the World and United States Foreign Policy, 1943–1945.* New York: Random House-Knopf, 1968.

Krock, Arthur. *Memoirs, Sixty Years on the Firing Line.* New York: Funk and Wagnalls, 1968.

Lawes, Walter and Francis O. Wilcox. "The State Department Continues Its Reorganization," *American Political Science Review,* 39 (Apr., 1945): 309–317.

Leahy, William D. *I Was There.* New York: Whittlesey House, 1950.

Leuchtenburg, William E. *Franklin D. Roosevelt and the New Deal, 1932–1940.* New York: Harper and Row, Publishers, 1963.

Lippmann, Walter. *U.S. War Aims.* Boston: Little, Brown and Co., 1944.

Macdonald, Austin F. *Latin American Politics and Government.* New York: T. Y. Crowell, 1950.

McNeill, William H. *America, Britain, and Russia, Their Cooperation and Conflict, 1941–1946.* London: Royal Institute of International Affairs, 1953.

Mecham, John L. *The United States and Inter-American Security, 1889–1960.* Austin: University of Texas Press, 1960.

Millis, Walter (ed.). *The Forrestal Diaries.* New York: The Viking Press, 1951.

Moran, Lord. *Churchill, Taken from the Diaries of Lord Moran: The Struggle for Survival.* Boston: Houghton Mifflin Co., 1966.

Morison, Elting. *Turmoil and Tradition, A Study of the Life and Times of Henry L. Stimson.* Boston: Houghton Mifflin Co., 1960.

Notter, Harley A. *Postwar Foreign Policy Preparation, 1939–1945.* Washington, D.C.: U.S., Department of State, 1949.

Paterson, Thomas G. "The Abortive American Loan to Russia and the Origins of the Cold War, 1943–1946," *Journal of American History,* 56 (June, 1969): 70–92.

Pratt, Julius W. *Cordell Hull* (2 vols.), vols. 12 and 13 of *The American Secretaries of State and Their Diplomacy,* ed. Robert H. Ferrell. New York: Cooper Square Press, 1964.

"The Quarter's Polls," *Public Opinion Quarterly,* 9 (Spring, 1945): 71–81.

Riggs, Robert E. "Overselling the U.N. Charter—Fact and Myth," *International Organization,* 14 (Spring, 1960): 277–290.

Roosevelt, Elliot. *As He Saw It.* New York: Duell, Sloan, and Pearce, 1946.

Rozenman, Samuel D. (comp.). *The Public Papers and Addresses of Franklin D. Roosevelt* (13 vols.). New York: Random House-Knopf, 1938–1950.

Rozek, Edward J. *Allied Wartime Diplomacy, A Pattern in Poland.* New York: John Wiley and Sons, Inc., 1958.

Russell, Ruth B. *A History of the United Nations Charter; the Role of the United States, 1940–1945.* Washington: Brookings Institution, 1958.

Seton-Watson, Hugh. *The East European Revolution.* New York: Frederick A. Praeger, 1956.

Sherwood, Robert E. *Roosevelt and Hopkins, An Intimate History.* New York: Harper and Row, Publishers, 1948.

Smith, Gaddis. *American Diplomacy during the Second World War, 1941–1945.* New York: John Wiley and Sons, Inc., 1965.

Stettinius, Edward R., Jr. *Lend-Lease, Weapon for Victory.* New York: Crowell-Collier-Macmillan, 1944.

———. "Sovereignty of No Nation Is Absolute," *Vital Speeches of the Day,* 61, No. 17 (June 15, 1945): 524–528.

———. *Roosevelt and the Russians.* New York: Crowell-Collier, Macmillan, 1949.

Stimson, Henry L. and McGeorge Bundy. *On Active Service in Peace and War.* New York: Harper and Row, Publishers, 1948.

Strang, Lord William. *Home and Abroad.* London: A. Deutsch, 1956.

Stuart, Graham H. *The Department of State.* New York: Crowell-Collier-Macmillan, 1949.

Truman, Harry. *Harry Truman Speaks.* New York: Columbia University Press, 1960.

———. *Memoirs.* 2 vol. Vol. I: *Year of Decisions.* New York: 1955.

Tsou, Tang. *America's Failure in China, 1941–1950.* Chicago: University of Chicago Press, 1963.

Ulam, Adam B. *Expansion and Coexistence, The History of Soviet Foreign Policy, 1917–1967.* New York: Frederick A. Praeger, 1968.

————. "On Modern History: Re-reading the Cold War," *Interplay Magazine,* 2 (March, 1968): 51–53.

Vandenberg, Arthur H., Jr. and Joe Alex Morris (eds.). *The Private Papers of Senator Vandenberg.* Boston: Houghton Mifflin, 1952.

Walker, Richard L. *Edward Reilly Stettinius,* vol. 14 in *The American Secretaries of State and Their Diplomacy,* ed. Robert H. Ferrell. New York: Cooper Square Press, 1965.

Webster, Sir Charles K. "The Making of the Charter of the United Nations," *History,* 32 (Mar., 1947): 342–345.

Weinberg, Sydney. "What to Tell America: The Writers' Quarrel in the Office of War Information," *Journal of American History,* 55 (June, 1968): 73–89.

Welles, Sumner. *The Time for Decision.* New York: Harper and Row, Publishers, 1944.

Werth, Alexander. *Russia at War, 1941–1945.* New York: E. P. Dutton, 1964.

Westerfield, H. Bradford. *Foreign Policy and Party Politics: Pearl Harbor to Korea.* New Haven: Yale University Press, 1955.

Wilmot, Chester. *The Struggle for Europe.* New York: Harper and Row, Publishers, 1952.

Woodward, Sir Lewellyn. *British Foreign Policy in the Second World War.* London: Her Majesty's Printing Office, 1962.

Dissertations

Campbell, Thomas M. "Edward R. Stettinius and the Founding of the United Nations." Unpublished doctoral dissertation, University of Virginia, 1964.

Francis, Michael. "Attitudes of the United States Government toward Collective Security Arrangements with Latin America, 1945–1960." Unpublished doctoral dissertation, University of Virginia, 1963.

Herring, George R. "Lend Lease: Experiment in Foreign Aid." Unpublished doctoral dissertation, University of Virginia, 1965.

Interviews

Lynch, Robert J. Interview with author, Nov. 5, 1962.

Reston, James. Interview with author, June 12, 1962.

Other Sources

Dulles Oral History Collection. Princeton University.

Stettinius, Edward R., Jr. Transcript of College Record, Office of the Registrar, University of Virginia.

Index